Time to Lay By

Time to Lay By

JAY MONDY

Order this book online at www.trafford.com
or email orders@trafford.com

Most Trafford titles are also available at major online book retailers.

Printed in the United States of America.

ISBN: 978-1-4269-4818-3 (sc)
ISBN: 978-1-4269-4819-0 (e)

Trafford rev. 11/29/2010

Trafford PUBLISHING® www.trafford.com

North America & international
toll-free: 1 888 232 4444 (USA & Canada)
phone: 250 383 6864 ♦ fax: 812 355 4082

The family of the late Jay Mondy would like to dedicate this book to him. Unfortunately, he did not live to see his book that he finished right before he passed away published. Therefore, his family had it published for him.

Jay wanted this book to be dedicated to his late and lovely wife, Doris Layton Mondy and to her good friend, Judy Brannan. The two of them encouraged him to take up the pen.

Foreword

Author's Biography

Jay Mondy was born near Fisk, Mo, in Butler County, grew up in the cotton fields, attended a two-room elementary school and graduated from the Broseley High School. He received degrees from Arkansas State University and a specialist degree from University of Missouri at Columbia. Jay's early life witnessed fistfights on Saturday night and hitchin' posts in front of the general stores in Broseley, Fisk, and Quilin, MO. The next 30 years, except for a tour in the military, were spent teaching students in the elementary grades, working as a public school principal and superintendent. Jay was married to the late Doris (Layton) Mondy for 44 years. They were blessed with three lovely, good children, Kerry, Derek and Charisse. Concerning his military experience, he is quoted saying, "I went to bed one night with my window open and woke up the following morning in the draft -a military draft, and it resulted in a two-year experience in the United States Army."

Time to Lay By comes from a life-long fascination with the true, unique and unusual stories of people in the Ozark Mountains. Some of the stories, he wrote, but the vast majority of them were unearthed through countless hours of research. Most of the stories were discovered in the Ozark Mountains. Some are from the foothills of the Ozarks and a few are Ozark related stories.

In addition to searching thousands of feet of microfilmed old newspapers, Jay visited many cities and county libraries, court houses, and historical societies in search of true, but unusual, tales that otherwise might have been lost in the pages of the past.

Preface

Jay Mondy has crossed and re-crossed the Ozarks, which covers parts of Missouri, Arkansas and Oklahoma. He has stopped in old towns (Potosi, MO; est. in 1763), libraries, churches, courthouses, historical societies, stores, and in people's homes. He has listened to the loggers, peace officers, Ozark grandmothers, farmers, historians and teachers. In all locations where real folk heroes and outlaws were born, he has listened to people tell their tales. He has researched old newspapers, microfilm, old manuscripts, plus actual court records and legal documents. In the process, he has been able to uncover the truth concerning court trials, old style lynching's, gunfights and murders in the Ozark Mountains.

Bob Sifford
Potosi, Missouri

It is with a great deal of enthusiasm that I recommend this book filled with true and authentic stories to the reader. The author has spent three years in devoted research in uncovering these interesting tales which have been lost in the pages of history.

Mr. Mondy's many years of formal education as well as his experience of teaching in and administering to public schools make him eminently qualified to do painstaking research and to communicate his findings to others in an informative and sometimes humorous manner.

The reader should take this book, *Time to Lay By*, sit back, relax and enjoy theses revealing stories. The tales should stir memories and may shed some light on where the reader came from and what hardships the characters involved underwent. There are stories of legal hangings, western men, moonshiners, bootlegging and many other topics too numerous to mention in this preface. If however, I am positive that the reader will find every story to be a mixture of humorous, interesting and unique occurrences.

Mr. Mondy's research included extensive viewing of old microfilms, visiting various libraries and reading published news items relating to each story. He also consulted with historical societies, county sheriffs and with many individuals he felt could shed more light on the story at hand.

The long ago stories are presented in this book as they occurred back in days lost in the pages of time. The book contains approximately one hundred forty five stories on a wide variety of topics of interest for all readers. The vast majority occurred in the Ozark Mountains with a few found in the foothills. They are all Ozark related. Please look at the second story in *Time to Lay By*. The title of this true story is "Faithful as a Yellow Dog". Then I am sure you will be eager to find out more, just as I was.

Jack Lincoln Ph.D.
Poplar Bluff, MO

"Reading Mr. Mondy's stories brought back fond memories of tales told to me on my grandfather's knee. Imagination couldn't be any more bizarre than true life.

I know readers of Mr. Mondy's collection will be amazed and very appreciative of his efforts in researching and compiling these great, old, true stories."

Pat Higginbotham
Friend and Teacher
Lamar, Missouri

"This book is a collection of great stories that takes you back in time and lets you relive many events we have all experienced. It is exciting and easy reading. Jay Mondy has given us an enjoyable book. This book will certainly have a place on my bookshelf. I recommend "Time to Lay By" without hesitation. This collection of true and exciting stories is pure history of our times.

Jay Mondy's background fits many of the stories. Jay married his childhood sweetheart, Doris Layton Mondy. She gave Jay great encouragement throughout her life and they raised three great children, Kerry, Derek and Charisse.

Jay was an outstanding basketball player in his youth, the star of his high school team. Because of his height he could really rack up the points. Jay spent most of his life working for the children of Southeast Missouri. He began as a teacher and later a principal and then superintendent of a large reorganized school district.

You will enjoy this book. It will bring back many happy memories."

James J. Rickman
Superintendent Emeritus
Fox C6 School District
Arnold, Missouri

"From the beginning, man's history was passed from generation to generation via the storyteller. The first stories were told and retold through word-of-mouth. Eventually, the storyteller wrote them down, functioning as the only reliable source of man's history.

As man evolved becoming more sophisticated, the contribution of the storyteller has been devalued. Yet, the preservation of man's history through storytelling is as important to man's future as the preservation of one's natural resources to man's existence.

The stories told here add to our knowledge of a fascinating region and a way of life nearly forgotten. Jay Mondy should be congratulated for compiling these stories that preserve this part of our history."

Carolyn Smith
Poplar Bluff, Missouri

"Time to Lay By has about 140 stories for entertainment and enlightenment. There are stories for all occasions, stories lost in the pages of the past. You will enjoy them."

Delores Pratt
Harrison, Arkansas

Table of Contents

Introduction

The Ozark Mountains contain natural beauty, a wilderness and a rigorous lifestyle. It was formed from ancient sea beds and now rest on a vast plateau, touching seven states: Missouri, Arkansas, Oklahoma, Kansas, Kentucky, Illinois and Tennessee. The highest range is the Arkansas's Boston Mountains, within the Ozark Range, measures only 2,578 feet. The Ozarks contain fifty thousand square miles of rugged and lovely landscape. Southern Missouri has the Lion's Share, more than thirty thousand square miles. The vast, remaining square miles of the Ozark Mountains are located in North Central Arkansas and Eastern Oklahoma.

"The Ozarks begin in Illinois and Kentucky and stretch across two states to almost Tulsa, Oklahoma. Five major rivers (Mississippi, Osage, Missouri, Neosho and the Arkansas) form their boundaries and there are more free-flowing streams here than anywhere in the United States. The limestone nature of the soil makes possible other wonders – a vast bubbling fresh springs and more caves (at least seven thousand are known) than any other place in the world.

There is no place on earth to match this area. The pioneer lifestyles that exist off the main roads and back in the hills are not for everyone. The Ozarks, in fact, are for something almost lost to fast-paced Americans – the slow, enjoyable sipping sights, sounds and scenery. Late April finds hill tapestried with white dogwoods and pink redbud trees, while the earth sparkles with a million floral jewels: Verbena, Golden Rod, Jack-in-the-Pulpit, Tiger Lily, Wild Roses and Wild Sweet William."

There have been many true and authentic stories printed in many newspapers, books and magazines about Ozark Mountain people. This book will cover many of those stories going back years and years. The vast, vast majority of the stories found in this book are in the confines of an in the foothills of the Ozarks and are worthy of publishing. The stories in this book awakens us, the readers, to some unique and unusual history of by-gone days.

Jay Mondy, Author

Chapter One

UNIQUE STORIES

I CAN READ YOUR MIND

Fisk, Mo.

During a teacher's tenure in public school education for thirty years, any teacher will meet unique and unusual students at sometime under unusual circumstances. Let's roll the clock back to the school year 1951-1952, fifty years ago. It was my good fortune to have been involved with a marvelous student in a most unusual way.

A fifth grade student, Sharon Hughes, moved from California into the home of her grandparents on Route 1, Fisk, Missouri, and into the Pleasant Hill School District, a country school, grades 1-8. The school contained two rooms. The student was a beautiful, intelligent girl with charcoal black hair, dark brown eyes and a warm and pleasant personality.

The first day in our school Sharon was reserved, somewhat shy, but she slowly got acquainted with other students in my room. I soon discovered the California student was even or above the grade level in all subjects except Arithmetic.

Sharon was about three weeks behind, according to where she was in arithmetic, when she departed California and where my fifth grade students were working when she arrived. I explained to Sharon about our Arithmetic text and workbook. I told her I lend her a workbook. She could work in it after school hours, turn in her book to be checked and, if she had any difficulty, she was to let me know.

The following day, shortly after the school bell had sounded and classes commenced, Sharon approached me and said, "Guess how many pages I worked in the book last night?"

The first number that entered my mind was four and I said, "Four."

Sharon said, "That's right. How did you know?"

I immediately decided to have some fun with the young lady. I told her about ESP (extra sensory perception) and about mental telepathy and said, "Don't ever think any unpleasant thoughts about me for I'll know what they are. I can read your mind."

Sharon replied, "No, you can't." Later in the morning she approached me again. As she was nearing my desk, her eyes went to Washington's and Lincoln's pictures hanging on the walls just

1

above the blackboard. She stopped immediately in front of my disk and said, "If you can read my mind, tell me what I 'm thinking of now."

I immediately pointed to the two pictures and said, "Those pictures on the wall." I really had gotten her attention this time. Again I remarked, "Don't ever think any evil thoughts of me, for I can read your mind."

She asked, "Mr. Mondy, seriously, how did you know?"

I attempted once again to remind her of my ESP. Later in the day, I looked at her and knew she was questioning my ability and was going to catch up with me and my imaginary ESP. It was a matter of time. When?

It was a warm, sunny day with a fine mist of rainfall in the air. I knew Sharon's grandparents lived on a sand hill, three-quarters of a mile from the old school. She was so intrigued and suspicious that she once again raised her hand and asked if she might speak with me. I granted her permission and she quickly hurried to my desk.

Sharon immediately stated, "I'll believe you can read my mind if you can tell me this time what I am thinking."

I replied, "I know what you are thinking about. When you get home today you're going to change clothes, go out on the hillside and play in the sand while the misty rain is falling."

I had scored again! A feather would have knocked Sharon to the floor! It was all in fun, was fascinating and perhaps enjoyable for the two of us. Shortly the school year ended. Sharon spent the summer months with her grandparents and then moved back to California.

Since 1952, I have neither seen nor heard from the beautiful, young lady with the inquisitive mind, but my ESP tells me Sharon has had a successful and rewarding life.

> Jay Mondy
> Wappapello, Mo.
> December 2000

FAITHFUL AS A YELLOW DOG

The Graphic But Devoting Tribute of an
Arkansan to His Deceased Wife

Ozark Mountains, Ark.

Rev. Sam Jones is not a stickler for clerical dignity and can see much from piety even among the loudest of those about him, says the Chicago Chronicle. A friend traveling with him recently asked, "What was the sweetest funeral sermon you ever heard?"

"Well," Mr. Jones replied, "I was riding along a bridle path in Arkansas and off the road a little ways I saw a number of horses tied to the scrub trees near a little log cabin back a ways from the road. They were mostly saddle horses, though some were hitched to buckboards and wagons.

I dismounted and tied up. I knew it was one of two things, a funeral or a wedding. As I entered the cabin there were a number of natives sitting around the four walls of the rooms and in the middle near a plain board coffin, which had been hewn out of a natural log, was a man I knew. He was the husband, for I knew their habits, and it was the fashion for the husband to make the funeral oration in the absence of the preacher.

"I was unknown and did not care to disturb their services."

Presently he arose and said: "Fren's, you all know I'm not much on speakin', but you all kno'd Suke. She was jest as faithful to me as a yaller dawg under a wagon," and he sat down in silence and tears.

"There is a certain kind of dog in Arkansas, which trots under the wagon of the natives whenever they go to town and when they hitch up to the rack, the dog is told to watch the wagon and no one, except the master, can come within 30 feet of the wagon without being bitten to the bone.

"A few weeks prior to the occurrence related, a man had been summoned on the jury at the county seat. He expected to be excused on account of a sick wife but was made to serve, and when he started, he told the dog to "watch the wagon". The men of this town managed to take the horses out and put them in a livery stable, but the dog would not stir and ten days later, when the master returned, he found his dog dead under the wagon.

"So when this husband said his wife was as faithful as a 'Yaller dog under a wagon' he paid her the highest compliment he possibly could."

The Daily Republican

Poplar Bluff, Mo.
September 7, 1900

MOUNTAINEERS KEEP PLEDGES

Harrison, Ark.

Out of the Boston Mountains of Newton, Arkansas' single county not touched by railroads, sometimes drift strange tales concerning the unbroken faith of pioneer ancestors – and of the swift justice of simple home loving people, whose knowledge of things "outside" is little and whose curiosity of such is even less.

One of these tales was related recently by United States Deputy Marshall Lark Shaffer of this city on his return from Newton County with four brothers, Bob, Columbus, Verlin and Levis Farmer, charged with the manufacture and sale of liquor.

The brothers, all men with families, and their father, Tom Farmer, a well-to-do but eccentric individual, live in Red Rock neighborhood on Big Creek in the ragged western portion of Newton County. The officer entered into the neighborhood as far as possible in his Ford, but finally was obliged to forsake the car and proceed on foot. The men lived at different places and when Marshal Shaffer had made his round, he found himself in charge of four strapping mountaineers, accused outlaws but uncontentious. Darkness was falling; he was several miles from his car and many miles from home.

Spends Night With Men's Father

Under these circumstances, the officer felt he could not do otherwise than seek lodging for the night for himself and his charges. With his party, he turned his steps toward the only farm house in sight to ask for hospitality and was not deterred by the information, for this residence was the home of the father of his prisoners.

To the senior Farmer was explained the circumstances and lodging was asked. The officer was received kindly and invited into the house, a small rude structure, to talk the matter over. The request for quarters was granted with apologies for the lack of facilities for comfort. The housing of five for the night, in addition to the aged couple, presented something of a problem, was self-evident.

After offering to render such accommodation as was possible, Farmer Sr. ventured a seemingly impertinent suggestion to the officer – the man who held in the toils of the law his four and only sons. He suggested the marshal release them for the night, each to return home and spend the night with his family and to accept the word of honor of each son and the father. All would report early the next morning. Mr. Shaffer would spend the night in the only spare room in the father's home.

The officer was confronted with an unusual circumstance, and on him was the responsibility of making no mistake in his decision. With an ability to judge human nature, gained from many years experience in dealing with me, he was led to believe he would accept at par the pledge of honor of his newly made acquaintances, and he accordingly complied with the suggestion.

Prisoners Report Back

Arising early, after a comfortable night's rest, Marshal Shaffer received into custody anew the first of his paroled men at 5 o'clock and the last of the four reported an hour later, all prepared to accompany "the law" to Harrison to answer the charges placed against them. After breakfast, the party started on the journey over the long tedious miles to the foothills and on into Harrison, where they had not been for years past and doubtless had not expected to be for years to come.

They were presented before Federal Commissioner Stapleton, and each told his own story in his own words. Of the four, one pleaded guilty, two pleaded not guilty and the fourth was discharged for lack of evidence. Satisfactory bond was made by the three, and the long wearisome trail "Home to our Mountains" – back to the heart of the Bostons was taken up.

Last January, Mr. Shaffer started one day for the same neighborhood and armed with a warrant of arrest for one Joe Farmer, charged with the same offense – the making of and dealing in liquor. On reaching a country store in the Red Rock vicinity, the officer made inquiry after the man sought and there learned from the mountaineer merchant how the man named in his warrant, a youth several months previously had come home on day, crazed by the effects of drinking moonshine whiskey and armed with a loaded shotgun and threatened to kill his aged parents. While leveling the gun at his hysterical mother, the youth was shot down by his own father in his own home, and his lifeless body lay where it fell – a quotation of the price at which mountain-made liquor is bartered.

Joe Farmer, the fifth and youngest son of Tom Farmer, was buried in the neighborhood burial ground, and the warrant of arrest on which his name appeared was returned unserved.

The Daily Republican
Poplar Bluff, MO
April 28, 1924

"BLUE MAN OF SPRING CREEK"

Strange Legend of Ozark Mountains

Douglas County, Mo.

The story of "The Blue Man of Spring Creek," has been current in the rough regions in the eastern part of Douglas County, MO, for 60 years. It is a genuine Ozark legend, and, if the testimony of scores of men during all these years is to be accepted, the legend is absolutely true.

It was in the winter of 1865, a noted hunter of that part of the Ozarks by the name of Sol Collins, was on the ridge that forms the watershed between the Big North Fork and Spring Creek. There was snow on the ground and Collins, was utilizing it to trail the game, with which the hills abounded. Suddenly, among the many tracks with which he was familiar, he came upon one such as he had never seen before. There were bears in the Ozarks in those days, and the hunter had trailed and slain many a one of them in his time. This track looked somewhat like that of a bear, but if it was made by a bear then certainly here was the largest of the tribe that ever roamed the Ozark hills. In the deep snow the great foot prints were longer and broader than those of any bear Collins had ever seen, and at each side of the tracks were marks in the snow such as might have been made by long claws.

The hunter at once took up the trail, determined to kill the biggest bear in Ozark history. For hours he kept on tirelessly following those great foot prints. Far away to the north, almost to Indian Creek, then in a wide semi-circle to the west, until he was close above the Big North Fork. Still up hill and down, the seemingly endless chase continued.

At last, he was climbing the north slope of Upper Twin Mountain, he heard a noise on the hillside above him, and looking up, was barely in time to leap to one side and allow a great boulder to seep past him and crash into the depths of the valley. Another quickly followed the first, and Collins was glad to spring out of its path and shelter himself behind a big post oak. As he did so, the third boulder struck fairly against the tree and was hurled with such force, it was shattered into fragments. The startled hunter ventured to peer cautiously from his shelter, to learn from whence this avalanche of boulder came. That which he saw fairly froze the blood in his veins for there, on the hillside, towered a gigantic figure shaped like an immense man, stark naked except for the skin of some animal around its wait and other wrappings around its feet. The creature was covered from head to foot with a tightly curling coarse of short black hair which, as the sun struck upon it, took on a dark blue hue. Collins always claimed the giant was not less than nine feet tall, and his estimate is among the least of many made by other men in the years to follow.

Fled For His Life

The hunter stared only long enough to make these observations before the creature cast aside the great ten foot club he carried and tore out another boulder from the frozen ground and hurled it with such deadly aim that, again, the tree was struck and the rock shattered and, as he hurled the rock, the giant lifted up his voice and made the hills echo and re-echo with an ear-splitting scream more terrifying than ever came from any wild beast that roams the woods.

This was enough for Collins! He was no coward and had creditably borne his part during the years of the Civil War, but he never denied that after this one look and that horrible scream, eh took to his heels and fled for his life.

The hunter made it his business to gather several of his neighbors, sturdy hill men like himself, and for several days they put in most of their time following the tracks of the giant. Time and again they caught glimpses of him at a distance, going through the woods at a speed that once left his pursuers far behind, but no man was able to get within rifle shot of the creature. For two or three weeks the hunt continued almost every day without result. The wild man was seen by numbers of people and the occupants of more than one lonely cabin were awakened at dead of night by the most blood-curdling yells and shrieks in the dark woods, and when day dawned would find sheep had been carried away or a pig stolen from the pen. The hunters found bloody fragments of the animals thus carried off, but the giant himself was never found.

After the first appearance of the "Blue Man", as he was now called, he disappeared for nine years. Then, when most people who had not seen him had decided the whole story was a fake, in the autumn of 1874, the work passed through the hills, the "Blue Man" had returned. Again sheep and swine were caught and devoured, again did men organize and hunt through the hills in a vain endeavor to capture or slay the creature and, again he escaped them all and after creating a reign of terror for a week or two, disappeared as mysteriously as before.

Seen and Heard By Many

During the next sixteen years he made two or three visits to the hills along the Big Fork. Always he was seen or heard by many and, always he caught and devoured some of the smaller farm animals, but although hunted with greatest vigor, he escaped unhurt as before. Evidently, however, the hunters had made it too hot for their strange quarry, for this time he remained away for many years and from 1890 to 1911 nothing was seen of him. New corners in the region ridiculed the fearsome tales told them by the old settlers and probably a majority of the inhabitants were of the belief that the story was the invention of some superstition.

But suddenly he was again in the hills. Many an unbeliever in his existence saw with their own eyes the old timers were undoubtedly true. More men than ever joined the hunt this time and it was reported they had discovered the creature's den in a cave in a remote valley and the floor of the place was strewn with the bones of the animals he had eaten and his bed of dried leaves was seen in a corner. But, then as before, the mysterious creature disappeared.

One Settler's Explanation

What then is the explanation, if any there is, for this legend which has endured among the hills for sixty years? Old Uncle Jerry Hilterbrand, who settled in what is now Douglas County in 1820, and who died there in 1885, used to tell the following story which had been told him by yet older residents of the hills.

Some years before the American Revolution, while Missouri was still part of the French Colony of Louisiana, a French fur trader came into the Ozarks bringing with him a very beautiful Spanish woman. The trader soon tired of his fair companion, bartered her to an Indian chief for a goodly package of furs, and slipped away leaving the woman a captive. The poor woman, thus abandoned in the wilderness, lost her reason and lived for years a demented creature of the woods.

From her sprang a strange race of people, half Spanish, half Indian. They never mingled with either French or Indians, but hid away in remote and inaccessible places where they increased in numbers and were known to exist for many years. When the pioneer settlers poured into the Ozarks form 1820 to 1840, the strange half breed race disappeared and it was generally supposed by those who knew anything about them, they migrated into more remote and unsettled depths of the wilderness. The Boston Mountains in western Arkansas were thought to be the place to which they retreated. From these people, probably the last of their race, came the "Blue Man of Spring Creek". That was Uncle Jerry's explanation of the legend.

The Daily Republican
Poplar Bluff, Mo.
November 20, 1924

WINS A HUSBAND BY PITCHING HAY

Kansas Student, Her Mate in Harvest, Picks Her For His Maud Muller

Unusual Romance Told in Court

Young Woman Also Wins Suit for Back Pay When She Still Was a Farm Hand

Wichita, Kan.

Maud Muller, according to John Greenleaf Whittier, raked the meadow sweet with hay, and forgot all about her briars torn gown and her graceful ankles, bare and brown, as she won the heart of the judge. But Mary L. Bennett, a Kansas Maud Muller, won her sweetheart while wielding a pitchfork and wearing blue denim overalls.

This is the story Mary told, and she has a husband to prove it. She made her word good enough for a court to order her employers to pay her $52, which she had earned by making a "hand" in the hayfield. Mary Bennett is an orphan, with a sister living in Texas. At the death of her parents, she went to live with neighbors, Mr. and Mrs. Peter Jason, in Sedgwick County. She grew to young womanhood in their home, and during the summer she was pain the regular wage of a farm hand. She was strong and young and as good a farm hand as the average man.

For three years, Mary Bennett pitched hay alongside the men. Last summer, Charles Lee was one of the workers in the field. The girl and the young man worked side by side. He was a college student working to earn money to help pay his way through school. They got along so well at their haying and in their wheat field that Lee decided they would be an exceptionally good team mating for life.

When Mary left the Jason household, she said the Jason's owed her $76 in wages, which they refused to pay. So the young husband hired a lawyer, and suit was brought in Judge Grover Pierpont's court for the money. Mrs. Lee, as a witness, told how she had pitched hay 12 hours a day, day in and day out, for three years, and blushingly admitted to the court that she and Lee had made love over their pitchforks.

The Jasons maintained they had helped rear her and had taken care of the girl when she was ill. Judge Pierpont decided that Mrs. Lee should pay for care during her illness and awarded her $52 in cash and told Jason he did not want any delay in payment, for the young couple needed the cash for furniture.

The Poplar Bluff American
Poplar Bluff, Mo.
September 18, 1917

LITTLE GIRL'S HEART IS LOCATED ON RIGHT SIDE

Poplar Bluff, Mo.

If you should ask little Willie "Peaches" Myhre, who will be three years old on August 7, where her heart is, she would say-

"Wite dare," and with a cute little believe-it-or-not-smile point to her right side.

"Peaches" would be telling you the truth, odd as it may seem, but it makes no difference in her young life which side her heart is on, so long as one of her pet chickens do not peck her on the finger or nothing else goes wrong to mar her happiness.

Lives on Farm

This little girl is the daughter of Mr. and Mrs. William Myhre, who moved to Butler County about three months ago from Hartford, Ill., and established a home on a farm near Beaver Dam, 12 miles west of Poplar Bluff.

If, in future years, she should say "no" to a suitor, he may accuse her of having her heart in the wrong place, but never can he say truthfully it isn't on the right side.

Not long ago when Dr. C.H. Diehl, the family physician, was called to the Myhre home he decided to give the little girl a close examination "just in case-"

When he listened to her heart, his face took a puzzled expression. He couldn't hear it on the left side. Her parents became anxious when they saw the expression on the Doctor's face. He then turned his ear to the right side. There was the beat as clear as anyone's.

Close Study Made

He told Mr. and Mrs. Myhre his suspicion and a close study of the heart was made. He was a former president of the Illinois Heart Association, and had given much study to the human heart. It was decided to take her to a hospital in St. Louis, where an X-ray photograph bore out his original theory, and also showed the liver to be on the left side.

The girl balked at taking barium to show more clearly the outlines of her internal organs in the X-ray, so she is to be taken back to St. Louis one of these days soon, at which time a close examination of her physical make-up may be studied.

Perfect Physically

Nothing else is wrong with little Willie (she was named after her grandmother). She often impresses her will upon her brother, Thorvald, who is nearly four years her senior.

She is a well developed child, with chunky, but nevertheless wiry legs, as strong a body as any two-year-old could desire, and a disarming smile that sends gleams out form her chubby little face which is thatched over with golden, curly hair.

She is Bashful

It is really boring to little "Peaches" to discuss her heart. People look at her so funny-like she is a freak or something. She is just a pretty little girl and prefers not to be discussed, particularly when hearts are mentioned.

Dr. Diehl learned from consulting specialist in St. Louis that statistics gathered so far showed dextracardia occurs in about four persons in every million, and cases were especially extraordinary among females. The combination with the other reversals, which have been indicated, truly make little Willie one in a million-or perhaps more.

The American Republic
Poplar Bluff, Mo.
July 31, 1931

FOOTNOTE

I received a nice and informative letter dated January 14, 2001 from Mrs. Clara Smallwood, who was little Willie "Peaches" Myhre on Cane Creek, July 31, 1931. Mrs. Smallwood retired in St. Louis in 1988 and then moved to Newport Richey, Florida.

She told me why she was nicknamed "Peaches". She said her mother peeled peaches until 3:00 a.m., and she was born at 9:00 a.m. the same day. Mrs. Smallwood stated the nickname remained until her teenage years.

In the first examination, the family doctor discovered "Peaches" heart was on the right side of her body. This was referred to as Dextra (right) Cardia (heart). She was sent to St. Louis for further testing. There it was determined her organs had been reversed. This was referred to as Situs (site, location) Inversus (inverted, backward), and organs reversed. The heart and spleen were on the right side of her body and her liver an appendix were on the left side. She had her appendix removed during her teen years. Yes, it was removed from the left side of her body.

Mrs. Smallwood stated she had lived a normal life, having had two brothers, a sister and three children, all normal.

She had undergone a mastectomy more than five years before, but the cancer returned before the fifth year after surgery. She stated her body was now ravished with the dreadful disease and she was fighting for her life. Her spirit was as admirable as her lovely handwritten letter. Clara "Peaches" (Myhre) Smallwood passed away on August 29, 2001.

Clara "Peaches" (Myhre) Smallwood
August 7, 1928 – August 29, 2001

Chapter Two

WELL, I'LL BE

SELLS WIFE FOR $100

Extraordinary Deal Separates Children

**Bill Ogle Said to Have Liquidated Note and Debts of Aleck Foust,
Paid Stipulated Sum in Cash and to Have Acquired Human Property of Man,
Who Takes Son and Goes to Texas – Inquiry Probably Will Be Made Shortly**

Melville, Mo.

A deal in which Mrs. Aleck Foust, a prepossessing woman, was sold outright like a bale of hay or a bolt of calico by her husband to Bill Ogle, a night watchman for a railroad, is reported to have been consummated Monday at Melville.

This report, given out by responsible persons influential in Melville's civic life, was received here today and it is likely that Prosecuting Attorney Ing will take immediate action with a view to having an investigation instituted by the Grand Jury.

Aleck Foust's wife cost Ogle and even $100, according to Melville advices. Foust owed some money and several small bills about own, one account being a not for $25, all debts totaling about $50 in cash, receiving in return for the money and settlement of the obligations Foust's rather attractive wife.

The Foust's have two children and they were separated by the transfer of their mother; a young son being taken by Foust and a young daughter being given into the custody of Mrs. Foust. These latter two are living with Ogle at Melville, it was reported here today.

Foust took the money acquired by sale of his wife, it is alleged, and departed shortly after the transaction had been completed, for some point in Texas, taking his son along. The arrangement is reported to have been made without any difficulty or hitch whatsoever and appeared to outsiders to be eminently satisfactory to all vitally concerned.

The men are reported to have got together on the negotiations after Foust had reported his indebtedness. Ogle agreed, it is said, to take up Foust's not and the accounts hanging fire at several

11

business houses and pay some cash besides if Foust would give his wife, whereupon the husband acquiesced and the agreement was carried out to the letter.

Mrs. Foust is said to be a prepossessing woman of about thirty years of age. It was reported by telephone from Melville this afternoon the owner and his property, together with the latter's daughter, were living together in perfect amity and in blissful ignorance of the sensation the deal created.

The Daily Republican
Poplar Bluff, Mo.
April 4, 1913

WIFE PULLS HARROW

Unharnessed Mules and Fastens Wife to Implement

Missourian in Notable Case Confesses and is Given Thirty Days in Jail for His Act

Lafayette Choate of Liberty, Mo., charged with beating his wife and tying her to a harrow in a field on a farm near Birmingham last July, pleaded guilty and was sentenced to thirty days imprisonment by Judge Trimble yesterday. Prosecuting Attorney Simrall suggested Choate had been punished sufficiently. He has been in jail four months.

Choate was arrested after his wife had revealed his cruelty toward her in the Juvenile Court in Kansas City. It was shown he became enraged because she talked to another man. He fastened a rope around her waist and tied it to a team of mules he was driving and pulling a harrow around the field. She was driven around the field four times and, when she stumbled over the clods, he beat her with a club until she regained her feet. Her arms had been tied behind her.

After the mules were unharnessed, the husband tied her to the barn while he fed and watered the mules. Another time, the wife said, he took a chain and padlocked her hands together. After he went away, she found the key and released herself.

After the harassing episode, Mrs. Choate took her two boys and went to Kansas City. She since has applied for a divorce.

The Daily American Republic
Poplar Bluff, Mo.
November 22, 1911

48 LBS. OF FLOUR AND 8 LBS. OF LARD

Desha, Ark.

If you have not awakened three mornings in a row without food for breakfast, and very little or no food during the day, you may not comprehend the full meaning of this short note.

My father was in an automobile accident in August, 1930. He almost lost his left foot. He never regained much walking ability. We moved to the Dr. Jeffrey Farm in December, 1930. Few, if any, knew of my dad's disability. We had lost every penny we had in the bank, when they went broke in October, 1929. No one in Desha knew us. They had their own problems. We experienced a very difficult three years.

After three mornings without food, I decided to try a little search for some. I cleansed myself and put on my best clothing. They were not good, but they were clean. Then, I walked up to Floyd Massey's Store. He was a warm, friendly, straight-forward gentleman. I waited until everyone had gone out of the store. Then I gave my request for credit in the amount of one 48-lb. sack of flour and one 8-lb. pail of lard. The total was $1.75.

Mr. Massey responded by asking, "Is your dad home?"

I replied, "Yes, sir."

Mr. Massey came back sharply with, "Well, I don't think much of a man that would send his kid up here to ask me for food on the credit."

I said, "Sir, my dad did not send me. He doesn't know I'm here. If he did, he would be up here with a razor strap. I'm here on my own. We have not had a full meal in three days. We desperately need food."

He asked, "How do you plan on paying for this food?"

I explained, "At the moment, I don't know, but I will tell you I will pay for the food."

Mr. Massey said, "Well, my truck is not here now. Can you carry a 48-lb. sack of flour and an 8-lb. pail of lard?"

"Yes, sir! Yes, sir!" I said.

He helped me get the flour on my shoulder and placed the pail of lard in my hand. There was a feeling of exaltation, jubilation I had never experienced before. We lived one-half mile from the store. It seemed with every step, I became stronger, more mature.

When I came into sight of our house, my brother and sister ran out hollering, "Dick, Dick! Where did you get the flour and lard?"

I explained, "Floyd Massey let us have it on credit."

They exclaimed, "We can eat! We can eat!"

Wanda A. Rider, Ph.D.
Chester G. Rider, Litt. D.
Desha, Arkansas
Eastwind Press
Memphis Tenn.

100 YEARS WITHOUT A BATHROOM

As a young confederate soldier from Georgia, John Hinkle heard of golden opportunities in Arkansas. There were promises of free land for those willing to inhabit and improve it. He received information about plentiful jobs involving the timber industry and railroad construction.

The roads, even those considered main routes, were little more than trials through the forest; folks struggled to get their horse-drawn wagons through the rutted quagmires. This rugged way of travel would be considered all but impossible by modern standards, yet around 1890, John Hinkle and his family packed up their gear and set off to stake their claim. They took in the North Central Arkansas Ozarks in what is now Van Buren County, and claimed 160 acres as their homestead.

John felled trees to build his family's new log cabin home. With a broad-ax he hand hewed each one of them. He skillfully notched each log so the corners fit snug and tight. John's finished product – a cabin that for over a century has proved to have the same strength, form, and longevity as he himself exuded. The small cabin consisted of one main room, and a lean-to that may have been used as a kitchen or sleeping area. Above the main room, John built a loft. A crude ladder of white oak branches nailed to the wall led to the sleeping quarters overhead. This primitive cabin, without a bathroom or running water, must have seemed lavish when compared to life in a covered wagon.

Local legend holds that John Hinkle's craftsmanship was proven when a tornado descended – reaching in like a cookie jar thief – lifting the roof right off the very rooms that it faithfully and gallantly protected. The regain storm contemplated relocating the roof to another nearby county. Upon observing the cabin's interior integrity, the swirling tunnel of wind reconsidered. It instantly returned the weather guard – though a tad mangled and about half bubble off plumb – to its previously mounted sentry duty atop the cabin.

The Hinkles went on to raise eight children in this tiny cabin. Eight of them! To remember the names and hierarchy of their offspring, they composed a little ditty that went something like this, 'William, Lize, Jane and Than – Simm and Nome – Ike and Dan.' That rhyme, to this day, is the family's memory-stoking method of ancestral recollection.

The character-laden cabin in the woods served four generations, being lived in continuously until the 1940s. It was then abandoned for human habitation and was subjugated to serve as a barn for storing hay until the late 60's. One Hinkle descendant, Roy Hinesley, cleaned up the cabin and made it livable again. 'Uncle Roy,' as he was referred to by the local population, could be seen daily walking or hitching a ride six miles down Highway 9 into the town of Shirley, where he would sit on the porch at the general store and visit with folks all day long.

During the 20-odd years that Roy lived here, there were some renovations made. He added electricity and running water. He built a less archaic stairway leading to the loft, which is now a finished room.

Neither signs nor travel booklet write-ups point to this little structure's existence, yet an astounding number of people are drawn to stop, marvel at and photograph it. John Hinkle would be proud to know that the wonderful little homestead would be a landmark in time. He would be pleased to know that when caught by the public eye, this time capsule of his would set into motion the imaginations and emotions of those who appreciate the strength and craftsmanship of those of that long-gone era.

Roy Hinesley's nephew, Wendell, who was born in the cabin, currently owns and takes care of its upkeep. Wendell has plans to refurbish it and maybe add a bedroom and a bathroom. Would this be progress or a travesty? You be the judge. I myself can only answer this question with another. After one hundred years, a bathroom? Who needs it!

Dana J. Leason
The Ozarks Mountaineer
June/July, 1997

SOAP TIME

Poplar Bluff, Mo.

Soap making time on the farm in Missouri Ozarks has come and gone. In the pantry of many homes today you could find layers of large cakes of hard soap, and many containers filled with soft soap.

Despite the fact that modern times have changed many housewives, there are still quite a number who save all scraps of meat, grease and meat rinds until soap making time comes.

Those who have made soap for family use declare the best times to get good results is in the dark of the moon in the month of March. Others declare it as superstition, and one farm wife declared she did not believe in the "bunk" but she always made her soap during that time because she preferred not to take chances.

How It Is Done

Soap making is an art of which few persons are well versed. Scraps of meat are saved all year. In March, that meat is placed in the yard kettle, under which a good fire is started. Two or three cans of lye, about 16 pounds of meat, ten gallons of water and a handful of salt are all that may be required to make soap.

The combination is boiled until the meat dissolves. A chicken feather is then stuck into the liquid and the cooker counts ten. When the feather is removed, it may be burned and it may not. If the feather is burned off, the soap is too strong. If it does not burn off before another 10 and 20, the soap is just right and the fire is pulled.

Make Own Lye

The more resourceful women even manufacture their own lye. It is a simple process. Put some wood ashes in a hopper and let the hopper remain outdoors in the rain until the ashes begin to sour. Then add more water gradually. As the water seeps through, catch it in a bucket. Chemicals have already done their work, and in the bottom of the bucket will be found lye and potash.

It is not so much the financial condition of a farm family that figures in homemade soap. Many farm wives with plenty of money for "store bought" soap, prefer their own make. They consider it a wife's duty to help her husband in her part of the farm life.

Daily American Republic
Poplar Bluff, Mo.
March 21, 1935

MAKING MOLASSES

West Plains, Mo.

When autumn leaves are falling and there's a hint of winter in the air, you'll find the children of the late George and Maudie Bradford busy as the bees that swarm around the sweet, crushed stalks of sugar cane. They are carrying on a tradition started by their great-grandfather, Warren Boone, more than 100 years ago, a business carried on by their grandfather, John Bradford, Sr. and then by their father, George Bradford. They are making molasses.

"We're the fourth generation making molasses, "Ella Bradford Sherrill recalled. "We thought we could go ahead making molasses without a hitch, but the first year we made molasses without Dad, we found it wasn't that easy."

Not that easy for Ella meant getting up at 3:30 a.m. to cook a large dinner to take to the Gene Bradford farm where the molasses is made. Then she helps strip the knife-edged leaves from the cane in the fields by hand and usually stands over the hot vat of boiling juice, stirring or skimming as it cooks down into the thick, golden product.

Her three brothers, Elmer, Emmett, and Gene, plant cultivate, and haul the cane to the home place where Gene lives and where great-grandfather Boone (born in 1818) homesteaded.

The cane stalks are fed into a mill where huge steel rollers crush out the greenish juice that is strained into a cloth-covered barrel. The mill is powered by a mule, horse, or tractor.

"Mules are best," said Ella, "they work slow and easy."

Tales of getting clothing caught in the mill press or losing a hand or arm make the Bradford's extra cautious when feeding the stalks into the mill.

The pummies (crushed stalks) are thrown into a pile and buckets of the cane juice are poured in one end of the nine-foot long molasses pan mounted on waist-high steel legs over a roaring firebox. This is enclosed with tin and walled up with native rock to protect those standing over it against the intense heat.

The molasses pan still used is a steel one bought by great-grandfather Boone which was made in Chattanooga, Tennessee right after the War Between the States.

The pan is sectioned so that as the juice thickens, it is moved from one compartment to the next by a trap door like device. Someone has to stand by the boiling mixture constantly to stir and keep the green scum skimmed from the top. The molasses can burn very easily so it needs supervision all the time. Testing is done by holding a ladle aloft to 'drip' the juice to see if it falls slowly into large, thick drops. When it does, it is ready to pour into clean glass jugs.

Depending on the ripeness and sugar content of the cane, it takes 10 to 20 gallons of the green juice to make one gallon of molasses. It's best to get the cane when the weather is hot and dry before frost. Frostbitten can be used but the quality of the molasses isn't as good.

Ella's father, George Bradford, used to haul barrels of sorghum into Willow Springs by team and wagon from the farm about 13 miles northeast of town. The molasses brought 35 cents a gallon in those days compared to $12.00 a gallon now.

A lot of hard work goes into the sweet, sticky business of molasses making. But Ella finds it worthwhile when she takes a pan of hot biscuits and a jar of the amber syrup to a friend and discovers other friends want some too.

Katherine Bryan Cummines
West Plains Gazette
West Plains, Mo.
Winter, 1983

OUTHOUSE, CATALOG A NATURAL PAIRING

Cabool, Mo.

The February wind was howling and creating its own unique wind song through the cracks. Snow had drifted slightly through these same cracks.

I could barely keep my mind on my business. The familiar Sears-Roebuck catalog lay open beside me. Even the women's lingerie section held no appeal for this 12-year old farm boy on this cold morning. After using the indoor facilities at school and in the homes of a few friends who lived in town, I had come to believe that perhaps warmth and convenience could offset the quiet solitude of our outhouse.

In fact, I'm sure it was on this cold, snowy morning that I pictured a warm bathroom.

Our town of Cabool got electricity in 1928. The main reasons electricity didn't reach our farm until 1949 were the high cost of bringing electrical service through the rugged Ozark hills, delay due to World War II and the sparse population out our way.

We got electricity (the normal power for water pumps) in 1949, but due to the droughts and hard times on the farm in the early 1920s, we didn't get an inside bathroom on our farm until 1957.

We kept our outhouse for a year or two after that because Dad still preferred its quiet and solitude. I believe it was after the cold winter of 1958 that he decided the inside version with pre-softened paper was going to be OK after all.

The Sears Catalog

It would be difficult to measure the impact of the coming of the Sears Roebuck catalog on Ozarks hill folks. The catalog started coming in the early 1900s.

The radio came in the late 1930s and television in the 1950s. Each of these brought hill folks more into the mainstream of American life. These major steps opened us up to a larger world, but each also led to taking away our uniqueness.

Prior to the 1950s, the Ozarks dialect and terminology were alive and well. We had been protected by the late arrival of rural electricity and natural isolation that existed in our sparsely populated area of the Ozarks.

The colorful Ozarks language and rugged individual style of those who made a hard living in our hills always made my home area so rich and meaningful to me. With progress, this life has now been lost for all time.

The Sears-Roebuck catalog made us aware of all the wonderful items that existed in America. Most of these we would never have – we could only "wish".

We had a huge mailbox over by the main road. We could hardly wait for our orders of basic needs and farm supplies to show up at our box. Even baby chicks came to our mailbox by way of Sears-Roebuck. My dad also ordered all the electrical supplies he needed to wire our house when electricity finally got to our farm.

But the final use of the Sears catalog was in our outhouse. Since we got a spring-summer catalog and a fall-winter catalog, we had new pictures to look at every six months. And we also had a new supply of toilet paper.

Leroy Walls
Springfield News-Leader
Cabool, Mo.

Chapter Three

THE GOOD OLD DAYS

THE OLD COUNTRY STORE

Growing up on a farm fifty years ago, I looked forward to summer. On Friday night, I wished for a "gully washer" because it usually meant a holiday from Saturday's chores. After a heavy rain the horses, mules, plows and hoes stood idle and boys like me donned clean overalls and headed for the country store. We walked because that was our only means of transportation.

"Let's foot it", we'd say, and skip off on bare feet, "splitting" every mud puddle between our homes and the country store.

Any boy who wore a pair of blue jeans was considered rich. Those of us in overalls were usually without hats and were wearing nature's shirt. If we were fortunate we carried a thin dime. The dime would purchase a large Pepsi and a Baby Ruth candy bar. This, to us, was "eatin' high on the hog!"

The old stores were usually constructed of cypress wood, had a gas pump and a kerosene tank out front, had a few ad signs in the windows and carried the bare food necessities. The center of the stores had seats consisting of blocks of wood and nail kegs. The seats would be filled and "spillin' over" with men and boys from the neighborhood.

It was taboo for a young boy to smoke for we were told, "It will stunt your growth." The men rolled their smokes from the contents of a Prince Albert can or from the sacks of "Bull Derm." Some men carried their plugs of tobacco others had only a "chaw."

The store was a social gathering for the men of the community to catch up on news, to settle world problems and a place to air out their daily frustrations. It was a place for a boy to listen, not to be heard. On news, the men were usually three days ahead of any daily newspaper. The old stores were places for the men to "chew the fat", rest, relax and tell some tall stories. I'll never forget the man who boasted of having the fastest running car ever to roll of the assembly line, a 1935 Chevrolet. He said he once drove from sunrise to sunset in one hour and fifteen minutes.

Another notorious yarn spinner told of taking his old L.C. Smith shotgun and plenty of shells, using a raft to cross the St. Francis River and entered the "Bottomlands" one early, fall morning for a duck hunt. At 10 o'clock he'd killed enough ducks to make two feather and one straw bed.

We head another fellow who believed he was the fisherman of all fishermen. He told he had been fishing in the St. Francis River below Fisk, Missouri using a trotline and green, puckering persimmons for bait. He told something kept stealing his bait and he kept replenishing it with more persimmons.

He finally landed a big flathead catfish. He estimated the fish to weigh 50 pounds. He put the fish in the back of his old truck, drove straight home, got the old cotton scales out of the shed and the fish only weighed 6 and one-half pounds.

The good old days weren't too easy for our parents for they had all the worries and responsibilities. We seldom ever got in a hurry. If we did it was to go to another gathering place. We certainly weren't in a hurry to get back to the farm chores which started before daybreak and ended after dark.

The old country store was a highlight of my childhood. I can see the tanned, lined faces of the men and hear their discussions of life as they knew it. I can remember the tall tales, the hearty laughter, the young wide-eyed boys sitting on nail kegs and drinking Pepsis, all part of a Saturday ritual. We only had ten cents to spend, but the memories are priceless.

Jay Mondy
Wappapello, MO
June 3, 1997

Old Magill Store
Hendrickson, MO
Butler County

HOG KILLING TIME IS HERE

Folks go to country after backbones and spareribs at this season

Butler County, MO

This is the time for all good city folks to go to the country—after backbones, spareribs and country sausage. The advent of freezing weather has opened the annual seasons for hog killing, and not a few farmers have taken advantage of the prevailing cool spell to lay in a supply of roast beef and round steak, utilizing the proverbial fatted calf.

Butchering methods haven't changed much in the decade or two just past. For the most part city cousins still wait until all of the work is done before they show up to claim their part of the hams, the shoulders, or perhaps just a helping of head cheese or a potful of cracklins.

In one respect, there has been a change. A growing number of Butler County farmers are taking advantage of special facilities in the way of a chilling and curing room. Farmers kill their hogs at home, bring the carcass to the local plant, and there carve the meat as desired. Each customer is assigned a space were his individual supply of meat may be kept at unvarying temperature throughout the curing period. Superior texture and flavor, less shrinkage and absolutely no spoilage, are some of the features claimed for this system. Several thousand pounds of meat were processed by farmers last fall and winter at the Ark-Mo plant, and more is expected during the present season.

Methods Unchanged

While the underlying methods of butchering have not changed much, there are two separate schools of thought with reference to starting the works. Some farmers, reflects the county agent, F. H. Darnell, still swear by the time-honored custom of tapping the squealing porker on the head with an axe or a sledge to stun it before sticking.

Others have adopted what they consider a more modern and direct method of sticking the hog without benefit of stunning. As one old-timer explained, "You can't tell 'em" all about it on paper, but unless you're on to your job, you're liable to have a lively rasselin' match on your hands." For the sake of those whose proximity to hog killing has been limited to a plate of pork chops in a restaurant, the latest approved method of sticking hogs is herewith described by County Agent Darnell:

Immediate sticking is preferable to shooting or stunning, as it is just as humane and you can be sure the hog will bleed out well. You can draw the live hog up by one hind leg with a block and tackle, or you can throw the hog on its back and straddle it with your legs pressed against its sides just behind its forelegs. Grasp each foreleg near the foot and pull up slightly.

With the hog squarely on its back, the man who is to do the sticking stands squarely in front of the hog, pushes down on the snout, inserts a six to eight-inch sticking knife about two inches in front of the breast bone and directly over the midline. He then works the point of the knife downward and underneath the front edge of the breastbone, the cuts straight downward toward the backbone and forward toward the head.

Sticking in this way will cut the veins and arteries where they leave the heart. No attempt should be made to stick the heart, since it should be allowed to remain in action as long as possible to clear the blood from the smaller vessels.

You see, it's really very simple. Just a single swish with the family butcher knife and the job's done.

Next Step

Next step, as every good farmer and hog sticker knows, is scalding. And even this apparently simple process is made more or less difficult by the experts.

It is best to keep the scalding water below 150 degrees if the weather is not too cold. A temperature of 140 to 144 degrees F. is considered best, except in the fall of the year when winter hair is beginning to grow, when the temperature should be 146 to 150, advised Darnell.

Then go ahead something like this: If the air temperature is below freezing, start scalding at 170 degrees as the water usually cools too fast at a lower temperature. When the Barrel scalding method is used, a reserve supply of boiling water should be kept in two small kettles so that hot water may be added as needed.

It is always best to have a thermometer to determine the exact temperature of the water. This will prevent setting the hair on the hog. In the absence of a thermometer, a rough estimate of the water temperature may be determined by dipping your finger in the water three times. The third time it should burn. Sometimes some wood ashes or lye may be added to the scalding water to help loosen the dirt or scurf.

Wash all mud and blood from the hide before scalding. Insert a hog hook or hay hook in the lower jaw under the tongue and scald the hind legs first. Keep the hog in motion so that no part will rest against the side of the barrel. A scraper is mighty handy in removing the hair and scurf.

Air Meat

Now the job is about half done, but there isn't a pork chop in sight yet. Our farmer-butcher next removes the waste and then permits nature or the Ark-Mo plant to chill the carcass thoroughly. Some farmers claim the "animal heat" airs out better in the open, but regardless of the fact, chilling is considered and essential step before proceeding with the actual carving.

Here again individual taste, size of the family to be fed, as well as the size of the now-dressed porker, enter for consideration.

A 225-pound moderately fat hog produces the best "family" size cuts, advises the adviser, Frank Darnall. Such hogs will yield hams and three-rib shoulders weighing about 16 pounds each, and bacon strips and loins weighing about 10 to 12 pounds. These cuts are of desirable size to cure and store after smoking, and can be cut into satisfactory economical slices for roasts for cooking. Heavier hogs normally produce a greater proportion of lard. They also produce bacon and hams that some families consider too fat.

Then a few more pointers and the family can enjoy its first mess of fresh "ham'ans"

Cut Them Longer

Hams that are to be held-through the summer should be cut reasonably long and the protecting covering of the fat should not be trimmed off. Where a good quality of sliced bacon is desired, the ribs should be removed and the pieces given a smooth trim. Whether used fresh, frozen, cured or canned, loins should be cut rather short and most of the back fat removed from them. Loin roasts carrying a smooth, even covering of fat will cook more quickly and satisfactorily than those that have been trimmed so as to expose the lean. Most of the fat should be removed from loins that are to be boned or canned. If large quantities of lard are needed, all the cuts should be trimmed rather closely.

Center splitting the hog carcasses—which is sawing down the center of the backbone—makes it possible to use the loin in any of several ways. Where the backbone is chopped out, the remainder of the loin muscle is usually available only for sausage. If the backbone is a much-demanded delicacy, it is often desirable to split one or two hogs that way but to center split the other carcasses so as to produce a maximum amount of curing meat.

Daily American Republic
Poplar Bluff, MO
December 24, 1934

PICKING COTTON

Cotton picking was a damnable job for man, woman, boy or girl-a hated task. In the early thirties cotton brought six cents a pound in the lint. The picker received from fifty cents to sixty cents per hundred pounds picked. Pick sacks manufactured out of ten-ounce, white ducking came in two sizes: seven-and-one-half feet and nine feet. The seven-and-one-half foot sack sold for $1.40 to $1.60. The nine-foot sack cost $1.80 to $1.95. Seventy-five per cent of the sacks sold were nine-foot sacks. An average picker could pick two-hundred pounds in nine hours. There were some 250 and 300 pound pickers, but they were very few. I picked 232 pounds one time. My day was usually 210 to 215 pounds.

Cotton picking took its toll on the fingers and back. One lady told her husband that a man who loved his wife would not let her pick cotton. The husband replied, "How can a wife who loves her husband so cruelly embarrass her husband in public?" There was a big laugh and the cotton picking continued.

A cotton picking day was long- a long day while picking, a long day before going to pick while getting everything ready, and a long day after getting home, getting dinner and getting ready for tomorrow.

When the picker started in the morning, there was usually the dew to contend with. The dew penetrated the fingers. They were soft and vulnerable to the sharp points of the cotton burr. This picker, early in the season, would get one or two burr points under the nail and it would remain sore for the duration of the season. There were also insects and stringy green worms to harass pickers. In the early picking season, the hot sun on the back made prickly heat an old, painful buddy.

I could not get a big thrill by switching my thoughts to my lunch time because I always had three biscuits filled with fried potatoes. With the biscuit and grease on cold potatoes, it was not a great lunch but at least it was fuel for the body. I was happy to have it. There was never enough water. Thirst, hunger, and tiredness made very poor companions.

The cotton rows were usually a quarter of a mile long and the cotton wagon was parked at one end. The pickers would carry their empty sacks to the far end and pick toward the wagon.

To make a cotton scale stand, the wagon tongue would be raised and propped up by the neck yoke. The hook o the top of the scales would be hooked onto the metal attachment at the end of the wagon tongue. Only the farmer or someone assigned by him weighed the cotton. The individual pickers had to keep their weights written down also or they did not have any gripe coming. All of the men and boys emptied their own sacks. The girls would beg the boys to empty their sacks. The boys would tease that they were not going to empty them, but they were happy to have the girls' attention.

Pickers outside the family paid on the weekend usually. I would have $5.00 to $5.25 coming. This was a massive amount of money to me.

23

My mother would encourage me to keep an eye on school needs: a pair of shoes at $2.00, two pairs of overalls at $1.75 a pair, two Chambray Shirts at 79 cents each, one knit cap at 79 cents, and one heavy coat at $3.00 to $4.00. School books were a large item. The cost was an average of two dollars per book with five books being required for each grade. At this time there were no free textbooks. I could never buy more than two textbooks. I always tried to buy the English and the history books. I could remember from the lesson or borrow the other books long enough to get most of the assignments.

My family could usually spare me about four weeks in the fall with the firm understanding that my money must go for my school clothing and books.

I worked on Saturday if the farmer would let me. Over the four week period, I would get to work two or three Saturdays. I did not see this as a burden. It was a grand opportunity. I was happy to have it. After school started, I would get to pick cotton two or three Saturdays. This always helped me out of the last minute pinch for a book or a pair of overalls.

Wanda A Rider, Ph. D.
Chester G. Rider, Ph. D.
Desha, Arkansas
Eastwind Press
Memphis, Tenn.

OLD COUNTRY SCHOOLS

As one travels through the countryside of this great land of ours, important landmarks of a vital part of our heritage are sadly missing – <u>OLD COUNTRY SCHOOLS.</u> While some few have been saved and serve as museums, county churches, community centers, homes, etc. others were allowed to fall into disrepair and nothing remain – not even the foundations, which would have been carried away to make room for farmland or other modern buildings.

The "little red school house" was a very important factor in the development of this nation. In many instances it shared its place with the community church until there were ample resources to have both buildings. It was a focal point for the meetings held to guide community development. Even though the little school house was primitive and very simple in its operation, it was the backbone of the development of the sophisticated educational institutions one sees today. <u>SOMETHING MUST HAVE BEEN VERY RIGHT ABOUT ITS SYSTEM BECAUSE JUST STOP AND CONSIDER THE GREAT PEOPLE WHO CAME FORTH FROM THESE LITTLE HAVENS OF LEARNING.</u>

An early school day began with the resonant sound of the huge iron bell hanging in the school belfry which sat atop the school building. If there was no big bell, the teacher used a hand bell which she shook vigorously from the front steps. The children lined up before marching into the schoolroom, where they stood beside their desks until after completion of a morning ritual. This usually consisted of the repetition of the pledge of allegiance to the United States flag. The sound of the ringing bell was the signal to the surrounding community that all was well and that school business was going on as usual.

One does not often thing of this, but school houses had their own characteristic smell, especially on opening day when the building smelled of stacks and stacks of dried out books mingled with that of the light coat of oil applied to the wood floors to keep down dust. In hot weather there was the piney smell of hot resin melted or the tangy smell of cypress planking both baking by the sun's heat. Spicy smells from children's lunches permeated the room along with the clean smell of freshly washed and starched clothes and freshly scrubbed heads, hands, and faces. Then there was the ever-present chalk dust which accompanied students working at the blackboards.

Earliest schools on the fringes of the frontiers were log cabins of the simplest sort. As a community grew, so did the school. Most of them were one room buildings with a bell tower perched on top. Some grew into two rooms or more as the community population grew. In earliest times they were painted red – hence the term "little red school house" with gradually the hue changing to white. Many times one side was a bank of windows (Pity ALL in summer if that bank of windows faced the west!)

Water was pumped from a squeaky old-fashioned iron pump or from a well. In the cold or winter, the pump had to be primed during school hours and the prime had to be let out to keep the pump from freezing up. (A job that required special knowledge which most country kids-even girls – were born with.)

In winter the building was heated by a huge wood or coal stove with a metal jacket around it. On extra cold rainy days steam rose in the air as this stove jacket was draped with wet coats and gloves – sometimes with wet stockings if someone had fallen or been pushed into a nearby pond. Many times the warmth never reached the floor, and our feet were often cold the whole day through. On those days the children were grouped as closely to the stove as possible. Conversely, in the hot summer time (no air conditioners existed then!) all windows were thrown open to catch any errant breeze. Even so, in the very hot part of the day the teacher might take her students to the cooling shade of a tree where lessons were recited just as if inside.

Outdoor privies with their accompanying wasps, spiders, spider webs, snakes and lizards were the rule rather that the exception. My mother relates excitedly of the time a blue stripped lizard ran up a girl's leg causing all kinds of pandemonium. It was the janitor's duty to keep the wasp, dirt dauber nests, and spider webs knocked down and to regularly dump lime down the toilet holes to keep the smell down. (This not so successful).

Regardless of the lack of modern amenities there was much fun and laughter emanating from these old buildings. We had spelling bees and ciphering matches; other schools challenged us and we challenged back. Everyone looked forward to these contests – and, must say, those old schools turned out some very efficient and brilliant citizens. Little ones learned from listening to the bigger ones as the recited.

Sports consisted of soft ball, volley-ball, and dodge ball and sometimes track sports such as high jump, broad jump, and foot races. Much friendly and unfriendly rivalry developed between neighboring schools. Many memories were made and cherished for years to come.

And **PIE SUPPERS!** Who can forget those? – With their cake walks, spooniest couple and prettiest girl contests. Even though money was really scarce the community really came together to raise funds for the school's much-needed equipment.

Communities were held together by school events, and the schools marked the joyous and solemn occasions. Once, when Mr. McWilliams died, (He lived about one forth mile from the school). Miss Mamie had the school children bring flowers from their homes in the morning of the funeral. The flowers were made into a large bouquet. A delegation of the older girls took the bouquet to the family home as a tribute to the deceased and his family from our school. Then Miss Mamie had the younger children to carefully watch the road to see when the funeral procession started to leave the family home. Then they were immediately to run back and tell her so that when the procession started down the road for the cemetery she could toll the school bell for Mr. McWilliams. She said "Now, everybody must help me count to 46 as she slowly tolled the bell one time for each of his 46 years. A very moving tribute. This event happened when my mother was one of the little ones watching in the road. She is now 93 years old and remembers it vividly.

Gone are most of these early school buildings, but with us will always remain the influences which they left behind them.

Therma Glass
Broseley, MO

Chapter Four

THEIR WORK WAS DEVINE

OLD-TIME CAMP MEETING

St. Joe, AR

Hell fire and eternal torment or eternal bliss with a harp and crown, or is there a sort of middle ground for those of us who wouldn't feel at home in either place?

The hill farmer has laid by his corn and cotton. His stock is on the open range and needs no care. The early fishing season is past, and he either has had his fill of fish or quit with the conclusion there are no fish I the streams anymore. The hunting season is still in the distant months of November and December. The harvest of 25 bushels to the acre still allows eight weeks for guessing the yield at 75. The budget of the hill farmer does not include the expense of vacation travel beyond Farmers' Week at Fayetteville.

So with every other task performed, and nothing else to occupy the farmer, the weeks will drag wearily before the commencement of fall plowing, he will now devote a season to his spiritual rehabilitation. For this is "camp meetin' time", this is the season of revival meetings, of protracted meetings and the shouting of "Hallelujah!" is heard in the land.

The camp meeting from "time immemorial" has been one of the characteristic institutions of the rural community in America and England, and in the hills of Arkansas. It has been preserved in all its pristine glory. "Glory" is a fitting word to use because it is heard so often now, even if the Republicans are not talking about it. When the capacity of meeting houses is small, and the nights are not, the outdoor arbor is now, and from pioneer days has been, the ideal auditorium. Posts are set up in an open space, the top is latticed with poles, and the whole covered with leafy boughs cut from trees and bushes. Rude benches of rough sawed boards serve for seats, and at one end a raised platform with a little table on which reposes the Bible, makes the pulpit.

Sometimes the arbor is so low and the pulpit so high, the preacher is hidden from view of those at the rear and seems to speak from out of the leafy boughs, giving his words a sort of sepulchral tone. This sometimes has a disastrous effect on the inebriated, if any, who congregate at the rear of the crowd, if at all.

The meetings are just beginning, yet within a radius of five miles of St. Joe there are six separate revivals in progress now, and a person kept by illness from attending, may sit on his porch and hear the sounds of three or four of them borne in on the still night air. Sickness is about the only misfortune that will prevent anyone from attending. The voices of the night are now happy voices filled with religious fervor, and often they are shouting voices and some are weeping.

So numerous are the camp meeting places that each largely serves its own community, and there is not much need for "camping out". There are some preachers, however, who have a side circle of admirers, and visitors come a great distance to their meetings. Such visitors either "make themselves at home" with some friend in the neighborhood, or camp by a nearby spring. There are clear, cool springs everywhere in the hills.

This is the season of bountiful feasting. Too, "Springers are ripe". Their raves reaches that blissful age midway between the joys of chickenhood and the cares of henhood known as "fryin' size". Watermelons and red tomatoes are "laughing on the vine", and the best of all, roasting ears are blossoming in every corn field. The visitor who camps out either brings a week's supply with him, or is welcome to reach out his hand and partake of the bursting stores of the neighborhood.

The Real Arkansas Preacher

What about the preachers? Magazine and news writers from the East seem to have rare sport in characterizing the Arkansas preacher, and coining an imaginary dialect. The Arkansas preacher, in the main, is not different from the New England preacher, the Iowa preacher or the California preacher. We name those three sections because three preachers reared and trained here now have pastorates in those states. The most illiterate is far ahead of the Indiana preacher who said to my ox, "Come Ah, Buckah". Many hill preachers have an assortment of perfect English of which any college graduate might be proud.

Of two whom we have in mind, one was a pioneer preacher near St. Joe, who died a few years ago. His name was George Davis. Another is Jesse Rose, now living east of Marshall. Neither was able to boast of much schooling. Both farmed for a livelihood. Yet both preached sermons which, judged by the accepted rules of logic and literary excellence and dramatic power, might have been credited to Phillips Brooks and passed as his own.

"How know these men letters, having never learned" one visitor asked, and a student answered for them. "Their English is the English of King James. They know their Bible from cover to cover. They can quote whole chapters from memory, without the mistake of a syllable. One of them could recite all day passages he has memorized, and not repeat. The grammar of the Bible has become their grammar".

But all the preachers of the hills are not this gifted in the mother tongue, and it is from the language of the more unschooled that the literary contortionists have constructed an imaginary language.

And while these writers have in this manner raised many laughs at the Arkansas preacher, the objects of their ridicule have "come right back at 'em," to use their own expression. We heard one of them "lashing out" in the following style this week:

The Morals Issue

"They sent a feller in here named Davenport. Now I know there is a heap of Davenports here, and he may be kin to ye, but I want ye to think no hardness of me, fer I'm talkin' of what he sed and not him. We had a dope head come in here once, with his needle and his little budget of morfin. He talked jes like this feller writes. He makes light of weuns and we make light of him. Down in New York they're one people and out here we're another. I read his paper and them stories thar. Weuns have the old time idea out here thet a gal's first kiss from a man should be the engagement kiss, but from their stories of nekin' and pettin', it seems their cigarette smokin' gals is mauled over by every young feller in the town before they is married, which is six or eight times before they is thirty."

The old preacher stroked his long beard, and then bit on a suitable chew of "home grown" and spat over the pulpit while waiting for his words to soak in.

Squelching the Scoffer

Camp meetings are generally orderly. They are a favorite gathering place for the young folks, and perhaps there is a little quiet courting, at least some "getting acquainted", but few rowdies get far. The reason is that hill people have an old fine noting that religious meetings should not be disturbed, and every man in the assembly will, at once, give effective aid to quell an outbreak. His family is there, and it must be respected. One overgrown fellow, the neighbors called him a "big old boy", crowned himself with a girl's hat, and leaned against a supporting pillar at the rear of the arbor, making a cigarette and plainly annoying the old preacher.

It was not long until the old preacher got around to his case. The story of the Prodigal Son was recited. "I imagine he was a leerin' lout, and I imagines she thought the gals said he was purty. I imagines he was given to immorality." The preacher said "immorality". "And I imagines after the old man had filled him up on steaks and he put what was left of the fatted calf into a basket and said: 'Take this home to your wife and younguns, which you run off from, which ain't had a decent meal in two years'."

The bonnet-decked Smart Alec had faded away into the outer shadows.

Now the least interesting feature of the religious gatherings at this season is the joint debate. And, incidentally, the marathon preachers reported from other sections have nothing on the hill preacher. Many of them will deliver two-hour sermons three and four times a day. The debates often last all day and far into the night.

An interesting series of debates is advertised for the latter part of this month at an outdoor meeting near Deer, in Newton County. Rev. Walter W. Lemon, Christian preacher, and W.S. Tucker, a Bible student, will be the debaters. One theme will be "The Suffering that Shall Never End." Other themes are advertised. These joint debates are generally good natured and free from unfriendly references. Each debater has his Bible, while the adherentness of the rivals take opposite sides in the arbor. Many sit with their Bibles handy, follow the references quoted and often interrupt when there is a misquotation. Sometimes an adherent will help his champion by interposing with Bible passages.

Of course, the climax of the meeting is the "call for converts". In the ordinary small community it is a matter of neighborhood concern as to "who will go forward". Will this old toper, groggy from many about with John Barleycorn. Finally give up and "surrender"? Will this old sister who helped exterminate the buffalo race, by pinching nickels, finally come to love her eternal future more than her money?

"Watch the backsliders coming up for rejuvenation." Over in Newton there is a man who proudly testifies he has backslid and been reconverted 36 times, but this time he knows it will stick.

One claim can be supported by the records of every community where meetings are held, and after a meeting there is always a season of "good works" – of generous giving to the poor, a forgetting of old scores, a general meeting is the season when people get together for their community interests – their schools, their church, their lodges, and even "business is better".

Following religious professions by the previously "ungenerate", there are unique demonstrations. Sometimes playing cards, rouge and other alleged "agencies of sin" are brought to the penitent bench. A few years ago a woman brought an old forests and tossed them in the pile of "denials". Two years ago a splendidly equipped copper still was hauled out in the night and left in front of the meeting arbor on Highway No. 65, south of St. Joe. A note placed on the boiler stated the former owner had been converted in the arbor, and was forsaking his evil ways forever.

After the meeting, there is the public baptizing of the new additions to the church. In this section are many places which have been known for generations as favorite baptizing places – in Buffalo River, Mill Creek, Dry Creek and Richland. These places are graveled-bottom holes in the stream, where the depth is well known and where there is no danger. Once, years ago, a convert grabbed Rev. Stephen Still, then an aged preacher, while he was conducting a baptizing by immersion, and the two were almost drowned before those on the shore could reach them. However, such accidents in the water are rare.

The Missionary Baptist has perhaps a larger following in the hills than any other denomination, although the Christian, "Holiness", and other denominations have many disciples. In Searcy County, the M.E. Church, South, and the M.E. Church of the North have separate organizations.

Sister Helped Him Out

What of the pay of the preacher? That has always been a big "bone of contention" among church folks in the hills. Should he work for the money, or should he work for the "Lord".

An old preacher led up to the subject in a rather adroit manner this week. "Ye almost left us on sufferance last winter", he added. "I wuz down on my back sick, and no medicine in the house and nothin' to eat. Once sister brung me a half bottle of carditt and I took that, and some brung some turnips and we cooked them, and then the Red Cross came."

He concluded a long description of the privations he and the "old woman" had endured with the bright hope that all of his church members would prosper and would be minded to help this winter.

Generally, the preacher lives as well as his flock. They share whatever they have in meat, flour, fruit and vegetables, and pound parties and box suppers help out with the clothing problem.

The brush arbor-camp meeting will soon be over this year. Then the crops will be layed by and, once again, it will be "Hallelujah" time!

The American Republic
Poplar Bluff, MO
July 27, 1931

PIONEER PREACHING IN MISSOURI

How a Service Was Interrupted by the Live Stock

Pike County, Mo

Doubtless no pioneer had more vicissitudinous experiences in the early settlement of Missouri than the itinerant pioneer preacher, who labored, generally without pecuniary recompense, to spread the gospel among the inhabitants of the then sparsely settled country. His duties were arduous and often attended with a great degree of danger.

Perhaps among the many reminiscences of these days the following incident related by Judge Fagg, one of Pike County's prominent citizens, will illustrate the vicissitudes of the preacher and the period in which he lived.

One of the earliest settlements in Pike County was made by John Mackey, and was about one mile west of the line of bluffs near the Mississippi River, which marked the western boundary of the well-known Calumet Creek Valley.

The Mackey home was on the old trail from St. Louis to the Salt River settlements, along which all the "rangers" and settlers passed until the war of 1812-14.

"Aunt Nancy" Mackey, wife of the well known pioneer, was a woman of extraordinary courage and inured to the hardships of the time. She was the first to reach the O'Neil cabin after the historic massacre of the household, and assisted in collecting the mutilated remains of the wife and children and prepared them for interment.

The house of "Brother John" and "Aunt Nancy" Mackey was a noted meeting place in those days for those religiously inclined, and nearly all the pioneers were. It was a characteristic dwelling place of the time. Built of logs, which were un-hewn, the floors were made of "puncheons," and naturally the structure was well ventilated in the summer season, but which in the winter time afforded the entrance of chilling blasts that were uncomfortable to even those hardy folk. Sometimes an undressed plank was laid un-nailed upon the "sleepers" and then the crack through which the wind blew, were both plentiful and capacious. One room – in fact, there was seldom another – was an all-purpose place for the whole family. The "loft," or low-ceilinged apartment above, was the sleeping place of some members of the family, usually the older children. However, despite the primitive conditions prevailing, happiness pervaded the scene, and sickness was less frequent than now.

"Brother John" Mackey's domicile was just such a structure as has been described. On the afternoon of a bitterly cold day in 1821, a visiting brother came to the settlement, and "Aunt Nancy" prevailed upon him to preach at her cabin that evening. The preacher consented, and despite the snowstorm that was raging, couriers went out through the sparsely settled neighborhood, inviting the settlers to assemble that night at the Mackey home, in order to worship. They were rigid in their customs relating to attendance at religious meetings, and nothing less than severe sickness was considered a sufficient excuse for absence. The wind grew more furious and the snowflakes fell faster, but a goodly number trudged or rode through the snow to the appointed meeting place.

All the hogs on the place were in attendance, too, having crawled under the "puncheon" floor to seek shelter from the storm, and when the preacher got u to read his text, the "porkers," in their eagerness to congregate near the fireplace, fought, bit, and squealed with such uproariousness as only twenty or more can produce, that the attempts of the preacher to make himself heard were for the time unavailing.

Finally the hogs settled down to some degree of quietude, and the sermon progressed. A little later, however, the door, which was insecurely fastened, was blown down by a gust of wind, and a large sow walked in with that nonchalance that indicated her familiarity with the premises. Before she had reached the fireplace, a small boy, a member of the family, in joyful welcome of some opportunity to break the monotony of the tedious sermon, seized the opportunity – and the sow by the ear – jumped on her back and, holding her ears, rode the swine, which was squealing vociferously all the while, around the room, through the congregation creating consternation in general, particularly among the female contingent of the assembly. At last, after several circuits of the room, the lad rode the animal out of doors.

In the meantime, a flock of geese had walked in the open door which had not been closed. Unlike the sow, they were obstinate, and, standing in the middle of the floor, stretched forth their necks and kept up a din of constant chattering. "Aunt Nancy," with rate tact and diplomacy, contrived to get rid of her uninvited guests. From the "jamb" she took an ear of corn. Then, walking backwards, shelled the corn, tolling the geese along and calling to them in the gentlest and most persuasive of tones. The flock outside, the door was closed, while the geese were fighting over the remnants of the corn ear left in the snow.

There was no tittering on the part of the audience over the interruption. They accepted the situation as a matter of course. The preacher's equanimity was undisturbed, while "Aunt Nancy" folded her arms complacently, as if such occurrences were nothing out of the usual routine of affairs – and the sermon went on.

The Saint Louis Republic
St. Louis, MO
August 20, 1900

Chapter Five

LIFE OF RILEY

OLD TIME HOBO TELLS OF HOBO LIFE

Poplar Bluff, MO
In Missouri Pacific Magazine

Where has the once huge army of railroad tramps gone?

The old-time boxcar hobo, only a few years ago so numerous throughout the country, has virtually disappeared. Since the World War the old-time railroad tramp has steadily passed along and no one seems to know just where he went.

As late as 1917 the hobo army numbered its members in the millions. Today it is doubtful if there are more than a few thousand tramps scattered over the wide territory, and the few tramps we see occasionally nowadays are not the genuine old-time ragged, bewhiskered hoboes of other days who rode freight trains and begged handouts at back doors. The few tramps who still beat their way on trains are mostly young men out to see the country or men who are broke and looking for work. The old professional tramps of days gone by, who didn't do a lick of work and begged all their goods at back doors, have disappeared as if by magic.

At the age of 14 the writer of this article got the wanderlust in his system and ran away from home in Missouri and became a professional tramp, spending more than 20 years on the road traveling and associating with tramps of the old school. He feels well qualified to write an article on the life adventures and disappearance of the once vast army of tramps and hoboes that, at one time, roamed throughout the United States and Canada.

The origin of the modern American tramp was in 1865. At the close of the Civil War, thousands of young men were released from both the Union and Confederate armies. These young men had had a taste of travel and adventure in the armies of the north and south and wanted more of it. Railroads were being constructed throughout the country at that time, especially in the western and Midwestern states and thousand of laborers were needed to build the roads.

That was the beginning of the modern tramp as we know him. The laborers who built the railroads got into the habit of beating their way from one construction job to the other on freight trans. As the railroads became completed and there was no more work for the construction workers, these men naturally became tramps, beating their way about the country, doing no work at all and begging and stealing for a livelihood. The ranks of the tramp were steadily increased by the new recruits – boys running away from home snared by the lure of the wanderlust and thrilled by the life of adventure. As the years passed by, the tramp army steadily increased in numbers until about 1907, the huge army of hoboes and tramps was estimated to number not less than 2,000,000 vagrants.

The death knell of the railroad tramp was first sounded in 1917 with the beginning of the World War. Thousands of young tramps were drafted or volunteered and were sent overseas. Next came prohibition – the tramps and burns now had no place to loaf and congregate. Steadily their number decreased.

When a tramp or hobo arrived in a city or town, he always headed first for the nearest jungle camp, where he could probably find other tramps and where he could boil out his clothes, eat his handouts, cook his mulligan stew and swap tales with his brother knights of the roads. Quite often the tramps would band together and go out on a mooching expedition. One tramp would beg nothing but bread from bakeries, another would beg nothing but meat from butcher shops, while others would beg vegetables, etc. Each would return to the jungle camp, where a grand mulligan stew would be prepared, everyone eating his fill, except the unlucky tramps who failed to bring in their share of the grub. Those who failed to bring in any supplies were denied any of the stew. The old-time jungle camps have disappeared along with old-time tramps.

Most of the old-time ramblers rode freight trains exclusively, as a freight was much easier to board and ride than a passenger train. It was the custom to catch freight trains just as the train pulled out of the division yards or at a street crossing. This was done to avoid the railroad police who were in all railway yards. The old boys liked to travel in comfort and would, if possible, crawl in to an empty box car, where they would curl up in a corner and travel in ease. The tramps generally did their riding at night, as it was easier to dodge train crews and police than in daytime. If there were no empty box cars on a train, a tank car, coal car, or even the rods, bumpers or on top the train would do.

Very few tramps, except young and nervy daredevils, road the passenger trains, because a passenger train was very hard to ride and there was no place for one to conceal himself except behind the baggage, on top the train or underneath the cars on the trucks, which was a poor place of concealment and a dangerous place to ride. Then, too, it was next to impossible to board a passenger train except at railway stations, where police were always to be found. Such being the case, none but daredevil young tramps, who were willing to take a risk, rode the passenger trains. Some railroads and some train crews were strictly hostile to tramps and put them off all trains and arrested them at every opportunity, while other road and train crews seemed to consider the vagrants a necessary evil and allowed them to ride almost at will.

The old-time tramps were migratory, like ducks and geese, spending the summers in the north and the winters in the south, but very few tramps entered Old Mexico, owing to the poverty of the country.

The railroad police or special agents in the railway yards were about evenly divided in heir regard for ramblers. Some railroad police seldom arrested tramps, confining themselves to easing the vagrants off railroad property, but others of the rail police were very hard on the "boss".

The road of other days produced many famous tramps. These men were the leaders and the outstanding men of the once great army of railroad tramps. Notables among the old-timers were: No. 1, greatest tramp the road ever produced, who beat his way more than 500,000 miles on freight and passenger trains; "Beef Stew Mike", the hardest-boiled hobo who ever rode the trains; "Back Door Slim", greatest panhandler the road ever knew, who was never known to have been refused a hand-out; "Box-Car Joe", the millionaire tramp, whom rumor had it, had half a million dollars in the bank and in property, but in spite of his wealth, "Box Car Joe" preferred to be a hobo and ride on freight trains; "The Katy Flyer", "Denver Red", "Mover", "Rambler", "Penn", and "Seldom Seen". The monikers or nicknames of many of these old-time notables of the rail can still be seen painted or carved on water tanks, stations, and bridges in many parts of the country, although most of these are now dead or old and retired from the road, but like the buffalo, the Indian, the frontiersman and the cowboy, the old-time railroad tramps had their day, passed on, and are now almost extinct. Modern life, changing conditions, the motor car, and the continual and relentless warfare waged on the tramps by the police and railroads have had an effect and reduced the once mighty army of tramps, more than a million strong, to a mere handful of slinking and cowardly hoboes.

Today, we have a new type of tramp. This new brand of ramblers are called "highway bums". They beg rides from motorists on the highways, and usually have some sort of "racket", such as peddling, whereby they earn enough cash to pay for their food and lodging. Of course the highway bums are an unpicturesque and unromantic lot of vagrants and could never compare with the rough and ready old-time tramps who rode the trains, and the passing of these picturesque wanderers mark another closed chapter in the history of American romance and adventure.

The American Republic
Poplar Bluff, MO
October 12, 1928

THE SORROWFUL

Tale of John Meeks of Ripley County – He saw the Elephant And Was Saddened

Ripley County, MO

John Meeks of Ripley County was a steady young man. He worked on the farm and he grubbed and he hoed, and then he came to Poplar Bluff. Tucked away in a vest pocket was the wealth with which he had determined to set the metropolis of Southeast Missouri afire. He would paint the town the most glorious color of crimson that ever was seen of this earth, b'gosh. All this happened Thursday and along toward evening John Meeks' supply of paint purchaser was getting low. But he still had dollars to the mystical number of seven all in silver, too, for he was not going to have no bartender refuse him a drink because he did not have legal tender. But no bartender got that money.

John Meeks meekly wandered down toward the Frisco Depot after night had fallen and he was beginning to reflect. He would have repented, in all probability, but fate did not give him a chance. Fate, in fact, in the guise of a buxom Negro wench, was lying in wait for John Meeks, with a figurative sandbag in her hand, and the disguised fate got the silver. It was not done in a rough manner, either. Fate, still in the guise of the attractive wench, began to make love to the young man from the empire of Ripley, and while embracing him, shyly and slyly slipped the simoleons from his pocket. Then

35

Fate chuckled and vanished. Shortly thereafter John Meeks of Ripley missed his roll and sought the police. But John Meeks, though confronted with every wench in the town, could not identify, and it is supposed that he walked home.

Thus closes the sorrowful tale of John Meeks of the Empire of Ripley.

The Daily Republican
Poplar Bluff, MO
July 12, 1904

Chapter Six

BOOZE, BOOZE AND MORE BOOZE

"THEY'RE NOT GUILTY"

Harold Elliott and William Snodgrass were on trial in Circuit Court here charged with possession of eight bottles of home brew beer, and the evidence had been lugged into court in a basket and reposed on the floor beside the jury box. The defense attorney waxed eloquent in his plea for clemency.

"Gentlemen of the jury, "he thundered, "not one iota of proof has been brought forth to show this innocuous beverage is stronger than pond water."

He stamped his foot vigorously to emphasize his assertion, and the floor vibrated.

Bam!

Simultaneously eight bottles of home brew, its potency revived by warm air of the courtroom blew up. Judge, jury, spectators and attorneys, showered with flying glass and suds, with one accord scattered to the four winds.

When Judge Schmook had regained his composure and jury members had mopped the beer stains from their shirt fronts and combed glass particles from their hair, the trial proceeded.

Both defendants got nine months in jail.

The American Republic
Poplar Bluff, MO
October 9, 1931

56 BOTTLES OF "MULE" TAKEN IN 4TH CROWN RAID

Poplar Bluff, MO

For the fourth time in several months a successful raid was made upon the barroom of the notorious Crown Hotel, resulting again in a heavy haul of bottled moonshine whiskey. The raid was conducted at 4 o'clock Wednesday afternoon by D.W. Carter, chief of police; Clyde Hogg, chief deputy sheriff; C.M. Bolton, railway special agent and deputy sheriff and Henry Drew of the city police force. Fifty-four half-pints were found in a hole in the floor over which stood a showcase.

Sheriff J.R. Hogg was "tipped off" some few days ago. One of the Crown force had bragged every time there had been a raid conducted. The real hiding place of the whiskey had never been found. By airing the location of the whiskey in a brazen manner, it came to the sheriff, resulting I the raid.

Two half-pint bottles were taken from Lucas' pockets. It is said, when he saw the officers enter, he picked two bottles from under the bar and put them in his pockets. The move was not quick enough for Deputy Clyde Hogg's eyes, and he forced Lucas to be searched.

This morning Lucas pleaded guilty in police court and was fined $25 and costs. He was allowed to go free upon promise to raise the money. Prosecuting Attorney F.M. Kinder will file information against Lucas this week.

Poplar Bluff American
Poplar Bluff, MO
February 16, 1922

75 GALLONS "WHITE MULE" IS DESTROYED

Poplar Bluff, MO

Many a covetous eye watched the operations of Sheriff J.R. Hogg and his men at 3 o'clock this afternoon, loading a wagon with contraband whiskey and moonshining equipment to be taken away and destroyed. The wagonload represented the moonshining raids, bootlegging and hip-pocket stocks captured during the past year. The wagon contained 75 gallons of whiskey in numerous sizes and kinds of containers, four captured stills and scores of feet of coil, some copper and other gas pipe.

Twenty-eight gallons were retained in the county jail as evidence against offenders whose cases are pending in circuit court.

The wagon carrying the contraband hauled it from the north side of the court square to the courthouse grandstand where, before a large crowed, it was emptied into a sewer catch basin.

Poplar Bluff American
Poplar Bluff, MO
May 6, 1922

PROMINENT MEN OF MARSHALL IN SEDALIA JAIL

Marshall, MO

Frank Campbell, Justice of the Peace, L. Rasse, a prominent local attorney, and five Negroes were arrested here yesterday and charged with the possession and sale of liquor.

The men, all residents of Saline County, were taken into custody by Sheriff S. Sewell of Pettis County and M.M. Wilcox, special federal prohibition agent.

All of the men are held in Pettis County Jail at Sedalia.

The Poplar Bluff American
Poplar Bluff, MO
May 1, 1923

FIVE MEN IMPERSONATE OFFICERS

Poplar Bluff, MO

Hijackers, who have pulled several jobs recently in this county, made a rich haul Sunday night.

According to the story that reached county officers, five men, with a big truck, went to a farm in the Cane Creek district, knocked at the farmhouse door, and when the owner admitted them, told him two of them were deputy sheriffs and three were federal prohibition agents. One of them introduced himself as Paul Toelle, federal agent who has operated extensively in this territory for some years. They read what purported to be a search warrant, and then, ransacking the place, loaded 350 gallons of whiskey into their truck and drove off.

Owned by Jones

The liquor belonged to Arthur Jones, local bootlegger. Jones told Sheriff Massingham of the raid. It developed that the alleged officers were imposters and were impersonating both deputy sheriffs and federal prohibition agents.

Hijackers have pulled several similar stunts during the past year. A truck load of whiskey was hijacked near Qulin not long ago. About a year ago, one man was shot during a hijacked feud just west of Poplar Bluff. Shortly afterwards, hijackers took a farmer living just over the Ripley county line for a ride, robbed him of several hundred dollars and made off with a large quantity of his whiskey. Many similar cases occur, reports of which never find their way to officers.

The American Republic
Poplar Bluff, MO
August 3, 1931

500 GALLONS OF WINE DESTROYED

Harview, MO

Having a gallon or so of wine about the premises for home use is one thing, but being in possession of 510 gallons of potent, fermented, sparkling grape juice is entirely different, Frank Kovach learned yesterday afternoon.

Members of the United States Revenue Department hauled the farmer living four miles south of Harviell, before U.S. Commissioner Arno Ponder, alleging they found a half thousand gallons of tax unpaid wine on the premises. Kovach admitted the charge, filled a $100 bond for appearance in federal Court and went his way.

Mouths about the courtroom watered and throats became unaccountably dry. The 510 gallons of what was said to have been wine of excellent quality, was destroyed. Three barrels formerly contained white wine, the kind from which an even more potent drink is brewed.

It was destroyed also.

The Daily Republic
Poplar Bluff, MO
November 3, 1934

CHEAP AND EXPENSIVE WHISKEY
ALL COMES OUT OF SAME KEG

By
A Bootlegger

Poplar Bluff, MO

The story of how I chanced to become a bootlegger, then found that I could never get out of the occupation how a bootlegger is protected by his associated and how the business is carried on in Poplar Bluff has been contained in my three previous articles.

Now, say, for instance, you wanted a quart of bottled in bond whiskey. Certainly I would take the order. I have the very thing you want. I will turn to a keg, pour out a quart, label it and place a seal on the bottle, and sell it to you for about $10. Bottled in bond whiskey comes high.

Then say the next fellow comes in with $2 and wants just ordinary moonshine whiskey. I pour that out of the same keg and place it in a plain bottle.

That trick is worked every day in Poplar Bluff.

Sell Anything

Not long ago a well-dressed man came in and wanted to buy two quarts of bottled in bond whiskey. I went to his room at a hotel to see if he was O.K. I found that he was a representative of a well-known university. That established my confidence in him and I went out and got his whiskey. It cost me $2 a quart and I placed the labels on the bottles and the tops on, so as to give the genuine appearance. First, though, I colored the liquor making it look just like bottled in bond stuff.

We have labels and tops for the bottles-just like the real stuff.

Collected $15

I took the two quarts to him and told him the price would be $12. He tasted the liquor, smacked his lips and said "That's fine." He paid me the $12 and gave me $3 for my trouble. That whiskey was about two days old.

We sell bourbon, rye and anything else they want, all out of the same keg.

Some time ago we ran out of beer. We couldn't get another batch quickly and our demand was heavy. We sent up and purchased several cases of Budweiser from the Coca-Cola Company. That beer contains less than one-half of one percent alcohol. We washed the labels off, put plain caps on the bottles, and sold them for 25 cents each.

Believe it or not, two drug store sheiks came in, purchased two bottles each of the beer, and before they hardly had time to turn around they thought they were dead drunk. I could hardly help laughing right in their faces.

The Daily Republic
Poplar Bluff, MO
May 27, 1928

POLICE FIND 700 GALLONS CORN LIQUOR

Thirty-one Barrels Containing Moonshine Booze
Found in Garage on Ninth Street

Biggest Haul Ever Made By The Police

Hundreds Stand Around and Watch Police
Knock Heads Out of Barrels and Feed Booze to Fish

Poplar Bluff, MO

Seven hundred gallons of corn whiskey, with a wholesale bootleg value of about $3,500 and retail "over the bar" value of about $22,000, was somewhere in Black River today as result of a visit paid by city and county officers to a garage in the rear of a house on Ninth and Poplar streets. The raid was conducted at about 6 o'clock Friday evening.

For about thirty minutes whiskey cascaded down the gutters in a stream approaching a small creek in proportions, while the officers knocked the heads out of thirty-one 30 gallon barrels, either full or partly filled with booze, and while about 300 spectators, some of them with their tongues hanging out looked on with expressions varying from amazement, joy and regret.

A Strong Odor

Officers have been receiving complaints from that vicinity for some weeks. It was claimed a strong odor of spirits emanated from the garage in question and residents were kept restless by this odor continually disturbing their quiet evenings at home.

About 5 o'clock Friday afternoon, Chief Davis, City Attorney O.A. Tedrick and Police Officer Charles Rose went out to investigate the case. Tedrick "boosted" Davis up to where he could peer in through a high window. Then Davis "boosted" Tedrick up so he could have a peep.

There, stacked in neat array, were the thirty-one barrels, while from the window cam an odor like the breath of a veteran bungstarter.

Back After Tools

Tedrick and Davis left Rose to guard the place while they went to Prosecuting Attorney Byron Kearbey and got the search warrant. Then the two, accompanied by Officers Bone, Ferguson and Vanderpool, and Sheriff McCown, armed with axes, went back to the scene of their investigation. They pried open the garage door, rolled out the barrels and one by one knocked out the heads, dumping the contents into the gutter.

Sixteen of the barrels were filled with whiskey, while aside from a few that were empty, the balance contained anywhere from two to 25 gallons. The bungs had been removed from some of the barrels, apparently with the idea of making the liquor age faster.

Owner Not Known

Just who the whiskey belonged to, officers do not know, although they are investigating, and expect to make arrests by night. The owner of the property were the garage is located is out of town. He has no car and some time ago sub-rented the garage to parties, the names of whom police do not as yet know. However, officers today thought they would have the guilty parties in custody by evening.

The whiskey confiscated Friday evening constitutes the biggest haul officers have ever made in Poplar Bluff. Bootleg whiskey purchased from the moonshiner, costs about $5 a gallon on an average. At this price, whoever owned the 700 gallons lost about $3,500. When sold by the drink over the bar, a gallon of whiskey brings about $32. At this price the retail value of the whiskey was $22,400.

The American Republic
Poplar Bluff, MO
June 24, 1928

MOONSHINE STILLS IN THE OZARKS

There were legal stills in these Ozark hills in the early days. These were licensed by the U.S. Government. Dan France operated a Government still at the mouth of South Bee Creek which emptied into White River. This was in southern Taney County near the Arkansas border. Another Government still was operated by Hensley on White River. Hensley also has the ferry at that point which carried the traffic across White River, traveling the old Springfield-Harrison Road. This was a regular stop for freight wagons. Hensley sold corn for the teams and also sold corn liquor. The freighters believed the corn whiskey enabled them to endure the rigors of outdoor camping.

The taxes on whiskey grew and grew. This brought the price of whiskey at the Government stills to the point where moonshining became prevalent in the hills and drove the licensed stills out of business. Then came prohibition, and again the moonshine still became a way of life for many hill men.

The moonshiner in the Ozarks operated in the remote sections. Cold water was a necessity. The moonshine still was set up by a spring with a big flow of cold water. Wooden barrels held the mash for souring. When the mash reached the proper stage of fermentation it was put in the big cooker and boiled. Proper distillation required three essential parts; the boiler, the condenser (thump-keg), and the retort, in which the distilled liquid was collected. The condenser was actually the copper pipe called the "worm", in the vernacular of the moonshiner. The coiled pipe was inside a keg, or other receptacles, through which the cold water flowed, thus condensing the steam from the boiling mash. The old timers who made the best grade of whiskey ran the liquid through the worm several times, making the liquor stronger each time. The whiskey was put in charred kegs by the moonshiner for customers who were particular. Many times the raw whiskey was put in fruit jars. Federal and State officers caught many of the inexperienced moonshiners. However, the old ones were wily and had help from friendly neighbors in spotting the "Revenooers."

There is the story of the city fellow touring the Ozarks who was taking a hike among the hills, admiring the scenery. Suddenly he came upon a moonshine still. There sat an old hill man with a long rifle and a jug. The old fellow pushed the jug towards the stranger and said, "Take a drink", the stranger emphatically declined. The old man repeated his demand in louder tones. Still the stranger refused to take a drink. The mountaineer leveled the rifle at the fellow's head and said sternly, "I said take a drink." The frightened tourist took a hurried gulp of the corn liquor and strangled and gasped for breath. The old man watched him a moment and handed him the rifle remarking, "Now you hold the gun on me while I take a drink!"

The late C.C. Williford, longtime weatherman in Springfield, Missouri, told me this story. He and some friends were fishing near Flat Creek on one of those hot dry days that come to the Ozarks during a protracted drought. All the crops were ruined and the bag worms were eating all the leaves from walnut, hickory and many other trees. The grasshoppers were devouring all that was left. Williford and his friends needed drinking water after a long day and made their way up to a cabin where a mountaineer sat on the porch. A poor, boney hound dog slept under the shade of a dilapidated ancient automobile. The visitors made conversation with the man as they waited for the boy to draw water from the well nearby. Williford remarked, "Well my good man, times sure are mighty hard around here; crop burned up; bag worms and grasshoppers eating everything. You must be having a hard time getting the necessities of life."

The mountaineer gazed off into the heat waves with a sad and woe-be-gone expression and replied, "Yes, and when I do get the damn stuff it ain't hardly fitten' to drink."

Douglas Mahnkey
Hill and Holler Storied, 1984
The Ozark Mountaineer Publisher
Kirbyville, MO

TEMPERANCE AXES WRECK DISTILLERY

This Leaves A Scope of Dry Territory 100 Mile Long

Men, Women and Children Demolish Plant, Then Pile It In City Street – Workers Rejoice

Thayer, MO

There was great rejoicing among temperance workers of this section today when the distillery of R.R. Roberts, formerly located at Rink, Ark., was destroyed at Myrtle, Oregon County, MO.

For several years Roberts has operated the distillery on the State line between Missouri and Arkansas. It was difficult for the officials to strictly enforce the laws. In order to get the distillery out of the neighborhood, the temperance workers proposed to buy it and Roberts consented. He made the first donation, saying he was tired of the business. The proposition, to publicly destroy the still met with approval and was widely advertised.

Five hundred persons gathered at Myrtle to witness the destruction. W.T. Taylor, merchant, Postmaster and superintendent of the Baptist school had charge of the work. There was a parade by school children and women. Then the effects were piled in the street. Miss Margaret Parrott, teacher of the Myrtle schools, with an axe, struck the first blow. Scores of women with hatchets and axes rained blow after blow, which broke the apparatus into pieces.

The demolition of the distillery on the State line leaves a continuous scope of dry territory 200 miles in length along the southern border of the State.

The Daily Republican
Poplar Bluff, MO
December 5, 1911

POSSE LANDS MOONSHINERS

Alleged King of Illicit Whiskey Makers in Missouri
Lodged in Springfield Jail

Federal Officers Take Mountaineers by Surprise
Captives Never Had Seen Locomotive or Street Car-Thirty
Armed Men on Guard

Oregon County, MO

The Federal posse, a portion of which was in Poplar Bluff one night last week, which left Doniphan of Friday in pursuit of a band of moonshiners, chasing them into Oregon county, raided the gang early Saturday morning and captured five. There was no battle, as expected, the men being taken by surprise.

As a result of this first raid on Ozark moon shiners in fifteen years, George Conner, alleged to be king of the illicit whiskey business in Oregon and Ripley counties, and five of his companions, were taken Saturday night to Springfield by W.S. revenue officials headed by Deputy W.S. Marshal H.C. Miller of Kansas City.

Jim Conner, George Baker, Bill Anderson, John Davis and Jim Dobbs rough mountaineers and relatives of Conner, also were arrested, charge with moonshining. The men were placed in jail after a preliminary hearing. Conner, who is 60 years old, is supposed by Federal officers to have organized moonshine into a profitable business. He is said to have thirty employees and four stills.

Raising corn to supply illicit distilleries furnishes employment to scores of families in that section. The arrest of Conner and his chief lieutenants will strike a fatal blow to the last of illegal whiskey making in Missouri, Federal officials believe.

The men were surprised at dawn Saturday morning, quickly handcuffed and placed in a lumber wagon, on which they were taken forty-seven miles over rocky mountain roads to Thayer and thence by train to Springfield.

The men were frightened at the sight of trains. Only one of them had ever seen a locomotive and the entire party saw elevators, streetcars and modern buildings for the first time.

The Daily Republican
Poplar Bluff, MO
May 19, 1913

SHERIFF GETS INTO NEST OF BUSY HORNETS

Three Members of Family Brought to Jail When Officers Found Stills in Wagon

TWO SMALL STILLS AND MASH TAKEN

Youngest and Smallest Alleged Liquor Law Violator Was One Member of Hornet Family

Fagus, MO

Sheriff Ray McCown and his deputies when into the woods near Fagus to raid a still camp late Thursday night, but instead ran into a Hornet's nest. And, incidentally, they captured the youngest moonshiner, and the smallest in point of stature, in the history of the liquor traffic in Butler County.

The sheriff had been told a still that was in operation in the woods north of Fagus. "The still camp is on a ridge," declared his informant. About dusk the officers set out, but when they arrived at the campsite which, by the way was in a swamp, they found only the embers of a campfire and a few other evidences of recent activities or moonshiners. They searched the woods, but found nothing more. Returning through the swamps to their car, the party sighted a mule-drawn wagon, on the hurricane deck of which were perched three gaunt figured, silhouetted against the horizon. Wading water up to their knees, the officers approached.

The Hornet Family

"Who goes there?", called the sheriff.
"Bill Hornet", came the reply.
"Who's that with you?", asked McCown.
"Earl Hornet and Ernest Hornet", called a voice.
"It looks like we've stepped into a Hornet's nest," said the sheriff, as his party overhauled the wagon and started to search it.

Covered up in the back of the conveyance were two copper moonshine stills, of 15 and 30 gallons capacity respectively, and about 200 gallons of whisky mash. The mash was dumped out and the three busy "bees" and their stills were brought to Poplar Bluff, where the former were lodged in the County Jail. All three will be charged with possession of equipment for the manufacture of whisky.

The three Hornets are brothers. Earnest, the youngest, is only 11 years old and exactly 3 feet 6 inches in height. He steadfastly maintained that while he was riding on the wagon, he had no idea what was in it.

The American Republic
Poplar Bluff, MO
March 21, 1930

46

"REVENOOERS" LOCATE STILL UP IN TREE TOP

Qulin, MO

Federal Agents associated with the Department of Internal Revenue added one more moonshiner experience to their growing list of Southeast Missouri episodes when they pulled a complete distillery out of tree a in the Qulin district.

"We have found stills near springs, on houseboats, in log cabins, on the peaks of hills, and in hidden caves, but when they start building 'em on treetops" the agents ran out of words.

Then they explained. Everett Wilson and Harvey Philips they said, attempted to dodge the U.S. registry tax on stills by building a scaffold above the high water mark in a flooded area 10 miles south of Qulin. The waters of Black River had left their mark approximately 18 inches below the level of an elevated tree-top platform. Only by boat could the agents reach the sequestered spot.

Philips and Wilson had hauled a motorboat load of lumber, sawdust and other supplies to the distillery. They hammered, sawed and pounded, so the agents informed United States Commissioner Arno Ponder. When they were surprised by "Revenooers", they plunged into the swirling water and tried to swim ashore.

One of the agents "induced" the boys to swim back to the platform. "They wouldn't have made it anyway. Their boots were full of water", one of the "Revenooers" reported to the Commissioner.

Philips and Wilson were placed in jail this morning when they failed to post a $2000 Federal Court appearance bond.

Daily American Republic
Poplar Bluff, MO
December 14, 1935

INDIAN HELD FOR OWNING BOOZE STILL-
WILLIAM FORBAR ARRESTED WHEN OFFICERS SAY
THEY FOUND HIM AT STILL

Powe, MO

William Fobar, 29 years old Indian who traces his ancestry back to the tribes that once roamed in the state of Illinois is singing as Indian lullaby in the Butler County jail today. Or perhaps it is the Indian Love Call. Anyhow, William is singing and it may must be the blues.

William was all set to become the best equipped Indian medicine man in the business last Monday. He walked the streets of Powe, Missouri, with his chest thrown out as if he owned the town.

Two old friends of William met him on the street. He recognized them, as he had a most vivid picture of these two gentlemen in mind, as most Indians do when suspicious of any of their paleface acquaintances.

"How's tricks, Willie? What do you know? Are there any new stills around here that you know about?", the men who happened to be two of Uncle Sam's liquor control agents queried.

"None here," he says.

"Don't know of a one, in fact, I'm positive there are none to be found in the county," William answered. The Federal agents smiled at Willie and replied, "Well, so long, old boy, we'll be seeing you."

And they did. Just 12 hours later as William walked up to a triple steam still outfit capable of producing 150 gallons of whiskey at a "run". The agents concealed themselves in the weeds near the Stoddard County line at 3 a.m. yesterday morning. About 8 a.m. Willie, armed with a high powered German rifle, walked up to the still. The agents stepped out into the open and startled him. William said, "Well, here I am boys. You said you'd be seeing me, but I didn't think it would be this soon. Here's my gun and that's my still. It's all over now."

Willie's still was the fifty-seventh taken by federal agents in this section since the first of the year. Since August, 1935, 102 have been taken and destroyed.

57 Taken This Year

"No. 57 was a dandy and Willie is one of the most amusing bootleggers we have ever captured," agents said last night. "Willie told us he made a much finer grade of firewater for the white men to drink that the white men used to sell to his forefather," agents quoted the prisoner as saying.

Willie, who gave his occupation as a farmer, had 110 barrels of mash in his possession and was booked.

Daily American Republic
Poplar Bluff, MO
August 6, 1936

Chapter Seven

LIGHT SIDE OF LIFE

GOIN' BAREFOOT

West Plains, MO4

My best friend had been tantalizingly barefoot for a whole week already because her mama gauged barefoot weather by the return of the butterfly. I had to wait for a cousin of the Capistrano swallow, the purple martin, but finally there they were, sailing and darting around the martin box in our backyard.

"Can I, Mama? Can I now? Ple-e-e-ease?"

"May I."

"May I, please."

"Oh, I guess so." It had been a long week for her, too.

I sailed out the kitchen door and kicked the once proud, Red Goose oxfords as high as I could send them. The shoes with knotted strings, run-down heels, grinning toes, and flapping rubber soles were fit only for puppy toys. Anyway, there would be new shoes come fall, and I did have the black patent leather slippers for funerals and weddings and such. I sat down, yanked off my long, faded cotton stockings, flung them to the breeze, and stood up to feel the cool, green earth caressing my pale, tender feet. And tender they were! I carefully picked my steps across the bare spots and avoided the graveled road for several days, but eventually, the soles of my feet were nearly as tough as the soles of the worn out shoes I had thrown away, and nearly as brown.

It was fun to walk barefoot in the smooth furrow behind Dad's turning plow picking up the long, wiggling earthworms and the short, fat grubs that would dangle from my fish hook later in the day. I would rinse my bare feet in the tepid pond water as I waited for the electrifying little tug that told me to jerk!

With my feet bare, I no longer had to skirt the puddles when it rained but could squish the soft mud right up between my toes.

I could build dams in the little rivulets and never hear Mama call, "Don't get your feet wet!" I could also get a better grip on a tree limb thirty feet above the ground without shoes on.

Oh, the joy of naked feet!

John Greenleaf Whittier recalled the barefoot days of his youth in the famous idyll, "The Barefoot Boy." These lines from the poem convey a testimonial to the innocence and freedom of childhood to which I can only say, "Mr. Whittier, touché!"

> Blessings on thee, little man,
> Barefoot boy, with cheek of tan!
> With thy turned-up pantaloons,
> And thy merry whistled tunes;
> With thy red lip, redder still
> Kissed by strawberries on the hill;
> With the sunshine on thy face,
> Through thy torn brim's jaunty grace;
> From my heart I give thee joy, --
> I was once a barefoot boy!

I must, however, warn the young, would-be-barefoot types that there is a squishes between the toes is soft mud, and oh, how a stubbed toe can smart! Things dropped take the shortest route to the big toe. Rusty nails and pieces of jagged glass position themselves to catch the unwary. Stones love to bruise heels. Splinters and burs and stickers of all kinds delight in seeing a lad or a lass hop and howl in pain.

By late September, after a long summer replete with "down-sides" and the martins with broods in tow had headed back to warmer climes, I was quite ready for my new "....prison walls of pride."

"Mama, when am I going to get my new shoes?"

"Just as soon as your daddy sells the pigs," she promised.

In a few days we were off to the Williams Shoe Store in West Plains. Row upon row of beautiful, aromatic, new leather footwear confronted us. So many to choose from!

After Mr. Williams or the handsome young clerk, Alvan Squires, had patiently dragged out every style of shoe in stock in my size, I laboriously made my selection, and having made it, was contented until the martins should come again to dart around the back in our back yard.

Shirley Carter Pilano
West Plains Gazette
Summer, 1987

FALSE TEETH

A Set of China Grinders Found on 4th Street and Wonder Created

Poplar Bluff, MO

An advertisement appeared in the Republican last Friday stating that a set of false teeth had been found near Jim Wright's saloon on Fourth street, and that owner should call there for his or her property.

Now, isn't that a shame? The idea of having the poor man come and identify his property after perhaps having concealed the fact that he wears store teeth for years? Or perhaps it was some young miss, a beautiful girl with a splendid life who be reason of eating too much sweetmeats or through cracking nuts with her natural teeth was forced to resort to this deception.

Far be it from the advertiser, in the mind of the writer, to cause a pang to shoot through the heart of the loser of these decorations, for what else could he do but advertise? But now that he has done so who is it who realized that his cherished possessions, the one thing with which he-or-she-manages to sustain life, has been found by a mere man? Ah, my friends, the way of the transgressor is hard and when you are so careless as to lose your false teeth, beware lest you are forced to follow the example of the cranks and go through a prolonged fast.

Probably some dainty miss, tripped by the place with her thoughts on George's visit of the evening before, smiled-and dropped her teeth. What a shame!

The Daily Republic
Poplar Bluff, MO
June 27, 1904

"BILL BAILEY" COMES BACK; IN JAIL AGAIN

"Peg" Mitchell Also In Authorities' Clutches

Famous Little Negro Charged With Theft of Shoes, And One-legged Man Accused of Stealing

Poplar Bluff, MO

The famous little Negro, Bill Bailey has some back! He was caught yesterday by Chief Gardner and accused of stealing a pair of shoes from a clerk for the Allison Mercantile company. He made no especial denial in face of the evidence presented against him, so Judge Kershner fined him $5 and costs this morning. Bill is back in the familiar city jail to work out the assessment.

"Peg" Mitchel, also somewhat hazy in our memories because of neglect to do anything to provoke the action of the law in his case, again is in the toils. He was accused of stealing a monkey wrench and went to jail this morning, after seeing Judge Kershner, to work out or lay out a fine of $5 and costs.

We appear to be getting back to ye olden times, when such distinguished members of the police court coterie reappear upon the horizon and again participate in the activities of the day.

The Daily Republican
Poplar Bluff, MO
June 18, 1912

CORPSE ASKED FOR A TICKET

Train Auditor Shocked to Discover Dead Passenger On Fast Train South Today

Corning Man Succumbs While En route Home

R. Hicks, on way from Battle Creek, Mich., Dies Shortly After Leaving Poplar Bluff

Poplar Bluff, MO

As the auditor of train No. 3 of the Iron Mountain made his rounds this afternoon after leaving here, he requested fare from a passenger who did not answer. The man was dead, sitting up in his seat as though only asleep.

The dead passenger was A.R. Hicks of Corning, Ark., who was En route to his home from Battle Creek, Mich. The body was taken from the train at Neelyville and Coroner Davidson notified of the sudden death. The train proceeded on its way south.

Discovery of the man's death was made when the train neared Harviell. The auditor believing the passenger asleep tried to arouse him without receiving response and investigation showed the glassy stare of death in the supposed slumberer's eyes.

Headquarters was telephoned by Conductor Massey from Harviell and he was directed to carry the passenger to Neelyville and there get a physician. This was done. Hicks was pronounced dead and his body then was turned over to the county authorities, who will communicate with his family or relatives.

It is assumed that Hicks succumbed to an affliction of the heart.

> The Daily Republican
> Poplar Bluff, MO
> September 11, 1912

HOG SENT CHECK TO PIGG FOR PORK

GREASY TRANSACTION OCCURRED THIS WEEK

Bank of Poplar Bluff Received Peculiar Check This Morning-Both Men Live Here

Poplar Bluff was this week the scene of one of the greasy financial transactions ever recorded. The time honored story of Mr. Stone turning to Wood, Wood turning to Stone and both turning to "rubber" has not got a "look-in" with this tale that is being told on the streets today.'

The Bank of Poplar Bluff this morning, received a check from F. R. Hogg, payable to P.L. Pigg, with a notation in the corner stating it was given in payment for pork. If the statement was not sworn to by reliable parties, we wouldn't believe it, but anyone who doubts the veracity can go to the Bank of Poplar Bluff and see for themselves.

Both Mr. Pigg and Mr. Hogg are well known in Poplar Bluff. The pork in question was sold by Pigg to Hogg to be retailed as pork at Hogg's meat market.

The Daily American Republican
Poplar Bluff, MO
January 2, 1915

GLASS JUGS BY CARLOAD

Eight Thousand Gallon Jars in One Shipment Received By the Hogg Distilling Co. Made Especially to Order, With the Name of Firm and Trademark Blown Into the Glass

Poplar Bluff, MO

The Hogg Distilling Co. never does things on a small scale, when it comes to providing for the accommodation of the growing trade of this Butler County specialty of theirs.

The latest innovation introduced by this well known distilling company in the laying in of a supply of unique glass jugs in which to place for the trade of liquid products of the firm.

There has just been received by the distilling company, the biggest record of glass jugs were shipped to one firm in Southeast Missouri. Eight thousand individual pieces of glassware, each of a gallon capacity, is something one seldom sees nowadays, when business is not as lively as it was when times were better.

Made by the Illinois Glass Co., especially for the Hogg Distilling Co., blowing the name "Jas. Hogg Distilling Co.", and the "Jim Hogg Whiskey" trademark right into the bottle to give it a distinguishing mark, which not even time itself can efface.

The carload of glassware has been unloaded and stored away in the salesroom at the headquarters of the firm on South Fourth Street. It is so unusual a sight as to attract the attention of everyone to the fact this company is right up with the times when it comes to giving the public their money's worth.

The Daily Republican
Poplar Bluff, MO
June 8, 1915

GANDER WAS WORTH MORE THAN
WOMAN REALIZED

Excelsior Springs, MO

Mrs. Lester Hunt of this city claims the distinction of having had a more valuable goose egg than the gold egg-laying goose of Grimm's Fairy Tales.

Last fall while feeding her flock of geese, Mrs. Hunt lost a 1 carat diamond setting out of her ring.

During the winter, Mrs. Hunt sold or gave away all the geese, with the exception of one proud gander, which she reserved for herself. The bird was beheaded last week, and while dressing the last survivor, Mrs. Hunt found her diamond setting firmly embedded in the craw of the fallen leader.

Mrs. Hunt is soaking the stone in goose grease, preparatory to having it reset.

The Daily Republican
Poplar Bluff, MO
April 17, 1924

Chapter Eight

LOOKING FOR TREASURES

MANY LEGENDS ARE REVEALED

Stories of Buried Treasure Told by Old Citizens-Tales are Thrillers

Calico Rock, Ark

Buried in the Ozarks are romantic legends that have stirred the souls of men and women for more than three quarters of a century. Some of these stirring tales have been disproved, while others continue to run on and on, handed down from generation to generation, yet never losing their thrilling effect. And, because of these stories, buried away in the bosom of the hills, the Ozarks have always been a land of romantic dreams.

Believed to Be Huge Sum Buried Since Civil War

According to the story, during the Civil War a band of bank robbers held up a bank in Illinois, getting $150,000 in gold, with which they escaped and brought in boats down the Mississippi to the mouth of White River, thence up White River to Wild Horse Landing. Somewhere in that area, according to tradition, the robbers held their gold to await an opportunity to make a dash for safety.

For a time the robbers were unmolested. Then they began to pilfer through the neighborhood, resulting in a drive being made against them.

In a fight which followed, one of the robbers was killed and another wounded so seriously he died within a few days.

It is said before he died he drew a map of the location of the money and gave it to the man who was caring for him. The latter, thinking the story was only that of a delirious person, gave the map to someone else and it became lost.

Later on, as the story became more widespread, White Horse Landing was the scene of many hunting parties searching for the hidden money.

J.R. Burgess of Calico Rock, who has spent a large portion of his life in that section, says he has sent many hours in company with others, in a search for the treasure. He gave an account of some of his experiences a few days ago.

Search for Treasure With Mineral Rod

"About the time the robbers were hiding in the hills, a man was fishing in the White River one night and was attracted by someone hammering among the rocks up in the bluff," Mr. Burgess said. "The hammering," the man said, "sounded like someone chiseling in rock."

Uncommon sounds and maneuvers in the hills during the early days were not noticed as much as they are today, so the fisherman went ahead with his fishing, dismissing the incident from his mind.

Several weeks later when the robbers had been driven out and tales of hidden gold began to spread, the fisherman recalled what he had heard that night and concluded that, at that very hour, someone was hiding the money.

Years passed. Then one day a man with a mineral rod appeared and offered to demonstrate the instrument, which he claimed would locate gold or silver buried in the ground.

"The rod was first adjusted to silver, but it would not register. Then its owner set it to gold and it began to pull and, believe me, it pulled hard," said Mr. Burgess.

The prospectors followed the rod until it led them to the mouth of a large cave-like opening. The needle then began to center around the mouth of the opening instead of leading inside as they had expected.

Everybody was in high spirits as they began to dig where the needle pad pointed into the sides of the opening. They soon found, however, that nothing was there.

"Later a bunch of us went again to hunt for it," Mr. Burgess continued. "This time we moved higher up from the river to begin our work. Soon we came upon a deep hole straight down into the earth. We cut a long blackjack sapling and lowered it into the hole and found it would not reach the bottom. Then we cut another about the same length and nailed the two together and lowered them. This time we reached the bottom, which was about 60 feet straight down. Then we cut two more poles and fixed them the same way and lowered them beside the first.

Deep Cave Fails to Yield Treasure

"Before we ventured into the hole we made a light and dropped it down there. We could see there was no water and there was a solid bottom, so we slid down the poles, taking some pieces of plank with which to make a ladder when we started back out.

When we reached the bottom and made a light we found something that strengthened our hopes. An old windlass made of small saplings was lying in there.

We saw the hole was the outlet to a long tunnel. We began to explore it then, feeling sure that we were about ready to find the $150,000.

Alas, such was not the case. We crawled out as empty-handed as we entered.

There was one prong of the cave we did not explore thoroughly and I believe there may be a possibility that one prong which led back toward the first cave, where the mineral rod was used, may hold the secret we have so much desired."

Mr. Burgess and his son declared that even yet, they believe the money is hidden around there somewhere and they say they expect to search for it again some time.

Another story of a hidden treasure is centered around what is called the "Big Spring," inside the incorporation limits of Calico Rock. O.L. McGinnis, who now lives at Creswell, Ark., said he remembered hearing of people tell about a man hiding his money near that spring before he went away to the Civil War. The man was killed during the war, and no one ever knew where he hid it.

"A mineral rod was taken to the spring and an attempt was made to find the money," Mr. McGinnis said "But the man that was operating it said there was too much mineral in the rocks about the place for his instrument to get the desired results."

When asked whether he thought the mineral rod would really work, Mr. McGinnis said, "Years ago a man took a mineral rod to Newburg, in Izard County, and attempted to find some money that had been hidden.

The man did not know what kind of money it was, so he set the instrument on gold first, and it would not work. Then he set it on silver and still it would not work. Then he was asked what the money was supposed to be in, and was told that according to an old story it was buried in an iron pot. So he readjusted his instrument and it began to pull. The party followed the direction indicated and, sure enough, found an old pot that had been dug from the ground some time before. If the pot had anything in it, whoever dug it up had taken it. But one thing sure, the instrument found what it had been looking for."

Believed to be Money Buried in Cantrell Den

Then there is another story about a man named Cantrell staying hid out during the Civil War in what is known as Cantrell Den, at the mouth of Calico Creek in this county.

It was said the man was a horse thief. He was thought to have stolen horses and kept them in the den, the entrance to which was gained through a long tunnel a few feet wide. When it was convenient to do so, it was said he would take what money his victims had, and it was thought he hid it somewhere about the den.

During the past few months, since the depression has been on, someone had been digging around the den, evidently looking for the money, which he is said to have hidden there.

W.A. Churchill, of Calico Rock, tells of a man coming here several years ago to search for a large amount of money which, according to the man's story, had been hidden by the Indians. He claimed a dying Indian told him about the money which he said was buried at the foot of a large tree, near a natural bridge near White River, about 50 miles north of Batesville.

Mr. Churchill said a native of this section went with the stranger and took him to one natural bridge, which spans a hollow north of this place, but failed to find anything.

There are two or three other natural formations, resembling bridges near here, and it is thought the Indian might have meant one of them.

Mr. Churchill also recalls another incident of strangers coming to the hills, searching for hidden treasure.

He said one time he was plowing in his field and saw two strangers lurking about the outskirts of the field as if they half wanted to enter, but were afraid to do so. He said they were seen several times during the day.

Late in the day, as he was turning his mule at the end of the rows it shied at something in the tall grass. Churchill investigated and found someone had been digging there, evidently the night before.

Find Place Where Pot Was Buried

On Sunday following, Churchill and another man went to the field to look over the crops. As they passed down a little path through a thicket, they spied a large hole dug beside an old stump. Close examination revealed the prints of what was likely a pot that had been lifted from the bottom of the hole. He said they actually found scales of such metal in the hole where the imprint of the pot was.

Now many are almost confident the two strangers were looking for such when he was them lurking about his place.

Joe Marchant, section foreman for the Missouri Pacific Railroad, also reports finding evidence of someone digging up a pot, which likely contained something valuable.

He said he was hunting for cattle and came upon an old dilapidated barn, made of logs, way back in the woods and went inside, thinking perhaps one of the cows might have gone in there.

Instead of a cow, he said he found a deep hole, something like four or five feet deep, in the center of a stable and there in the very bottom was a perfect imprint of a kettle or pot that likely had contained money or other valuables.

Thus, storied of hidden wealth in the Ozarks continue to run on and on. Some are true, others false. Yet they are interesting tales that are left open for the succeeding generations to marvel at and try, perhaps in vain, to prove.

The American Republic
Poplar Bluff, MO
May 20, 1931

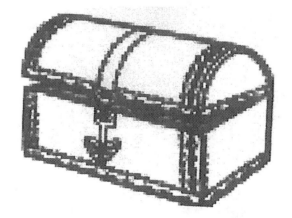

OZARK PEARL MEN HAD BIG YEAR IN 1922

Poplar Bluff, MO

It was a big year for the pearl fisheries of the Ozarks.

Approximately $200,000 was realized for pearls taken from the Black, White, Current and other rivers of the hill country during 1922. According to estimated here, it has been the most profitable year since 1909.

The summer of 1922 was ideal for the work of pearl fishing because of the low stage of the streams and the comparatively slight rainfall, thus making it easy to fish for mussels.

While pearl fishing in the Missouri and North Arkansas streams has always been considered little better than a gamble, some pearls found in the mountain russets have been sold for as high as $5,000.

Poplar Bluff American
Poplar Bluff, MO
March 3, 1923

FINDS PEARL VALUED AT $2,000

Almost Half Inch Thick

Poplar Bluff, MO

Lady Luck treated L.M. Younger, a farmer living about 14 miles south of Poplar Bluff, in first class style yesterday. Although pearl fishing has been worked "almost to death" during the past few years, and it has been reported that virtually all of the pearl bearing shells have been taken out of the rivers in the Ozarks region, Younger found an exception to this rule.

The man, while getting bait for a trotline, picked up the shell containing one of the most beautiful pearls ever seen in Poplar Bluff. It is about one-half inch in diameter and is almost perfect. It is fastened to the shell in two places and Mr. Younger has not attempted to remove it. He said he intended to send the shell, pearl and all, to a New York jeweler and let the experts remove the pearl.

Local jewelers said the pearl would bring $2,000 if it is perfect where attached to the shell. If not, it will likely run between $1,000 and $1,500, he said.

The pearl is perfect as a "ball pearl", Younger said. He declared that few of the valuable ones are now being found on Black River, the majority being very small and imperfect. He has done considerable pearl fishing and is more familiar with the art than probably anyone in this section.

The Daily Republican
Poplar Bluff, MO
October 17, 1924

Chapter Nine

FOR THE REST OF THE STORY

HE'S "DEAD" IN TWO STATES

Joplin, MO

John Frederick Bartels has been dead 20 years, but he never minded about that until just recently.

Legally dead, that is in two states. He was "buried" in Alma, Neb., in 1908, and also legally declared dead in Missouri in 1910. But he didn't care. Life can be pleasant for an active man of 75 even if legal papers no longer recognize his existence.

But not so long ago work came to the little Ozark town of Neosho, MO., that one John Frederick Bartels is heir to a valuable estate in Prussia. John Frederick Bartels? The records of the probate courts are that he is dead.

Complications Arise

A simple matter, you would say, for Bartels to go to the court, prove his identity and have the records changed. But not so simple. Bartels, when he left his prosperous strawberry farm near Neosho-30 years ago it was, back in 1901-left a wife behind him. They were never divorced. And she, when last heard from, was alive and well, somewhere in California.

But not so long ago the man who used to be John Bartels came back and married another wife. Laura Crouch. SO if he legally declared himself to be the John Frederick Bartels who is legally dead, he is a confessed bigamist, and there are laws about that.

Enoch Arden Leaves Home

There's a strange story of this Rip Van Winkle of the Ozarks. With his first wife, Etta Bartels, he lived on his strawberry farm and prospered. He has amassed property valued at from $60,000 to $100,000. He was successful.

But some taste of success was not sweet to Bartels. He quarreled with his wife and grew tired, somehow, of the eternal picking and shipping of carloads of strawberries. Suddenly, and to the complete surprise of all the neighbors, John Frederick Bartels went away. That was July 2, 1901. Nobody, least of all his wife and daughters, knew where he was. Years passed, and in 1909, in response to a petition of Mrs. Bartels, he was legally declared dead. The widow (as she thought) had a tombstone set in the cemetery at Alma, Neb., with the name of John F. Bartels cut in the polished granite.

"Bartels" is Buried

She had identified as John Frederick Bartels a man who had died in an Illinois asylum under the name of John Mitchell. The body, identified at the asylum by mailed descriptions and pictures from Mrs. Bartels, was sent on to Alma, and there buried, March 24, 1910.

Seven years later, Bartels turned up in Neosho. His wife, it is said, refused to receive him, and after some parlaying, he signed quitclaim deeds to her property. Homeless and nameless Bartels found Neosho something less than the pleasant place it had often been. So he once more drifted away.

It was last fall that he returned to the hill country. He sought out his old friends who had been pallbearers at "his funeral." The Ozark folk, mildly surprised to see and shake the hand of a man believed dead 20 years, accepted the fact that here he was, and let it go at that.

Begins All Over

Spry and active for his age, Bartels moved onto a little hillside on Indian Creek with his new wife, who cannot take his name because he hasn't any. He cannot vote, admit his own name, and not own his little farm, which stands in his wife's name.

But he didn't care. Life moved along just the same.

Bartels felt that all the tangled skein of his life had been unraveled, or at least that the knots had been cut. Then, suddenly, came word from Prussia recently that John Frederick Bartels was heir to an estate there. Memories came back to Bartels of childhood in Pomerania, on a farm 80 miles from Berlin. Memories of thrifty farmers and millers who were his forebears came to him. Memories of how, in 1869, he came out to America as a 13-year-old boy with the great wave of Germans, which surged across the sea about that time.

Wants to Live Again

After a short stay in Wisconsin, they had gravitated to Alma, Neb. Then all the family back in Germany died, and John Frederick Bartels was the last of the line, heir to their lands and money.

But John Frederick Bartels reflects, is not so bad, until suddenly you have a reason for wanting to be living again. So now he is going to ask the courts to revise their edict that he is dead, seek to straighten out the threat of bigamy charges and claim the fortune that may be his.

The American Republic
Poplar Bluff, MO
April 1, 1931

CLIPPING TELLS OF PUBLIC SALE

Poplar Bluff, MO

J.H. Walker, of 1202 Spring Street, possesses a clipping of a public sale on March 17, 1849, which contains some interesting information.

Contents of the bill follows:

An Old Sale Bill

"Sale! Having sold my farm and I am leaving for Oregon Territory by ox team and will offer on March 17, 1849, all my personal property to wit: All ox teams except two teams, Buck, Ben, Tom and Jerry; two milk cows, one gray mare and colt, one pair of oxen and yoke, tow ox-carts, one iron plow and good moldboard, poplar weather board, 800 to 1,000 fence rails, one 60 gallons soap kettle, 85 sugar troughs made of white 3 ft. clapboards, 1,500 ten ft. ash timber, 10 gallon maple syrup, 2 spinning wheels, 30 lbs. mutton tallow, 1 large loom made by Jerry Wilson, 300 poles, 100 split hoops, 100 empty barrels, one 32 gallon barrel of John Miller whiskey, 7 years old; 200 gallon apple brandy, one 40 gallon copper still, one dozen reap books, 3 scythes and cradles, one dozen wood pitchforks, one-half interest in tan yards, 32 caliber rifle made by Ben Mills, 50 gallons of soap, hams, bacon and lard, 40 gallon of sorghum molasses, 6 head of fox hounds, all soft mouthed except one."

"At the same time, I will sell my Negro slaves, two men, 35 and 50 years old, two boys, 12 and 18 years old; two mulatto wenches, 40 and 28 years old."

The American Republic
Poplar Bluff, MO
September 26, 1928

MAN DROWNS IN WATER SIX INCHES DEEP

William Earl Heck Victim of Unusual Accident at Father's Farm Home Was Subject to Epileptic Attacks Believed to have Suffered An Attack When He Started Over Ditch

Poplar Bluff, MO

William Earl Heck, aged 34, an epileptic, was drowned in about six inched of water in a ditch at the Heck farm about 8 a.m. today. The body was found shortly afterward by the young man's father, Lee M. Heck.

Heck and his father have resided on a farm about 14 miles northwest of Poplar Bluff for some time. At about 8 o'clock this morning they went to the barnyard to do the morning chores, and the young man went into a pasture to drive a cow to the barn.

When the cow came in alone, the father, who had kept a close and constant watch on his ailing son, started to hunt for him. The body was found lying face downward in the shallow stream, his hands on each side, and his feet on the bank. Apparently he had suffered an attack as he started to step across the stream.

Called Neighbor

The father worked for some time with his son, in an attempted resuscitation, and called two neighbors, O.L. Smith and Ira Ketchum, who also helped until they realized there was no chance to restore his life.

The Daily American Republic
Poplar Bluff, MO
June 5, 1937

FINE WASN'T FOR BEATING LITTLE WOMAN

Columbia, MO

The downtrodden male, rather a pathetic little figure these days, as his pleasures and privileges disappear one by one, may find cheer in this intelligence from Culture Cove.

It's still not against the law – in just so many words – for a fellow to beat his wife.

It happened in Columbia last week – fellow slugged the little woman. He drew a $15 fine, but not for hitting his wife. The charge was breaking glass on the street.

She had her specs on.

Howard Cowan
The Daily American Republic
Poplar Bluff, MO
May28,1942

Chapter Ten

CHOOSE YOUR WEAPON

ONE OF MISSOURI'S MOST FAMOUS DUELS

One hundred and twelve years ago today the first dual between Thomas H. Benton and Charles Lucas in which Lucas was severely, but not fatally wounded, was fought in Missouri. Dueling was considered, in those days, to be a "gentleman's" way of settling disputes, and most of the duelers were lawyers or editors. Benton, it is said, was associated with duels in Missouri more frequently than any other man.

In the Mississippi river, not far from the Missouri shore, was a small island. It was here many of the duels took place and it was for this reason that it was known as Bloody Island. An Illinois law prohibited dueling in that state, but said nothing of men going to another state for the fight.

The challenge sent to Benton by Lucas, which resulted in the first Benton-Lucas duel, was as follows:

"Sir, I am informed you applied to me on the day of the election the epithet of 'puppy.' If so I shall expect that satisfaction which is due one gentleman to another for such an indignity."

Terms of the Duel

Before night that same day the terms had been arranged and the "personal interview" was to be at 6 o'clock the next morning, August 12, 1817. The terms were as follows:

1. The partied shall meet at six o'clock on the morning of the 12th inst., at the upper end of the island opposite Madame Roy's (Bloody Island).
2. Each party shall choose and provide himself with a smooth bore pistol, not exceeding 11 inched in length.
3. The pistols shall be loaded on the grounds by the friends of each party in the presence of both friends and parties if the latter shall require it.
4. The friends of each party shall have the liberty of being armed with two loaded pistols on the grounds if they please.

5. The parties, respectively, shall be examined by the friend of each other on the grounds to see they shall have no personal defense of any kind about them, or anything that can prevent the penetration of a ball.
6. The parties, previously to taking their ground, shall strip off their coats and waistcoats to their shirts respectively, and shall fire in that situation.
7. Each party shall have leave to take a surgeon with them, if they please, to the grounds.
8. Both parties shall stand at a distance of thirty feet and, after being asked if they are ready, and each having answered in the affirmative, they shall receive the word to "fire," after which the parties may present and fire when they please.
9. The friends of the parties shall cast lots for choice of stand and for giving the word.
10. The friends of the parties shall pledge themselves to each other there are no persons on the island to their knowledge except those seen.
11. If either party shall fire before the word "fire" is given, it shall be the duty of the opposite party to shoot him who has so fired.
12. The parties by their undersigned friends pledge themselves, on their honor, for the strict observance of the above articles.

LAWLESS

J. BARTON

Lucas was wounded after the first fire and Benton demanded if Lucas was satisfied. He said he was not so Benton demanded another fire, of a second meeting. It was finally agreed they would have another meet as soon as Lucas was able. Great efforts were made to call the second duel off, but it could not be done. More than a month later the two men met in a duel which was fatal to Lucas.

Distance Reduced to 10 Feet

The distance was reduced to 10 feet and the ball from Benton's pistol went through the right arm of Lucas and entered the body near the heart. Benton was challenged repeatedly in the later years of his life. Once, it is said by Judge J.B.C. Lucas, father of Charles Lucas, but he refused. He said that he had promised Mrs. Benton that he would not fight another duel.

By 1823, public sentiment against dueling was growing strong in St. Louis. The Missouri Republican said, "Two more persons have been killed in a vicious state of society in every controversy."

One of the earliest and most notable of St. Louis duels was that between J. Barton and T. Hempstead.

Duel at Belleville

In 1819, Alonzo G. Stuart and William Bennett fought a duel at Belleville, MO. The seconds had that, in order to prevent bloodshed, they would load the guns without bullets. As his weapon was handed to him, Bennett slipped in a bullet and Stuart was mortally wounded.

Bennett was tried for murder, was convicted and hanged. This made dueling unpopular in Missouri and it is said that was the last fight fought in the state by its citizens. Illinois did not consider its jurisdiction extended to Bloody Island.

The Daily Republican
Poplar Bluff, MO
August 11, 1925

HORRIBLE STREET DUEL

The Two Men Kill Each Other Instantly
Battle Was over a Woman

Ill Feeling and Quarrel of Long Standing Reached
Crisis on Highway

Bismarck, MO Feb. 7

John Hughes of this place, age 21, and George Ketchicide, age 26, of Leadwood, became involved in a shooting affray at Leadwood this morning in which a number of shots were fired and both men were killed outright. They were sons of well-to-do farmers and unmarried.

Ketchicide was the aggressor. He had been at the post office and started trouble. He went from the post office to the Baptist Church and created a disturbance. From there he started for the Huffman lead mill. He met Hughes on the street and, as the men had previously had a trivial disagreement, sharp words were exchanged and the street duel began.

Ketchicide shot Hughes four times, twice in the limbs, once in the body and between the eyes.

Hughes fired three shots into Ketchicide all of which took effect, the last one killing him instantly. Hughes lived twenty minutes.

Justice Adams impaneled a coroner's jury, the verdict of which was that each one came to his death by a gunshot fired by the other party.

The trouble, it is said, was over a widow that both men were wooing.

The Daily Republican
Poplar Bluff, MO
February 9, 1908

ANGRY EDITORS IN DUEL

Huntsville Writers Fight in Post Office

Third Man, Spectator, Injured – Clothing of
Two Perforated by Bullets

Huntsville, MO

Bitter personal differenced, engendered by the congressional campaign in Randolph County, resulted in a street duel late yesterday between Van Davis, editor of the Huntsville Times, a supporter of W.W. Rucker, and John N. Hamilton, editor of the Huntsville Herald, who is an ardent advocate of the candidacy of J.H. Whitecotten. Both men were shot and a bystander may die of a wound received.

Several hundred persons were passing the post office, where the fight began at 4:30 o'clock, when the mail is distributed.

Hamilton entered the post office, and was at the end of the line when Davis went in. Both men drew revolvers and the first shots rang out as one. Neither was effective.

Hamilton stepped toward Davis, and fired again. Davis, standing about ten feet off, backed out and rapidly fired every cartridge in his revolver. Davis staggered but steadied himself and his weapon, narrowly missing Hamilton and ran down the street. Hamilton followed, firing as he ran. It was while the last shots in the post office were being fired that Pearl Gunn who was standing in back of the two men was shot, the bullet narrowly missing his heart.

The Chautauqua audience, just dismissed, came down the street toward the post office and the bullets fired by Hamilton at Davis, who was staggering and soon stopped, whizzed over their heads. J.M. Morris, deputy sheriff, at the head of the crowd, ran up and took Hamilton's gun from him and arrested both men. Davis was found to be shot in the left hip, and Hamilton had a bullet wound in his left arm.

The clothing of both was perforated with bullet holes. Both were released under $1,000 bond for appearance before a justice today. Davis left the employ of Hamilton more than a year ago to become the editor of The Times.

The shooting was due to a quarrel over an article in The Times, which Hamilton said, gave him the "lie".

The men came face-to-face Saturday, but trouble then was averted.

The Daily Republican
Poplar Bluff, MO
August 5, 1912

TWO BROTHERS FIGHT A DUEL, BOTH KILLED

Tishomingo, Okla.

Brothers Nick and Ike McDonald were wounded critically today in what Sheriff L.W. Hamilton described as a duel with shotguns climaxing years of quarrels.

The brothers, in their 40's, were found by their families in a pasture shortly after daybreak. Nick McDonald had shotgun wounds to the stomach. Ike McDonald had wounds near the heart.

Hamilton said the shotguns of both men were nearby. Both had been fired.

The brothers lived on adjacent farms one half mile west of here, Hamilton said, and had quarreled for years.

Daily American Republic
Poplar Bluff, MO
July 26, 1938

SIKESTON MOUND DIGGER BRINGS IN THRILLING STORY

Sikeston, MO

Kenzie Kennett Baker or, if you please, Shawnee Tock Eagle, southeast Missouri's original, self made archeologist and curator of Indian relics came to town today and with him the story of a double tragedy dating back to the time when logging camps and sawmills dotted this territory. Baker might be envied by any number of outdoor boys. He spends weeks and months each spring and early summer investigating Indian mounds, and from bits of flint and stone, pieced together interesting tales of the past.

This particular time he comes in from his rambles with a rusty revolver, the stock alone bright and shiny. It is a green tinted bond and carries the insignia of its makers.

Baker's diary reads: Wednesday, April 22. A cold windy day. I went to the McBride farm near the White Oak School to the home of Harry Peevyhouse to eat dinner. Then went over in the fields where Alfred Gossett was planting cotton…A short time later Curtis Gossett gave me several nice arrow heads, and an old Smith & Wesson revolver, condition very rusty and out of repairs, which he found while plowing on the McBride farm at the old White Oak logging camp site near which White Oak school house No. 2 is now located.

Duel Shooting

This calls to mind a duel or shooting affair thirty-five years ago between William Fetters and Charley Hogg. Neither lived to tell the tale. A Himmelberger tramway (railroad logging road) ran through this strip of woods from the Morehouse sawmill, and Fetters was foreman and scaler. The two men fell out over a woman at Morehouse. A few days later Hogg came down to the White Oak camp on a handcar. He and Fetters met near the feed barn, and there the affair was settled once and for all time.

Hogg used a shotgun to pay his respects to Fetters. The latter replied with five shots from a revolver. There was absolutely nothing wrong with the marksmanship of either. Fetters died on the spot, and Hogg drilled through and through the chest with five lead slugs, died two days later in Morehouse. Fetter's revolver, a Smith & Wesson, according to other workmen about the camp, was never found. It was lost where it fell in sawdust and leaves.

"I believe," concludes Baker, "that this is Fetter's gun."

The American Republic
Poplar Bluff, MO
April 28, 1931

Chapter Eleven

WHOA NOW

THE MULE WHICH IS SLOWLY GIVING WAY TO MACHINERY

Poplar Bluff, MO

Now speaking of mules—

The mule is the most maligned of all domestic animals. He is laughed at, sneered at and used for purposes of odious comparisons.

It is said, and it true, that he is one of the homeliest of God's creatures. He is stubborn and slow. Sometimes he is sullen, sly, vicious, restless, and wayward. He is the offspring of the male ass and the mare and his proper name is Equus Asinus, variety gamma, if that means anything to you.

It is true that the mule is among the most useful of God's creatures. He is more intelligent than either of his parents; usually he is willing, docile, faithful, and hardy.

Until the comparatively recent advent of the machine, the south was built and operated by mule motive power.

Is the mule vanishing?

Figures about the mule

In asking a number of Poplar Bluff fans this subject, some answered in the affirmative and others in the negative. It seems that opinions differ, but here are actual figures on the mule.

In 1910, when the automobile and the tractor were still rich men's toys, the mule population of the United Stated was 4,210,000. In 1928 it was 5,566,000.

In Missouri the mule population in 1922 was 377,000 and according to a survey made by the state agricultural department. The 1930 invoice shows 300,000 head of mules, which proves the animal is on the decrease. That is attributed to the fact the tractor is slowly and surely taking his place.

The decline in mules continues heavier than horsed, mostly in yearling mules compared to a slight increase in mule colts. The five leading mule-owning counties in Missouri now are New Madrid, Dunklin, Mississippi, Stoddard, and Saline.

Now What She Used to Be

The old gray mule ain't what she used to be, says Jeff Woods, who had been dealing with mules in Southeast Missouri for the past 35 years. Years ago Mr. Woods went to St. Louis and bought his mules by carloads. A drove of mules clopping along the downtown street of Poplar Bluff was a sight as common then as a summer Sunday procession of flivvers now—well, almost as common.

In addition to buying at the big markets, Mr. Woods sometimes would go over the Southeast Missouri territory and buy mules as he went. He would then have what he called a private auction sale and auction them all off.

The Mule State

There may be a good number of mules in Missouri today, but, take it from Mr. Woods, they are a sorry breed. Time was when a self-respecting farmer took pride in his mules. If he had a team, he wanted a good one, a matched pair with some life to them. He wanted mules with deep bodies, broad chests, full flanks, short backs and well-sprung ribs with height about 15 hands, but it's different now.

"The trade," mourns Mr. Woods, "want cheap mules and they get plug-uglies—scrawny beasts of no more than inferior or common grade, with keg heads, long backs, waspy flanks and sloping hips. The farmer uses his car to come to town and he thinks there is no need of the mules being of the highest grade, since they stay on the farm all the time."

Can't Buy Them

Mr. Woods, in relating some of his experiences in past years, stated that in 1915 he went to Doniphan and bought 200 head of mules and shipped them to the St. Louis market. "Now," he said, "I'll bet you couldn't buy 200 head of mules in Ripley County." He also said "in the year 1917, I bought range horses and mules out of the St. Louis market, amounting to 55 cars, and sold them at auction over Southeast Missouri and Northern Arkansas. But now (he gave a big sigh) you couldn't sell that many horses and mules in Missouri and Arkansas in five years."

While talking to Mr. Woods, he said trucks and tractors had both taken the place of the mule. "I'll bet there isn't more than five mule colts in Butler County," he said. "The farmers have quit raising them, and the raising of horses isn't much better."

All Poplar Bluffians will agree they seldom see a horse drawn dray in the city. In fact, we are of the opinion there is only one of this kind and that is the dray of William Randies. But for a mule-drawn vehicle, that is almost a thing of the past.

While we are talking of mules, just what kind of a critter is this animal called a mule? It is known he is a hybrid of a jackass, but what else do we know about him?

Least Romantic

The mule is probably the least romantic of all animals. You never see a gallant movie hero whispering pretty nothings in a movie mule's flapping ear. The mule wins no spectacular raves, rescues no heroes or heroines, pulls no smoke-belching fire wagons to alarm fires, poses for no

71

beautiful pictures to be hung in one's living room, and bears no brave generals into battle. None of these glamorous adventures have been no brave generals into battle. None of these glamorous adventures have been his in the movies or in real life.

The mule lives, works, and dies, unwept, unhonored, and unsung – and doesn't give a hoot.

Despite the drab existence of the mule, he is one of the most interesting of domesticated animals. He is the hardiest of work animals. In comparison with the horse, he lives longer, endures more work and hardships, requires less attention and feed, is less liable to digestive disorders, lameness and disease, and is more easily handled in large numbers.

He does not like to be hurried, worried, or cuffed about. Forcing him to do things against his will is one of those things that can't be done with safely. He must be understood and gently persuaded to do things out of the ordinary. He is naturally suspicious of everybody who comes around him and never takes his eyes off a stranger. If his ears begin to wag a little, the stranger had better seems to be able to read his handler's intentions, be they kindly or cruel.

Have you ever seen a man face a mule and tug at the halter line? He never gets anywhere. But if he turns around and starts off in the direction that he wishes to go, the mule will follow quietly.

The mule is quite fond of rolling in the dust and he always likes company.

He Is Intelligent

A large number of stories to prove the intelligence of the mule are told. You can turn him into a lot at night with access to a tank full of water, a trough full of grain and a rack full of hay and he will not overeat nor over drink. When he has satisfied his hunger, he stops and goes to sleep. Under the same circumstances, a horse would kill himself.

If a farmer is plowing a team consisting of two mare, one with a mule colt and the other with horse colt, this will happen: The horse colt will follow its mother up and down the rows all day waiting for time to suckle. The mule colt, after the first few rounds, will lie down at the end of the rows and wait until dinnertime.

The gate-opening talents of mules are well known, which show that they are quite intelligent, as all farmers will agree.

But few mules are raised in Missouri any more, and eventually there will be none raised, according to Mr. Woods.

The American Republic
Poplar Bluff, MO
February 5, 1930

MAIL CARRYING MULE IS MARVEL

St. Joe, AR

Tom Mix and his horse, Tony, have very little on Sam Allen, St. Joe mail carrier and his mule, Maude. In fact, his owner thinks Maude would be equally proficient in the stunts of the movie horse if given equal training and opportunities. As it is, the mule's training has been in the rural postal service, and in that field he has done almost everything but read the postal cards.

Allen is the carrier on the route traversing the rugged hills west of St. Joe, and Maude knows every box on the route. There is a confusion of cross roads and trails, and yet last winter when Allen was incapacitated for a day or two, and was forced to send a substitute, his only instructions were to let Maude travel the route. The mule did not pass a single box without stopping and faithfully carried the substitute over every bend and by-path in the long winding route.

Part of the mail carrier's daily load is carried to Wollum on the Buffalo River, where another received it and takes it on the Point Peter, Eula, Leigo and other post offices in Eastern Newton County. On one occasion, during high water, Maude, riderless swam the river with a load of merchandise and then sway back again.

During the time of the heavy snows in January, when the road was impassable for automobiles and wagons, Maude traveled the route daily, the owner carrying mail and groceries to snowbound families. One day the faithful Maude became affected with snow blindness, but Allen remedied that by manufacturing a bonnet such as was used to protect dray horsed from the hot sun in the cities 10 or 15 years ago, and equipping it with green goggles.

Maude can count too, at least to 11. That is the number of ears of corn apportioned for each meal. When the feed box is opened she will pick 11 ears out – one at a time – depositing them in the manager, always stopping when 11 are picked out.

Maude is a good plow mule, but from her actions in the harness the job has no "appeal" for her and is drab and uninteresting. She is a different mule when saddled for the mail route, and appears to enter spiritedly into the faithful and punctual delivery of the daily mail.

The American Republic
Poplar Bluff, MO
April 10, 1930

OLD GREY MULE NOT WHAT HE USED TO BE

Williamsville, MO

His name is Jim, but he is familiarly known as Old Jim in his home neighborhood. He has spent his entire life on the farm of a well-known citizen near Patterson. Although his hair, once a beautiful silver grey, is now snowy white, he can still outwork anybody on the farm, according to the man whom he has served all these years. He never gets off the farm any more since the advent of the automobile. In his younger days he made regular trips to the post office, grocery store, etc., and sometimes even accompanied the boys when they went to see their best girl, but time has wrought change in the life of even Old Jim. However, the depression has not affected him. He still has comfortable quarters and three square meals a day. A family? Oh, no!

If you'd ask him his age, he would probably kick up his heels and race to the farther side of the barn lot, thinking you were going to slip a halter over his head, for Old Jim is just an old gray mule belonging to Jonathan Meador, a prosperous farmer of the Patterson neighborhood.

Although Old Jim was 30 years old last March, he has helped to make 29 crops, and Mr. Meador says can keep pace with anything on the farm, the boys not excepted.

So proficient has Old Jim become in his years of service, that no check lines are needed when he is in the harness. In laying off a hillside piece of new ground for corn this spring, no lines were needed. He seems to know by instinct or habit what is required of him. The same is true in plowing corn or truck patches. He seems possessed of an intelligence above the average in many respects.

He never jumped a fence in his life, yet no rail fence ever built would hold him if he wanted over it. He simply lays it down nosing off one rail at a time, thereby liberating himself and any other stock confined with him. However, it is said just a single strand of wire fence will hold him. He also has a habit of opening gates unless they are chained.

In some respects he has grown quite contrary in his older days. Mr. Meador says if he goes to the pasture to bring Old Jim in, he had to pretend he is after some other animal. If the mule thinks he is not wanted, he is sure to follow and he is first in his stall. In turning him out of the barn lot you must open the gate and try to prevent him from passing through. He will then go out in spite of you.

Nevertheless Old Jim is almost like one of the folks and is highly esteemed by the entire family. Money could not buy him.

The American Republic
Poplar Bluff, MO
May 28, 1932

Chapter Twelve

THE DAY THE ROOF FELL IN

TORNADO RIPS POPLAR BLUFF APART

Monday, May 9, 1927, about 3:17 p.m., the worst destructive tornado to ever strike this part of the state, hit Poplar Bluff with a powerful force, wrecking practically every business building, snuffing out scores of lives and injuring hundreds of other citizens.

The tornado hit on Fifth Street and veered slightly to the east and then north through the business part of the city, and then crossed the river at the Vine Street Bridge, wrecking several business buildings and many homes, leaving behind death and destruction.

Tuesday morning, May 10, the citizens of Poplar Bluff and assistance from far and near were busy locating and identifying bodies and clearing away the debris.

The May 11th issue of the Daily Republican listed the names of 89 dead and 3 unidentified bodies. The paper stated May 13th the dead had risen to 105, and May 17th issue stated the list had grown to 110. Some Butler Countians stated the final count was 114.

"In the hush that followed the temporary suspension of rebuilding operations, Poplar Bluff people today (Friday, May 13) paused for an hour to pay final homage to those who died in Monday's cyclone. Funeral services for the storm victims were conducted from the courthouse square, with the courthouse steps serving as a pulpit."

The citizens of Poplar Bluff and from surrounding communities joined together in their efforts and rebuilt a bigger and better city. The indomitable spirit and ingenuity of the people prevailed.

Jay Mondy
Wappapello, MO
October 20, 2000

VINE STREET, BETWEEN BROADWAY AND MAIN- Buildings now house Bay's Music, Vine Street Cafe, Boxx Barber Shop, etc.

AERIAL VIEW OF TORNADO PATH- View is Northeast with Fifth Street at bottom

THE DAY THE ROOF FELL IN

Poplar Bluff, MO

The date of May 9, 1927 may not mean much to many Poplar Bluffians, but for some of us it is a date we'll never forget. As for me, the roof fell on me. I was a sixth-grade pupil in the East Side School. When rebuilt it was named J. Minnie School. Our teacher was Miss Marcia Velvick.

I recently saw the book The Darkest Hours, which lists disasters over the world such as the Titanic and other boat accidents, train wrecks, tornados, typhoons, mine accidents, hurricanes and others. The Poplar Bluff Tornado was listed.

The tornado of that day started with a series of storms in Texas and Oklahoma and gradually worked its way east arriving in Poplar Bluff at 3:17 in the afternoon.

The next regular issue of The Daily Republican (later to become The Daily American Republic) on May 12 listed 105 dead. A community memorial service was held on the lawn of the courthouse, which had been destroyed. All churches and ministers participated. For days afterward, services and burials were conducted almost continually.

Two boys died in the East Side School. Three brothers, Stone, Bryan and Howard Bilkey, died when a meat market tumbled on South Fifth Street just south of the present post office. Another man died as a piece of timber struck him as he looked around the corner of the old Frisco Depot, which was rebuilt and later was a police station.

Victims said it seemed like an eternity as the vicious storm twisted across town from the 2500 Block of South 11th Street to the northeast outskirts of the East Side near what is now the Riggs and Barnes Wholesale area.

I remember the tornado as if it were yesterday. My room on the top floor of the East Side School. The entire second floor was blown off. I was buried in the debris as I failed to get out of the room and into the hall.

We had just returned from recess at 3 p.m. Our teacher, Miss Marcia Velvick, was conducting a class on the west side of the room. I was seated in the first row by the east windows. It suddenly got dark as night and debris started filling the air. The teacher started herding the pupils into the hall. I hurried to try to get into the hall, but didn't make it. I could hear the building timbers twisting and cracking. The next thing I knew, I was buried under the debris.

It rained a cloudburst. Water poured in on me and I wondered if I would drown. I was trapped and never did know how long I was buried. Sometime later rescue workers arrived. They started digging for a boy who screamed the entire time. The load on top of me felt like it would crush me.

That was when I started calling for help as some of the debris on the other boy was being piled on me. I do not know who dug me out or who carried me downstairs to a room. Sometime later my grandfather, Bob Gray of Rombauer, found me and carried me to an uncle's house at Peach and D Streets. Our home was blown away.

My head had knots where I was pelted with bricks. I was hit in the neck and back. It was the next day before I could stand up and it was the second day before I could start moving around to see some of the damage done by the storm. There wasn't any going to the doctor as there were not many doctors in Poplar Bluff at that time, and they were needed to care for those more seriously hurt. Churches were turned into hospitals.

The next day the newspaper put out a one-page handbill with the names of some of the casualties. The press had to be turned by hand as electricity had not been restored. The following day a page about the size of a newspaper was put out on a job press with a little more tornado news and more of the casualties.

The first regular issue was resumed on Thursday. It was my first trip to the newspaper office. I was going to have a paper route along with my brother, Earl. Miss Rose Saracini, circulation manager, was having a reunion with her boys. She had not been able to learn if any of them were casualties. There were none.

The paper was late that day. Residents were wanting to find out the latest news. My brother got his papers and started to his route in East Poplar Bluff. He sold out before he got to the bridge. He came back and got my papers as I wasn't able to make much speed. My papers were also sold before he got to the bridge.

Mrs. Frances (Deckard) Gamblin was a teacher at the East Side School. She had been my fourth-grade teacher. Students called her Miss Frances and I still do. I spent an afternoon with her recently, and we recalled that afternoon with the tornado struck.

She had a better view as she was in the room on the southwest corner of the building. "The first thing I knew, it was getting dark, and the wind was blowing birds into windows. The boys were laughing at their trouble. I was trying to get them back from the windows. Harry Rexford and Clarence Hastings, the two boys who died in the storm were my students", Mrs. Gamblin recalled.

"I was trying to move the children to the north wall of the room and a number of girls were around me. Then the building tumbled. I was hit with bricks, which brought knots all over my head and bruises on my body. I was covered and, for a time, thought I was dead. Sometime later, I saw a hand moving toward me. It was Mrs. Arnita (Githens) Key, who had the room next to me. She and Miss Velvick helped me out. One of the girls, Lucille Bragg, was seriously hurt, and I carried her downstairs", Mrs. Gamblin recalls.

The Bragg girl was operated on that night at the hospital set up in the First Christian Church. She recovered.

"One of the first persons I remember seeing coming to the wrecked school building was Dr. Bond. He had his shirt and pockets stuffed with medicine as he came to see who he could help," said Mrs. Gamblin.

Mrs. Gamblin recalled seeing Dr. J. Lee Harwell several days later. His daughter, Gladys, and Mrs. Gamblin were close friends. "We thought you were dead", said Dr. Harwell. Without any type of communication, people just waited to find out about friends and relatives.

Mrs. Gamblin's mother, Mrs. Laura Deckard, lived in the 900 block of Poplar Street. She made her way across the wrecked city to the school to find her daughter. With the help of Charles Hastings and another boy, they took her home.

It was a day that won't be forgotten by those who survived that tragedy. In the first newspaper publication there were headlines of "We Will Rebuild" and "We Will Be Back".

One year later, "Poplar Bluff Day" was held. It was a celebration where people came from miles around to see how Poplar Bluff was coming back. That celebration became the Ozark Jubilee and continued up to the period before World War II. The newspaper published a special edition showing how the city came back.

Out of the storm came a spirit that let the city through the loss of Galloway Pease Lumber Company and the Brooklyn Cooperage mill in 1928 as they moved to Sumpter, South Caroline. Both were located at Palmer Slough in East Poplar Bluff and employed up to 1,000 workmen.

That same spirit has continued in Poplar Bluff to make it one of the nicest places to live. The roof fell in, but I was lucky. Scores of others weren't.

Bob Gray,
Retired DAR Staff Writer
Poplar Bluff, MO
May 8, 1987

37 KILLED IN MYSTERY BLAST; 22 INJURED

Explosion in Garage Wrecks Dance Hall – Dancers Die

Mystery Envelops Cause of Explosion, Although Many Believe Gasoline Wiser Motor Co. Building Was Cause Dance Hall Wrecked; Flames Envelop Dancers and Only Few Escape

West Plains, MO

Thirty six or probably more people are dead and nineteen are injured, many of them seriously, as a result of a mysterious explosion which occurred at 11:05 o'clock last night in the garage of the Wiser Motor Co., on East Main Street, and which wrecked the Bond dance hall on the second floor of the building where a dance was in progress.

Nearly all of the dead and injured were those attending the dance, and members of a small orchestra who gave the dance and who were providing the music.

The blast, which was heard all over the city and which completely wrecked the building in which the Wiser Motor Co., and the Bond hall were located, came without an instant of warning. People in nearby buildings, who rushed out, saw the bodies and debris flying high into the air. In another instant the bodies were coming back down. Several of those who escaped and are now in the hospital were blown out of the building and were picked up in the streets.

A coroner's jury today will investigate the cause of the explosion, although many believe that a tank of gasoline in the Wiser garage was responsible for the tragedy.

J.W. (Babe) Wiser, owner and manager of the Wiser Motor Company, was in the garage at the time, and his body was picked up after the explosion in a nearby vacant lot.

Building inflames Instantly

Following the explosion the Wiser building and also the Riley building on the west, and the Adams building on the east of the Wiser building, burst into a mass of flames which leaped a hundred feet or more into the air.

The two adjoining buildings were badly wrecked and persons living in them had narrow escapes.

G.B. Owens and his family and Arnold Merk, who lived in apartments on the second floor of the Riley building, barely escaped with their lives and Charles Merk, young son of Arnold Merk, lost his life, his body being recovered today.

Aged War Veteran Saved

Frank K. (Daddy) Pool, an aged Civil War veteran, who also occupied rooms on the second floor of the Riley building, was rescued. Mrs. Martha Hawkins and her four children, who occupied an apartment on the second floor of the Adams building, also barely escaped with their lives.

Owing to the intense heat rescuers who rushed to the scene were able to do but little toward rescuing the victims from the debris, and only some of those in the front of the building were saved.

Scene is Horrifying

The scene was a horrifying one. Screams and groans issued from the wrecked building for a few moments following the blast, but soon the scene was quiet.

After the explosion only a part of the front wall of the building remained standing. The second floor and roof of the building and parts of the walls dropped to the level of the street. When rescuers arrived one youth who was hanging by his hands on a part of the wrecked wall dropped to the street and was carried out of danger.

Three injured boys were in a second story window of a part of the remaining front wall screaming to be saved. A ladder was put up to the side of the building and they were brought down.

Few Women Escape

One of the pitiable facts was only three women escaped from the dance alive, while sixteen men escaped. This obviously was due to the fact the men were stronger and were able to extricate themselves from the wreckage.

High School Athlete Rescues Woman

Mrs. Garrett McBride, one of the women who was rescued, was extricated from the debris and was carried out by Lester Blackiston, West Plains high school football star, who was one of the first to reach the scene. Mrs. McBride's husband, who also was badly injured, was trying frantically to rescue her when Blackiston reached them. She was pinioned under wreckage.

Mrs. McBride is one of the most seriously injured. It is feared her back is broken and she also is suffering from burns and other injuries. Her husband is suffering from internal injuries.

Charles Unger of Cabool, also is one of the most seriously injured. All of the injured are suffering from burns, cuts, bruises, broken bones and some from internal injuries.

Rushed to Christa Hogan Hospital

All of the injured, with the exception of Ralph Langston, Jr., were taken to Christa Hogan hospital, where doctors, nurses and volunteers worked with them all of the remainder of the night.

Neighbors rushed extra quilts, blankets and other bed clothing to the hospital.

Young Langston was taken to the new Cottage Hospital on Webster Avenue.

The men who escaped were too dazed scarcely to know what they were doing and probably would not have reached safety after they got out of the wreckage had not rescuers arrived in time to aid them. They staggered blindly about and some collapsed completely after they got to their feet.

A.W. Landis, who was one of the first to arrive on the scene, helped one large man to extricate himself. Then he and the man pulled out a woman, whom the man said was his wife. This evidently was Mr. and Mrs. Fitchett, although Mr. Landis did not know them.

Many of the town's young people were here for the dance, and within a few hours after the tragedy frantic relatives from neighboring towns joined the relatives of West Plains who were searching hospitals and morgues for their loved ones.

The bodies, as they were removed from the debris, were taken to the morgue of the McFarland Undertaking Company and the Davis-Ross Undertaking Company.

The first body removed last night was that of Paul Evans, Jr., son of Dr. Paul Evans of West Plains. The youth was found lying face down on the pavement in front of the wrecked building, his body covered with debris. The next body removed was that of Mrs. R.G. Martin, which was found in the wrecked stairway of the dance hall.

Three Buildings Destroyed

Three buildings were completely destroyed. The Bond building, owned by Mrs. Leland Ward of West Plains and which housed the dance hall and the Wiser Motor Co., the Adams building, adjoining the Bond building on the west, which housed the Laird Plumbing Co., and the Bell Café, and the Riley building on the east, which housed the G.B/ Owens Grocery. The Adams building was owned by Mrs. Ada Adams and her sons, Mat Adams of West Plains and Dr. Alford Adams of St. Louis. Nothing was saved from any of the three buildings. All of the buildings destroyed were of brick.

Other Buildings Damaged

Plate glass fronts and windows were blown from nearly every building on court square and East Main Street even the windows in the court house were shattered.

The Arcade Hotel, just south of the Bond building, the beautiful West Plains bank building, at the corner of East Main Street and court square, the Langston-Pease building across the corner from the bank, the Davidson Motor Company building, the Gray Garage building and the Commercial Hotel all were damaged by the explosion, the bank building and the Arcade hotel suffering the heaviest damage.

West Plains Weekly Quill
West Plains, MO
April 19,1926

Chapter Thirteen

THINGS DO HAPPEN

DEBONAIR JACK DESERTS CREDITORS

Cuts Quite a Swath in Gayest Society for Several Months, Accumulated Debts, Works Friends who Pamper Him in Belief He is Son of McKinley System President, Spends his Own and Others' Money Like Water – Then Departs Hastily Without Liquidating Accounts.

Poplar Bluff, MO

Gay society in Poplar Bluff, and even a more conservative and retiring social set will be stunned when it learns that dashing John R. Dew, peach-blown complected, silken-hosed, delicately aristocratic and lavish-spending "Jack" Dew is a prisoner in Denver, Colo., charged with posing as Adolphus Busch III, grandson of the late multi-millionaire brewer. Debonair Jack Dew was not posing as a merely rich brewer's grandson when in Poplar Bluff, but his eye was set on greater social heights than that. So while in this city he was the son of the president of the tremendous McKinley System, which controls hundreds of miles of the interurban railways in America. And the beauty of it is, Jack Dew had the personality and the brass to make his declarations stick as truth.

Several of Poplar Bluff's fairest and most highly respected young women "fell" for Jack Dew's magnetism, and one or two, it is said, were in imminent danger of losing their hearts to him. He was a royal host, entertaining with enthusiasm for expense, which was never questioned, but as later developments occurred, however, these expenses became huge and of vast annoyance to his erstwhile friends after he had vanished from the city's social whirl.

Spender he was, exhibitor of a fat bank-roll upon his arrival, having the fastidiousness in dress of a Berry Wall, purchaser of countless suits of delicately tinted and imported pajamas, socks, shirts, and various other most acceptable and wisely chosen articles of apparel, Jack Dew created a flutter among the young men of the town as he did among the young women.

He put up at the Wright Hotel. His appetite for the best liquors was voracious when in the company of friends and his capacity was abnormal. And he was host upon all such occasions. The money of all others was counterfeit. He was a high roller, careless, polished, dainty – and accounted for his idleness in the fact that his "papa" was the rich chief of a great system and the son's allowance was in keeping with papa's rating.

But after about three months of luxury, which finally was entirely at the expense of his found friends, the blowup came. A young fellow who had been touched for one hundred became suspicious and went to the McKinley System's headquarters. Nobody there knew a Mr. Dew. Nobody had ever heard of him. He might be employed somewhere in the shops, officials said, as a day laborer but he wasn't on the payroll.

And it was just about this time that Jack Dew decided he must tear himself away. He started with his two packed grips, but a squat and hard-fisted businessman met him on the depot steps and demanded return of the money borrowed and the total of a merchandise bill. Dew tried to sidestep, but there was nothing doing, so he smoothly explained the embarrassing situation to an admirer who wrote out a check for the amount due, and which the distinguished railroad man's son was to send by first mail.

The Daily Republican
Poplar Bluff, MO
January 18, 1914

RATTLER READY TO STRIKE GIRL

Buelteman Child Fascinated by Reptile at Time
C.M. Copeland Appears and Dispatches It

Snake Four Feet, Ten Inches Long; Bro't Here

Serpent Measures Seven Inches in Circumference –
Rears Head Two Feet Preparatory to Fight

Poplar Bluff, MO

A small girl named Buelteman narrowly escaped being a victim of a huge rattlesnake yesterday afternoon at a point about two miles east of Kinzer, on the Cat railroad. She was saved by C.M. Copeland, who dispatched the reptile, clubbing it to death.

Copeland was attracted to the scene by the attitude of the child, who was standing as though fascinated by something. When he arrived the great rattler was rearing its head almost two feet and preparing to strike. He dealt it a blow with a club and then beat it to death. The child had not budged.

The reptile was brought to Poplar Bluff and shown a number of persons. It was four feet ten inches in length and seven inches in circumference. It had twelve rattles and a button. The monster is said to be one of the biggest ever killed in this part of the country.

Death was certain for the child, it is believed, had not Copeland appeared just when he did.

The Daily Republican
Poplar Bluff, MO
July 24, 1912

VENOMOUS SNAKE AFTER FISHERMAN

Story From Piedmont, MO, That Must Be Taken For Its Face Value

Piedmont, MO

Snake stories are in order, the following from the Piedmont Banner being given for what it is worth:

John Wilkinson and Clay Bunyard were attacked in a skiff out on the river several days ago by a large and determined cottonmouth snake.

The snake had taken refuge between some rocks. Wilkinson prodded it with a gig pole and it came out and disappeared beneath the boat. Bunyard stood at one end of the boat with a shotgun watching for the snake to reappear, but it eluded his search and the first either man saw of it was when they discovered it in the boat with them. Bunyard, gun in hand took to the water for safety. Wilkinson was also about to take a header out of the boat when he saw that the snake was following Bunyard over the side of the boat. His courage returned and he managed to deal the snake a crippling blow as its head lay athwart the edge of the boat and he killed it with follow up blows.

The snake was five feet and two inches long. As is well known, cottonmouths have no fear of men and will fight rather than run any day.

The Daily Republican
Poplar Bluff, MO
September 27, 1914

CALF ATE HIS CHECK

Farmer Man Had Received It as Payment for Hog Killed, It went For Lunch

Says He Needs the Money and Will Railroad Company Please Send Another Check

From Monday's Daily

Disappeared from Stump

So after the farmer got his piece of paper, he laid it on a stump in the field. When he came back one of the calves was licking his chops as if to say that sort of fodder was rather good eating. The check was gone, and a piece of it on the ground indicated that the calf was six dollars in, while Mr. Farmer Man was six dollars to the red.

Then he went home, a sad man, indeed, until he thought maybe the railroad company he had abused so much would send him another check, which would be "calf proof." He thought it all over, then wrote the following letter to the company, which has just reached Mr. Collins:

The Letter From the Farmer

"In regards to that check you sent, I thank you for your kind attention. I received the check and taking it to the field and aimed to take it to be cashed and saw I was going to get it soiled and laid it on a stump and a calf got hold of it through a fence and ate it up, and I would be more than glad if you would help me to get another one and if there are any charges, I will pay you, and as I need the money very bad, I will certainly appreciate it if you will send me another check. I will sign anything to get it replaced. Let me know what to do about it."

"I remain as every."

Another Check is Sent

He has been sent another check, which it is safe to say, will be cashed as soon as it is received.

The Daily Republican
Poplar Bluff, MO
May 13, 1915

DROWNED IN A BUCKET OF WATER

Year-Old Daughter of Mr. and Mrs. Perry Tidwell of Near Harviell
Drowned Last Sunday Afternoon in Water Bucket
Father was Nearby and Hurried to Rescue
When the Child Was Strangled So Badly That She Died
Within Short Time, Father Reported

Harviell, MO

Little Minnie Tidwell, slightly more than a year old, daughter of Mr. and Mrs. Perry Tidwell of near Harviell, was drowned yesterday when she fell head first into a large water bucket at the Tidwell farm home.

Mrs. Tidwell was ill and was in the home in bed. Mr. Tidwell was in the back yard doing necessary chores late in the afternoon and the little child was playing in the yard.

The father chanced to turn around and saw the little child topple head first into the bucket. He hurried to her and pulled her out of the bucket, but she had apparently strangled to such an extent that she died within a few minutes.

Funeral services will be held tomorrow in the Tidwell home, and the little body will be placed at rest in the Cochran Cemetery, the Frank Undertaking Company reports.

The deceased child is survived by the mother, father and one sister. The entire community is grieved over the sad incident.

> The Daily Republican
> Poplar Bluff, MO
> May 16, 1924

Chapter Fourteen

WAS IT MURDER?

A MISSOURI MILLIONAIRE BETRAYED BY EMPLOYEE

Hiram N. Holladay, Lumber King, Married Two of the Haynie Sisters and Became Infatuated with the Third, Who was Employed by Him, and Her Husband, Monroe A. Johnson, Slew Him

Greenville, MO

Hiram N. Holladay loved the three Haynie sisters. Two of them he married. He ruined the reputation of the third. The second is now his widow. The husband of the third killed him. Monroe A. Johnson shot and killed Holladay when he found him in his wife's room. This was in Greenville, Wayne County, MO.

Holliday was wealthy. Some say he was worth a million. Johnson was the husband of Holladay's sister-in-law, one of Holladay's 600 employees. He had no property, and not enough money to mention.

Each of the men married a daughter of "Old Man" Haynie. Holladay's first wife was Ellen Haynie. She was his helpmate in the days when he needed help, long before he became the owner of a town, a railroad, and could boast of 600 employees and $100,000 worth of life insurance.

Ellen died and left him three children. After a while, he married her oldest sister, Mary.

His business increased rapidly and his wealth was soon numbered by the thousands. Holladay was industrious, frugal and shrewd. He had a good eye for business.

Thirty years ago, at the age of 20, Holladay was hauling logs with an ox team to a saw mill in Williamsville, Wayne County. "Old Man" Haynie then lived at Williamsville. He conducted a small general store, which is now operated by his sons, Charles and Asa.

After a while, Holladay became the owner of a small sawmill. In the meantime, he married Ellen Haynie. His business grew and grew until other lumber manufacturers in that district were forced out of business. Holladay built a fine house and Williamsville was very proud of it. It stands on a hill overlooking the little graveyard where he now lies.

Mrs. Holladay died and the villagers thought it would be appropriate if Mr. Holladay, the widower, should marry the sister of his former wife. Mary Haynie became Mrs. Holladay and the stepmother to her little nephew and nieces.

Holladay

Five years ago Holladay commenced building a railroad east of Williamsville. He extended it to the lonely house at Greenville, 13 miles away. He then moved his sawmill to the eastern terminus of his road. His 600 employees and their families went with him. Greenville became a thriving town. Williamsville, deprived of its stamina, degenerated into a railroad station with a handful of houses.

Holladay built scores of houses at Greenville, which he rented to his employees. The houses were all alike and looked as if shaken from a box of German toys.

He opened a big general store and turned his business into a corporation. It became the Holladay-Klots Land and Lumber Co. He extended his railroad further east into the timberlands of Wayne County. Over this road his employees had to pay fare whenever they desired to reach Williamsville or the Iron Mountain Railroad.

Holladay was never noted for paying high wages. Part of his employees wages were paid in cash, the remainder in checks good for so much merchandise at his store. In time, the authorities tried to enforce the anti-check law of Missouri against him. The Holladay checks are still in circulation.

Greenville was a one-man town. It was established and owned by one man. The town never got out from under his control until a bullet ended his life. The only people not directly dependent upon him were the few county office holders and the saloon keepers. But even they derived their votes and wealth from the Holladay corporations, and appreciated that fact.

For three or four years Holladay continued to live in his big house at Williamsville. Less than a year ago he completed a great mansion with a bay window, turrets and hardwood and moved his family to Greenville. The place was within sight of his big store at an equal distance, in the middle of a pretty acre of ground. It belonged to Holladay.

There lived Monroe Johnson and his wife, Nancy, the sister of the two Haynie girls whom the rich lumberman had married.

Johnson

Johnson was employed as a timber agent by the Holladay corporation. Mrs. Johnson acted as a cashier in the company office.

People at Greenville thought nothing of that; Mrs. Johnson was the rich lumberman's sister-in-law. Besides, the people of Greenville had no right to think. They were dependent upon Holladay for bread.

Johnson was a peculiar man. He was not popular. He wore a long mustache and his eyes were gray and cold. There seemed to be no warmth about them or him. His looks did not inspire familiarity. He went about his business quietly. He was not addicted to much speech. That eye of his made people think of unpleasant things. If the people of Greenville did not dare think, Johnson did. He suspected wrong-doing between his wife and his employer. Some say he spoke to Holladay and threatened him with vengeance.

The woodpile behind which Johnson hid, the house in which he lived

The Murder

Late in the afternoon, Johnson informed his wife that he was going to St. Louis. Apparently he started, but he did not go. After nightfall he returned to the house and sought the woodpile. There he remained and watched closely. He saw a figure approach the house. The front door opened. A woman's face appeared and the figure entered.

The Johnson arose and crept softly toward the house. He threw himself with all his force against the door, and it was broken in. The dim light revealed the forms of Mrs. Johnson and Hiram Holladay.

Johnson drew a revolver with which he had armed himself and fired. Holladay fell. Time after time the hammer clicked and half a dozen bullets entered the form of the prostate man. In a minute he was dead.

Johnson left the house like a man strolling downtown. He went to the little hotel. There he told the deed he had done. Soon afterward, he surrendered to the Sheriff.

From the first, there was intense feelings, pro and con.

Some men claimed the Johnson was justified by circumstance. Others said it was a deliberate murder. Johnson, having once warned Holladay, was actuated by a spirit of revenge. Some said the slayer should go free. Others said the law should take its course and the cold-eyed Johnson should to tot the gallows tree. Inside of an hour, the whole town of Greenville was divided on the question of Johnson's responsibility before the law. Men, who had not dared think while Holladay was alive, breathed more freely and were secretly glad that he was no more. He furnished them their daily bread, yet they considered him an oppressor, because they had to rent from him, buy from him, and work for him. It was the puerile resentment of the weak against the strong. Others upheld the memory of the man who had been their benefactor. They declared his death an outrage which should be punished to the law's limit.

Evidence was heard by a coroner's jury on the day of Holladay's funeral. They ordered Johnson held for the next grand jury of Wayne County.

The Woman

While all this was going on, Mrs. Johnson remained at home. Every night since the tragedy, she has slept in the room which is marked by the blood of her despoiler. He father and her 13 year-old son were in the house at the time the shooting occurred. She talks to them as calmly as though nothing had happened. She avoids the gaze of her neighbors as much as possible. She will receive no one to her house. The blood of her employer is still on the floor. But, on the second day after the tragedy, she sent her husband, the slayer – her wronged husband – a rocking chair, a pillow, and other articles to make his cell in jail comfortable.

Mrs. Johnson had no photograph of herself. At the request of a representative of the Sunday Post-Dispatch, without a great deal of persuasion, she consented to pose before a camera. She excused herself while she changed her waist and brushed her hair. She then stepped out into the sunlight of the backyard where she posed.

The attraction about Mrs. Johnson that lured Holladay is not apparent to the average observer. She is forty years old, although in justice to her it must be said she looks ten years younger. There is not a gray hair visible in the rather thin, reddish-brown locks combed plainly from an even part in the middle, and united again in a flat knob lob on the back of the head. Mrs. Johnson's eyes are dark. Her face is rather thin. Her teeth are not good. Her general demeanor was of a woman suffering physical pain, rather than mental anguish. She said her health was good. She declined a hand proffered to assist her to descend from the porch to the ground, seeming to shrink from the intended kindness.

Mrs. Johnson's voice faltered enough in refusing to discuss the tragedy to make it difficult to determine its quality. It is probably not musical. She does not look like a woman with a musical voice.

Mrs. Holladay refuses to be seen, except by a few close friends who are admitted to the Holladay mansion to console the window. Mrs. Holladay is two years younger than her sister.

The Haynie sisters, who are now the widow of Holladay and the wife of Johnson, Holladay's slayer, are the women of very ordinary attainments, living in different stations because of the difference in their wealth.

At Greenville there is no society, but one of that of respectability. All persons who can claim respectability are admitted. But there are no special affairs to attend, no theaters or places of amusement of any kind. People in society at Greenville simply visit each other's houses after the breakfast dishes are washed or neighborly lending of things to one another.

Both sisters are homely. Mrs. Holladay wears better clothes than the other. They are not burdened with education. Until the tragedy most people in Greenville thought the sisters very estimable people.

Mrs. Johnson worked in Holladay's store as a cashier. She has been employed there more than three years. That was all right by Greenville, even if she was married, for her husband was not a great money earner.

The Cause

This latter fact doubtless had much to do with the causes which led up to the tragedy. Holladay was a self made man. He had made a good job of it. Financially, he was worth between $500,000 and $1,000,000. His life insurance was worth $100,000. He worked more hours every day than his employees and went to church on Sundays. He seemed to have no amusements of recreations. He was thrown daily into contact with his wife's sister. She was the only woman he saw frequently. Socially their life was limited. He saw her more often than he did his wife. He became enamored of her. Holladay was caught in a trap of his own building, the Johnson cottage. The occupant killed him.

Holladay's chief characteristics was shrewdness. It was said of him, he never failed to make money on a deal. His chief business was making lumber. The railroad he built was necessary to that business. He never paid big wages. No one received anything from him that was not earned.

Holladay's hair and mustache were dark. There were few signs of gray in either one. He weighed about 190 and was tall enough to carry his weight comfortably. He dressed in cheap store clothes. He was not particular about his clothes. People looked up to him because he was successful and because he furnished them a living. Had he resided in a large city, he might have escaped the environment of loneliness, which induced the relations that led to his death.

Holladay was well known in St. Louis. Major C.C. Rainwater is president of the company owning the Holladay Railroad. Kit Klots of St. Louis was associated in business with Holladay for a number of years. R.J. Medley of St. Louis was vice-president of Holladay-Klots Land and Lumber Co. at one time. Other St. Louis men owned stock in the corporation. The corporation has an office in the Equitable Building. Alfred Bennett of St. Louis is the company's representative in this city.

**This Sixteen Room Victorian Home Was
Constructed in old Greenville in the Early 1890's
For Hiram Holladay and his Family**

Note: In August, 1900, a trial was held. The jury found Monroe Johnson
Guilty of manslaughter and fixed his punishment at a fine of $500.

Jay Mondy

A BRUTAL MURDER

Carnie Parsons, Wife and Three Children Are Victims

Licking, MO
October 18, 1906

Texas county is aroused over the most brutal and dastardly murder ever committed with its borders.

People, usually so peaceable and law-abiding, are worked up to a point of determination to take the law in their own hands toward a cold blooded murderer. A just penalty for one of the most brutal crimes ever committed, but it is now hoped cooler judgement will prevail and the law will be allowed to take its course, the public being assured the confessed murderer will fully suffer for his deed.

The first evidence of the crime came to light Saturday morning. Judge W.L. Hiett, Attorney Clark Dooley and L.L. Hodges, were on a fishing trip near Platter's Jam some twelve or fifteen miles north of Houston on Piney River. Messrs. Dooley and Hodges started out for an early fish, and when they climbed out of some rocks in the edge of the river discovered what they thought to be a rag doll in the water. Investigation showed it to be the body of a child and nearby another body was found. The alarm was given and neighbors were unable to first identify the bodies. Later a wagon was found in the woods nearby which was recognized as the property of Carnie Parsons, a man who had been making a crop on the farm of C.H. Cantrell. The children were recognized to be Parsons' and as the wagon was covered with blood stains, it was evident a foul crime had been committed. It was known that a young man named Hamilton had purchased the crop from Parsons and the latter was moving his family to his former home in Miller County. Suspicion was directed toward Hamilton and search for him was begun.

The Capture

Hamilton rode into Williams Livery barn here on a mule and asking for a saddle horse to go to Cabool, giving some excuse for his trip and stating he had been working near Raymondville. Nothing was known here of him being under suspicion of the crime at the time, but after he had secured a buggy and had gone on his way to Cabool, J.W. Cantrell, R.W. Williams and Deputy Sheriff Upton became suspicious of Hamilton's actions, knowing he had been at work on the same farm with Parsons and when Mr. Cantrell saw the mule he recognized it as one of Parsons'. Messages were at once sent to Simmons and on Hamilton's arrival there he was held by J.R. Simmons and Ben Sroufe until the arrival of Deputy Sheriff Upton and J.W. Cantrell, and after Hamilton saw there was no further chance for him to get away, he made a full confession of his crime. The prisoner was securely handcuffed and safely landed in jail here at 2:00 o'clock Sunday morning.

Hamilton is about 20 years of age youthful looking and rather small in size. He is a son of J.B. Hamilton, who formerly lived on the Millard farm; ten miles north of town. The young man has not borne bad reputation heretofore, but since his capture has admitted stealing a horse near Beulah some time ago.

The Bodies Found

Acting on the information from the self confessed murderer, the search for the bodies of the man and woman and the third was renewed and all were soon found but far from the place where they had been thrown in the water. Laid out on the bank of the river, the bodies presented a horrible sight; one never to be forgotten by those who viewed the remains. The man had been shot in the right leg just above the knee and the bone was shattered. Besides this he had wounds about the head evidently made with the gun barrel and with a knife. The woman was also badly cut and bruised about the head. Parsons was a man about 35 years of age and bore a good reputation as a hardworking man in the community. His wife seemed to be about 25 years of age. The three children were pretty little boys; Jesse, age 5; Frank age 3; and Edward age 1. These bodies presented the most pitiable sight of all. The two older ones had been struck on the head and their throats cut in a horrible manner. The Platter hone nearby were a postmortem was held under supervision of Prosecuting Attorney Hiett by Doctors R.B. Lynch, and then to the Cantrell graveyard Tuesday.

The Crime as Committed

Carnie L. Parsons had lived in that neighborhood for the past two years or more. He had been recently living on the farm of C.H. Cantrell and had made a crop there. Jodie Hamilton, as he is known , worked on the same farm. Parsons concluded to return to his former home in Miller county, and Hamilton bought his crop. Hamilton paid Parsons $25 a day or so before the murder. The prisoner has given very little reason for any trouble to have come up between the men, but claimed that it was some difference over a saddle. On Friday morning, Parson, with his family and household effects in his wagon, was on his way to Miller County. Hamilton claimed they had some little altercation but no difficulty. It seemed Hamilton then followed the family and overtook them some three or four miles west of the river. He evidently shot Parsons while the latter was sitting in the wagon from the fact the dead man was shot in the leg and blood was all over the side of the wagon. The gun used is a single barreled, breach loading shot gun and had belonged to Parsons. How or when Hamilton got the gun is not known.

After wounding the man he had evidently beaten him to death with the gun barrel. Those who visited the scene of the killing report evidences of a terrible struggle between Hamilton and the woman, as the surrounding bushes were covered with blood, and her comb and fascinator were found at some distance from the wagon. Hamilton claims to have killed the woman and children in the wagon.

After the inhuman deed was committed, the murderer took the harness from the mules and the dead man's money and started for home. One mule would not lead, so he turned it loose, taking the other back home.

Friday night Hamilton attended church and accompanied his girl home. After church he returned to the wagon, taking a team with him, loaded the dead bodies all in the wagon and started for the river. On the way he stalled and went to Ed Bates and borrowed a mule to help pull out. He was delayed until daylight and was recognized by James Ormsby as he passed the latter's house. Ormsby asked him what he was loaded with and he replied it was wheat. Driving on down to the river he threw the bodies in and drove the wagon a quarter of mile back in the woods where he stripped off the harness and left the wagon and harness and went on back home.

Learning of the discovery of the bodies, he became uneasy and started to get away, but owing to the prompt work of the officials was captured as stated above. When searched something over $32 was taken from him which he stated was Parsons' money. He also had a razor, some spectacles and other articles which had belonged to the dead man.

The crime is an extremely cruel and blood thirsty one, without a single redeeming feature to attract sympathy for the slayer of the family. His only motive was to secure possession of the dead man's property.

The Murderer's Tale

After being arrested Hamilton made the following statement to those who had him in charge. We are indebted to Mr. Cantrell for the statement as follows: "I am up against it; I did the killing. I overtook Parsons and family on the Success Road, west of Piney River, about 2 miles or more west of the Millard farm. When I overtook them we got in a quarrel over a saddle. Parsons then went out the road a short distance and we commenced to quarrel again; Parsons got out of the wagon and opened his knife and then I shot him with a single barreled shotgun. The shot did not kill him and Parsons and wife both tried to take the gun from me, but I got it away from them and knocked Parsons in the head with the gun barrel and then knocked the woman in the head and thought I had killed her, but soon noticed she was coming to, and I began beating her in the head again and finished killing her. I then killed the oldest boy by cutting his throat and the next oldest the same way and the youngest one by knocking it in the head with the gun. Then I drove the wagon off a short distance from the road and took the harness off the mules and saddled one of them and got on it; led the other mule a short distance, but it wouldn't lead, so turned it loose, thinking it would follow, but the mule left and I have never seen it since. I went back to the farm where Parsons had lived and that night went to church and after church took my girl home and then borrowed a horse from Alfred Decker and took the horse and the mule I was riding and went back in the night to the place where I had left the dead bodies. I harnessed up the horse and mule and struck out for the river and drove through the woods for awhile, but finally got stalled and couldn't get the horse to pull; I then went to Ed Bates and borrowed his mule to pull out with and then got with it."

"Daylight came before I got to Jim Ormsby's and he came out and spoke to me. I went on down to the river and then threw all them into the river, then drove back up the hollow and left the wagon, unharnessed the team, got on the mule and went back to the farm. I intended to go to church again that night and went out to Mr. Fowler's were my girl was. Then told me someone had found some children in the river and I knew then they would find out it was me that killed them. I told them I could not go to church that night, as I had to go to Licking on business. I got on the mule and rode east from there and went on to Houston, put the mule in Bob Williams' barn and got him to send me to Cabool."

Prisoner Taken To Springfield

Rumors of mobs being formed continued to be circulated. Sunday evening Sheriff Wood was in Licking when the crime was first discovered and was promptly at the scene and assisted in the search for and taking care of the bodies. Seeing the feeling that had been aroused in the neighborhood he came to town Sunday afternoon, and as rumors of a mob continued to come in he determined that it was for the best the prisoner should be taken away before any violence was attempted. Just after dark Sunday night he loaded Hamilton in a carriage and conveyed him to Springfield and placed him in jail to await preliminary.

There is not a man, woman or child in Texas county who does not believe the murderer should pay the full penalty for his awful crime. Circuit court meets next week and the trial will be a speedy one. In the meantime, let us hope that wiser counsel and cooler heads will prevail, and the awful crime will not be added by violence. No man will attempt to condone, the inhuman act but the fair name of out citizenship is at stake, and the unorganized violence of a mob will but add to the already disgraceful reports to the daily papers of St. Louis and Springfield, which describe our county as desolate and wild and our people as illiterate mountaineers. Hamilton will get justice: let the law take its course.

Reprinted
The Licking News
Licking, MO
February 3, 2000

Note: A few weeks after the trial a gallows was erected outside the county courthouse, Houston, Missouri, the county seat for Texas County. Jodie Hamilton was sent through the trapdoor and the rope broke. The rope was repaired in about five minutes and Hamilton was sent through the door once again.

Jay Mondy

THE SHOOTING OF SHERIFF KELLY

C. Roy Kelly, 1885-1931
Sheriff of Howell County
Shot and killed in the line of duty, shortly before 9 a.m.
December 19, 1931, at West Plains by members of the notorious
"Ma" Barker-Alvin Karpis gang
After 50 years – The Tragedy They Still Talk About in West Plains

West Plains, MO

"In Cold Blood"

It was early Saturday, December 19, 1931. Buss Barrett, who was 22 the time, happened to be standing on the sidewalk in front of the Davidson Motor Company garage on East Main Street. He saw Howell County Sheriff C. Roy Kelly drive up and park across the street in front of what was then the post office. Kelly got out of the car and went up the steps into the post office. Checking his mail box was one of his regular morning stops, after having coffee with his good friend, J.R. Bridges, the police chief.

Before moving to West Plains, Kelly had been in the restaurant business with his wife in Mtn. View. The Van Buren native had also been a traveling salesman for a Springfield candy company. It was during his travels through the country he saw the need for better law enforcement in the area and decided to run for sheriff.

A congenial, easy-going sort, he proved to be a popular candidate and won by a large majority. As a law officer, he won respect for his balance of firmness and friendliness. He didn't carry a gun as a habit, and never used force when he thought he could bring in an offender peacefully.

About the same time Kelly entered the post office, a blue DeSoto sedan with three men in it backed into the Davidson garage. The driver told owner Carac Davidson he had two flat tires needed to be patched. One of the passengers, a young man, got out to watch as Bill Tiner, a garage mechanic, repaired the tires.

In the middle of the job, Davidson suddenly recognized whither the car or its occupants as possibly being connected with a late-night break-in at the C.C. McCallon clothing store on the Square, December 17. $2,000 worth of merchandise had been taken. That was the latest of a series of unsolved burglaries and robberies in the area.

The West Plains Journal reported the crooks gained entry by removing two bars from a rear window. Evidently they were classy dressers, as "the stock was carefully selected, as shown by the fact only the winter shades were taken in the hosiery lines. Ties, gloves, sweaters and shirts were not taken in great piles but were selected carefully as to quality and the latest styles."

It may have been an article of clothing from the store that tipped Davidson off, or it may have been the tread on the tires, matching tracks left in the alley behind McCallons two nights earlier. For whatever reason, Davidson excused himself, got to a telephone and asked McCallon to come over for an identification.

Just as McCallon arrived at the garage, Davidson saw Kelly coming out of the post office across the street. As Kelly paused at the top of the steps to light a cigarette, Davidson hurried over and told him of his suspicions.

After this hushed discussion, Barrett saw Kelly go back to his car and put on his gun and holster, which he kept in the back seat. The gun was hidden from view by the sheriff's overcoat.

As the two men walked across the street to the garage, Kelly said hello to Barrett. McCallon and Barrett remained outside the garage, near opposite corners of the building. They were joined by Dutch James, who owned a building next to Davidson's.

One of the James' employees, Jess Thomas, walked up to Barrett while he was standing there and whispered urgently, "Something's hot!", meaning something was about to happen.

We can only speculate now what was in Kelly's mind as he entered the garage to investigate Davidson's suspicions. Did he expect to be confronting desperate outlaws? Was he thinking of the October 6, 1931 robbery of the People's Bank of Mtn. View, where several thousand dollars had been taken? Whatever the case, he showed no fear as he walked directly to the car and started questioning the men inside.

A moment later, Barrett heard shots inside the garage. A man came running out the front door, turned the corner and slipped down in front of Barrett. Barrett remembers seeing the man pop a clip of bullets into an automatic pistol he was holding before getting up and running down the alley between the buildings.

When the shooting started, McCallon looked in the door in time to see Davidson dive behind the service counter. At first he thought Davidson had been hit.

Another witness to this scene was Frank Ball, now of West Plains. He had hitch-hiked into town and was let off in front of the post office just as the shots were fired. Ball recalls seeing the gunman run down the alley, slip and fall, then continue running.

Seconds later, Ball heard the screeching of tires and the roaring of the blue DeSoto as it shot out of the garage. It bounced violently as its wheels hit the gutter and headed off down East Main Street. The right rear door was swinging open as the car headed out of town at a high rate of speed. The driver, the only person in the car, reached around and pulled the door shut.

While this was going on, Dutch James ran to his car, which was parked next to the post office, got out a .22 semi-automatic rifle and with Barrett's encouragement fired several shots after the fleeing car. Several shots hit a utility pole. Others seemed to strike the car, but with no telling effect.

Still another witness was Monroe Forbes. He and some other young men used to hang out behind an old building down in the alley, which they called the "Clubhouse to find help. Forbes says the gunman who shot Kelly ran right through the middle of a crap game there in the alley, the gun still in his hand.

M.C. Stephens, who was a city policeman at the time, recalls vividly what he saw when he was summoned moments after the shooting. The sheriff had been killed instantly. In addition to two bullet wounds in the middle of the chest, there were two shots in the left arm. Kelly's right hand was inside the front of this coat. Stephens believes Kelly was fending off the sudden attack with his left arm while, reaching for his own revolver when he fell mortally wounded.

The cold-blooded murder shocked and grieved the whole town. Not only had the gangsterism of the newsreels begun to stalk their own streets, but people had been very fond of their sheriff.

This could be seen in the reaction of Kelly's friends when they looked up from the limp body, and saw the young man who had been the third occupant of the fleeing DeSoto, still standing there in the garage. They angrily pounced on him, and it is said he was beaten up very badly before Barrett could persuade them to stop.

Later he told police he was just hitch-hiking from Arkansas to Springfield and had been picked up by the other two men that morning. He and friends finally satisfied authorities he was just a hapless victim of circumstances, but he still had to post bond to get out of jail.

With word spreading that armed killers were on the loose in town, there was a rush of gun sales at Aid Hardware immediately after the shooting.

Police Chief Bridges was still asleep at home after working overtime on patrol duty when Dutch James drove up in front of the house shouting. "They've shot Kelly. Let's go!"

Frank Ball also remembers seeing a tough band of policemen circling the downtown area after the shooting. He could see the barrel of a shotgun protruding from the rolled up front glass. The only sign of the man who had fled on foot was a red scarf he apparently dropped on Washington Avenue while circling the block to link up with the driver of the car.

M.C. Stephens led a posse as the search for the killers widened. Late into the night, throngs of people kept a vigil in the street in front of the police station, as reports from the posse filtered in.

As the dragnet widened and state law enforcement agencies were called in, the trail of the killers led south.

Late Saturday night, the missing car was found abandoned in a ditch near Thayer by a hunting party. They weren't aware at first of the importance of the find, but the bullet holes in the back end of the car convinced them they ought to report it.

Using this lead, the lawmen were able to locate the bandits' hideout near Thayer. On Sunday morning, the gangsters were gone, evidently having cleared out shortly before the raid. Otherwise, the officers might have gotten a warm reception of their own: An alarm was connected to the gate at the foot of the hill below the house, which sounded a bell in one of the bedrooms, should someone open the gate.

About half the goods from the McCallon store were recovered. An attempt had been made to burn some of the clothes in the wood heater.

On the table was a sketch of the floor plan of the First National Bank of West Plains, apparently the gang's next target – until Sheriff Kelly stepped in the way.

"Ma" Barker & Sons

The next question was, who were they?

The house and property had been leased three months earlier by a Mr. and Mrs. Arthur Dunlop of Oklahoma. A check of police files revealed she was the former "Ma" Barker, whose sons, Fred and Doc, had long police records as members of the Barker-Inman-Terrill gang of earlier years.

From a photograph found in the hideout, Bill Tiner, the garage employee, identified Fred Barker as the man who had shot Kelly.

At first it was thought the driver of the blue car was Phoenix Donald, another ex-con living in the Thayer area, who was a frequent visitor to the gang's hideout. A check of the abandoned car's registration turned up one of the aliases of Alvin Karpis, another gangster with roots in Oklahoma. He too was reported to be a frequent visitor to the Dunlop place near Thayer. From that time on, Karpis was sought as one of the Sheriff's killers.

Things were awfully hot for the gang in the Ozarks after that. (They had also shot and killed a night watchman in Pocahontas, Arkansas and a policeman in Monett, Missouri, it was learned later.)

While local papers carried article after article on the shooting and its aftermath, other dastardly deeds and names also fought for headline space. The most startling even was the Springfield shootout between more than a score of law enforcement officers and two outlaw brothers named Young. Surrounded in their home on January 2, 1932, they shot and killed Sheriff Hendrix and five other officers while wounding two others. Through the smoke of their burning house, the brothers got away, only to be killed in a Texas shootout a short time later.

These stories, accompanied by many other "normal" shootings and robberies, created near hysteria among citizens of West Plains and other nearby communities. Newspapers reported the formation of vigilante groups. With these bands of citizens patrolling the Ozarks it is little wonder a number of false leads, sightings and arrests made the newspapers almost daily. The thought of the $1,200 reward no doubt had its effect on the populace too.

Yet with all the armed groups roaming the streets and highways, somehow the Barker-Karpis gang eluded the law and escaped from the Ozarks. There were no further developments I the case for several years, and the incident left only an aching sense of loss among the townspeople.

It would be more than three years before "Ma" and Fred Barker would come to the end of the "outlaw trail" in a bloody Florida shootout with the FBI, and four and a half years before Alvin Karpis, as Public Enemy One, would be personally arrested in New Orleans by none other than FBI Director, J. Edgar Hoover himself.

A half century has come and gone since that December day when Sheriff Kelly was gunned down – time enough for an entire generation to be born, grow up to have children and even grandchildren. Many still remember that fateful day and we have passed on their recollections to their off springs.

Ron Pyron
West Plains Gazette
West Plains, MO
May-June, 1982

C. ROY KELLY, 1885-1931
Sheriff of Howell County, Shot and killed in the line of duty, shortly before 9 a.m., December 19, 1931, at West Plains by members of the notorious "Ma" Barker-Alvin Karpis gang.

SHOOTOUT IN SOUTH JOPLIN, MO

Barrow Brothers Escape From House Under Hail of Bullets

Two local law enforcement officers were killed in a shootout with gunmen at a South Joplin residence in April 1933, according to the Globe.

"A gun battle with two desperadoes at a residence in Freeman Grove, in the south part of the city, last night had claimed the lives of two officers," the paper stated.

"J.W. (Wes) Harryman, 41-year-old Newton county constable, was killed instantly by buckshot from a sawed-off shotgun, used by one of the desperadoes.

"Harry McGinnis, 53, Joplin motor car detective, died at 11 o'clock last night in St. John's Hospital as the result of shock and loss of blood from several wounds.

"The desperadoes, who have tentatively been identified as Ivy (Buck) Barrow, 27 years old, and his brother, Clyde Barrow, about 23, both of Dallas, Texas, known to Texas officers as 'bad men,' shot their way to freedom, although one of them, believed to be Clyde Barrow, is believed to have been wounded.

"Fleeing with the two men in a motor car were two women, one of whom, police apparently have established, is the wife of Ivy Barrow. Both young women are known to Dallas police."

While the first story did not identify the second woman in the shootout, it later was learned her name was Bonnie Parker, who subsequently became known as the cigar-smoking gun moll of the "Bonnie and Clyde" duo.

Charles E. Gibbons
Joplin Globe Archives, 1996
Joplin, Missouri

HANGINGS

In the 1880's, a man who had committed a crime was sometimes placed on a horse's back with a noose around his neck and the rope tied to a tree limb above his head. The horse was then driven from under him, leaving the victim dangling at the end of a rope. Other people, who committed terrible crimes, such as murder, and were found guilty of the crime, were placed on tall ladders or tree limbs and pushed off. Almost all the victims of the above hangings died from strangulation, not from broken necks.

In the 1890's, we became more sophisticated and built tall scaffolds, or gallows, consisting of two "A" frames with a strong, sturdy beam connecting the frames at the top. Some of the gallows had wooden floors near the ground level with fourteen steps (not thirteen), counting the top one, leading to the second floor were the beam was overhead and where a trap door was constructed. The trap door, in early days, was held in place by a rope.

At a legal hanging in the early days, a death warrant was read to the perpetrator of the crime by the sheriff of the county or his deputy. A minister usually spoke to the victim about this soul and issued consoling words for all present. The person who was charged with the crime was then placed on the trap door.

A rope with a noose was attached to the overhead beam, and the "necktie party" was nearing the end. The sheriff asked the condemned, "Do you have anything to say?" After the victim had spoken, his hands were handcuffed behind his back, and his legs were securely tired together. The sheriff and occasionally a deputy worked together placing the noose over the victim's head with the knot of the noose resting on the left jaw. Then a black hood or cap was placed over the domed man's head.

Shortly the sheriff would sever the rope (usually with an axe) holding the trap door, and the door would instantly fall to the side allowing the victim to plunge approximately eight to twelve feet toward the ground and then into the unknown world. The body quickly descended to the end of the rope and where his feet did not touch anything. Instantly the knot, from the jolt moved directly under the victims chin, giving the body a whiplash and dealing a devastating backward thrust of the head, breaking the victim's neck. Death usually resulted with five minutes.

Jay Mondy
Wappapello, MO
June 2000

A STEP TOWARD THE GALLOWS

Hiram, Missouri, is a small community located in Wayne County, northeast of the county seat, Greenville. It is also in the southeastern part of the lovely, rolling hills of the Ozark Mountains. In 1900 several families lived near Hiram where the men made ties for a livelihood. The tie makers were paid for their efforts by the firm, Holladay-Klots Land and Lumber Company. The making of ties was an art and was hard work during hard times.

Some of the workers and their families lived in pole cabins – shanties, sized 10' x 12' and 12' x 14'. Some of the shanties had earth floors, two or three pieces of homemade furniture and straw piled in corners for beds.

One tie maker, George L. Richardson, had worked hard, saved his money and was planning to take his wife, Anna (Ann) and head for the Klondikes in Alaska, where gold had been recently discovered. Incidentally, George and Ann had met in Mississippi. He had been visiting some friends. She was from Tennessee and was visiting a cousin. The two were married in Tennessee, September 19, 1899, and Ann moved with George to the Hiram Community around November 23, 1899. Ann was 18 years old, George, 42.

Around tie maker, William (Will) Shaw Grant, age 21, was from Indiana. He ventured to the Hiram Community in 1898 and moved into the home of his sister and brother-in-law, Sam Brown, age 28. Grant and Brown not only hewed ties together but were in each other's company nearly around the clock.

They soon heard Richardson carried a good sum of money in a concealed belt tied around his waist. As the days passed, Brown and Grant decided to relieve Richardson of his money.

On Tuesday, March 20, 1900, Richardson had worked until approximately 3:00 p.m., gone by his home, gone by the Holladay-Klots Land and Lumber Company and picked up a check for completed work for approximately $160.00, bought some groceries at the firm's store and was on his way home. The time was about 6:00 p.m.

Suddenly, two shots echoed through the hills and hollows near Hiram, and George Richardson was dead! He was relieved of his money belt, containing approximately $700, and was dragged by his heels into a vacant shanty, which was torched.

The pole cabin or shanty had been recently constructed of fairly green poles, so obviously, the cabin didn't burn well. The criminals apparently did not consider the consequence for their inability to totally burn the shanty.

Very early the following morning, Brown, wearing a heavy coat and gloved, along with Grant, went to the cabin and found a portion had not burned, and the body of Richardson was badly burned and charred, but it remained intact. Brown picked up the remaining parts and carried them approximately one-forth mile to a wind-uprooted tree. He deposited the body into the hole once occupied by the tree, raked leaves on top, threw on some dead wood and set fire to them. Once again Brown and Grant tried destroying all evidence. Instead, they left an abundant amount of clues. The body, below the leaves and wood, did not burn completely.

The Wayne County Sheriff, George S. Schlater, and several tie men searched the wooded area near Richardson's home. The sheriff found a pair of blood-stained, work gloves discarded in a hollow stump. After a short search both burned sites were discovered. The sheriff found evidence of foul play and talked with several people in the area.

About midnight, Thursday, March 22, 1900, Sheriff Schlater, after considering all the evidence, went to Brown's home and arrested him for the murder of George L. Richardson. Shortly, he arrested Grant as an accomplice to the murder.

While Grant was in jail, Sheriff Schlater interrogated him. Grant tried to turn state's evidence. He told the entire story about the shooting, getting the money belt, torching the cabin and moving the body to a second site. Grant stated he had to go along with Brown, for Brown had said, "I'll kill you if you talk!"

During the trial, Grant stuck to his story. He said Brown had threatened his life. He then told the story of what happened to Richardson. The jury did not believe him to be innocent of any wrongdoing, and Grant was later sentenced to the Missouri State Penitentiary.

There was an unusual witness in that case. Mr. J.H. Forbush, was unusual because of his expertise in small guns, rifles, sounds, distance according to wind directions and rifle calibers. He was thoroughly questioned and cross-examined. Mr. Forbush stated he heard two shots, and they were "a little south of west" of his place and were fired from a .38 or .44 caliber rifle.

"Will you go on record it was a .38 or .44 caliber rifle," asked the attorney for the defendant?

"Yes, sir," replied Forbush.

"Can you tell the difference?"

"No, they sound almost alike. I believe it was a .44 caliber."

"You said it was a Winchester. Will you go on record it was a Winchester Rifle?"

"Yes," replied Forbush.

The last witness was the defendant, Sam Brown. He, of course, denied all charges. The sheriff had taken an item from Brown's shanty and presented it as evidence in court. It was a .38 caliber Winchester rifle.

The evidence against Brown appeared overwhelming. He and Grant had been seen together on the same road about the same time Richardson disappeared. There was more evidence, such as: William Grant's testimony, the .38 caliber rifle with a trace of blood on it; a pair of blood-stained, work gloves, tracks at the burned cabin, tracks which were Brown's exact size according to the coroner, Dr. Charles Davis. Also, tow witnesses had seen a red discoloration in a tub of water where Brown had washed the heavy coat, the coat he had used in transferring Richardson's body. One witness was Ann Richardson.

The conclusion of the long trial ended as follows:

We, the jury, find the defendant guilty of murder in the first degree as charged.

Fred Henson
Foreman of The Jury

The Honorable Frank R. Dearing, Judge of The 21ˢᵗ Judicial Circuit Court of Wayne County, sentenced Sam Brown "to be hanged." Brown's attorneys made an appeal to the Missouri Appellate and Missouri State Supreme Court asking Brown be given a new hearing. Both courts denied the appeals.

"Sam Brown was a large, robust, brawny man weighing between 175 and 200 pounds. He was a very peculiar man, of a rowdy disposition, and shortly after being confined in jail, his health began to fail. During the last year and a half his physical manhood had been slowly and steadily giving away. For several months prior to his execution he was only a mere skeleton. His digestive organs had become so diseased he could hardly eat anything at all. He had perhaps not a well day in months. Yet, in his condition, and to the last, knowing the end was at hand, he kept perfectly calm, composed and most of the time, silent."

The gallows had been prepared at the courthouse, June 27, 1902, in the original town of Greenville. "About 9:00 o'clock in the morning, Brown was shaved, washed and dressed in a neat, black suit and prepared for the execution. Sheriff S.J. Malugen (newly elected) read the death warrant to him. At 11:50, Sheriff Malugen came out of the jail, followed by James Lee Shipman, James Bennett, W.G. Hartman and Harry Hays, who were carrying Brown on a cushioned chair.

"Brown was conveyed upon the platform, across the west end of the platform where a large window opened, and here he was presented to view the multitude of people standing on the ground. When the window was first opened, and he beheld the vast throng, he seemed somewhat surprised and embarrassed. His face momentarily colored and then paled. The Rev. Brooks of Greenville offered a short and fervent prayer. The guards were directed to raise Brown to his feet."

A black hood or cap was placed over Brown's head, followed by a rope with the noose resting on his left jaw, and his hands were tied behind his back. The sheriff asked, "Sam, do you want to say anything?"

Brown replied, "Not a word."

As the Sheriff stepped from the trap door, he said, "Sam, this is a hard duty to perform, but in the name of the law of the Great State of Missouri, I must do it. Good bye, Sam!"

As the Sheriff said the last words, he raised his right hand, and just as the feeble response 'good bye' came from the lips of Brown, he, the sheriff, came down with a hand axe in his raised right hand, and the rope to the trap door was severed. The door swung violently back and Brown dropped like a shot through the opening about seven or eight feet until the rope stopped him with a heavy, sickening 'thud!'

"No movements or contortions of the body were discernible for almost two minutes, when the shoulders were slightly raised as though a real effort was being made to breathe. At the expiration of nineteen minutes he was ordered to be taken down and turned over to the undertaker.

"The body was taken down. The rope and black cap removed, and the body placed in a coffin, where it was viewed by perhaps 1500 people, who thronged past, eager to get a glimpse of a man charged with being so remarkable a criminal."

After 32 years, 2 months and 17 days, the tragic life of Sam Brown ended. The final cost: Two lives for $700.

Jay Mondy
Wappapello, MO
July 2000

Note: Taken from the transcript containing 194, 8 ½" x 14" typed, double spaced pages of the entire testimonies. A copy of the entire trial is on file in the Wayne County Courthouse, Greenville, MO.

Everything in quotations was recorded from microfilm of the once Greenville Sun, Greenville, MO, July 3, 1902

THE HANGING TREE

Randolph Co., Ark.

Fact or fiction, the controversial old tree will soon be gone. The tree known as "the hanging tree" is deteriorating. Limbs are decaying. Some have fallen in the road and others beneath the tree.

The tree is in Randolph County near the Old Jackson site. It was well known years ago when Jackson, later called Old Jackson, was a thriving town. Located near Spring River, it is about two miles north of Imboden. Randolph County was part of Lawrence County until 1835. Jackson was the county seat of Lawrence County from 1829 to 1937.

Though some discredit it as the hanging tree of the early 1800's – possibly thinking a tree would not have lived that long, - descendants of those who lived in Jackson in early years provide some interesting information. Many state it was the tree on which the first murderer in Lawrence County was hanged in 1831.

When Randolph County was formed out of Lawrence County, it was necessary to move the county seat of Lawrence County from Jackson to Smithville. Evidently, it was customary to hand offenders considered worthy of death at the county seat. It is recorded that two men, who waylaid a stranger at Old Jackson, robbed him, and left him for dead, were hanged at Smithville on December 6, 1850. Thus, hanging at the county seat before 1837 would undoubtedly have been carried out in Old Jackson.

After an interview in 1988 with Homer Horsman, a long-time resident of Old Jackson and former school teacher there, he said, "Be sure and go by to see the hanging tree." He told me to take the road to the right at the fork where the early town existed and go about 200 yards. I thought I would not find a single tree of the description in the growth of trees all along the road. But, there it stood – an old white oak tree just as he had described it Mr. Horsman died in 1996 at the age of 96 years.

Another resident who has been told about the tree and the fact of the first hanging there is Mrs. Mary Dunham Van Winkle. Her information was passed down through descendants of the Songer family. One was the jail keeper there years ago, and his wife cooked meals for the prisoners. Also, the Dunham family lived in Old Jackson for many years. Mr. Dunham operated a saw mill there.

Another very knowledgeable present-day resident is Kathy Cude Morgan who lives near the fork in the road mentioned before. In 1979, while in high school at Sloan-Hendrix in Imboden, she wrote a paper on the History of Old Jackson. In her writing, she used information passed down through the Starling family, the Songers, and the Hendersons – supplied by Dalton Henderson. Also, her ancestors, the Cudes, were land owners in Old Jackson for many years. In her history, she records that the first murderer in Lawrence County, a slave who killed Mrs. Polly Hillhouse in Smithville, was tried in court, convicted, and then hanged at Old Jackson of Friday, December 23, 1831.

History books record there was an Old Jackson but interesting additional information comes from oral histories.

With the passing of the hanging tree, the location of Old Jackson will be known by a cemetery and foundation near the spring which is just below the old schoolhouse site, but the stories passes from generation to stories will include the existence of the old town alive. Undoubtedly, these stories will include the existence of "the hanging tree."

Pauline McKamey
Lawrence County Historical Society
Imboden, Arkansas
Spring 1998

The Hanging Tree
Randolph County, Arkansas

WORDS RECORDED ON A PLAQUE FOUND ON THE COURTHOUSE LAWN

The conviction of Samuel Helms, court records from the archives of the Powhatan, Arkansas Courthouse relate the brief story of one prisoner, Samuel Helms.

"We the jury, find the defendant guilty as charged in the indictment of murder in the First Degree."

"Samuel Helms: It is the judgement and justice of this court that you be taken hence to the jailhouse of Lawrence County and thereby safely be kept until Friday the 17th day of December, 1875 and then upon said last mentioned day you be taken hence, by the sheriff of said county of Lawrence and hung by the neck until you are dead! dead! dead!"

> Honorable William Byers
> Judge of the Court

"I hereby certify this transcript came to hand at 9 o'clock a.m., December 16, 1875, and that I executed the same at Powhatan on Friday, December 17, 1875, between sunrise and sunset by hanging Samuel Helms by the neck until he was dead! dead! dead!"

> W.G. Wasson, Sheriff
> Lawrence County

Those sentenced to execution were hung from a tree near the jail.

> Jay Mondy
> Wappapello, MO
> March, 1999

MISSOURI'S LAST, LEGAL HANGING

Galena, MO

Roscoe "Red" Jackson was convicted here on December 11, 1934, for the murder of Pearl Bozarth, owner of a poultry medicine company of Evansville, Ind. Bozarth, who spent part of his time on the road selling his products, picked Jackson, a hitch-hiker, up on the road from Springfield to Forsyth. He hauled him into Forsyth, paid for his meals and a night's lodging, and the next morning started out with him from Forsyth to Ava. Jackson had told him he was trying to get to his "folks" in Ozark county.

Just west of Brown Branch, in the northeast corner of Taney County, Jackson shot the man who had befriended him, threw his body on a side road exposed to the August sun, took his car and drove away. A farmer in the neighborhood found the body of Bozarth a few days later, badly decomposed, and the search for the killer started.

Bozarth was well known in Forsyth and residents of the town remembered seeing him in town a few nights before in company with the hitch-hiker, which gave officers a clue to the identity of the killer. About two weeks later Jackson was arrested in northeast Oklahoma in possession of Bozarth's car. He was returned and placed in jail at Ava. While awaiting trial he escaped from the Ava jail but was recaptured a few days later near West Plains.

When he was assigned for trial the defense took a change of venue from Taney County and the case was sent to Stone County for trial. He was tried at a special term of court in December, 1934, found guilty, and sentenced to death by hanging.

After his conviction here, Jackson confessed to the murder of Bozarth and also confessed to killing another man in Oklahoma a short time before his arrest. Jackson became penitent after his conviction and asked to be baptized before being taken to Jefferson City. The Rev. R.L. Whittenburg, then pastor of the Christian church here, was summoned by Sheriff Seth Tuttle, to conduct the baptismal service. Jackson was taken down on the banks of James River and was baptized. The next day he was taken to Jefferson City.

During his long incarceration in the penitentiary Jackson never wavered in his faith. He spent hours reading his Bible and praying. It is also understood that he preached to fellow inmates.

For weeks the residents of the town in particular and those of the county generally, have been excited and disgusted with the prospect of a legal hanging to be conducted in their midst. As Sheriff I.H. Coin and his deputies worked on the scaffold, people gazed with fearful eyes, dreading the moment when the peaceful quiet which ordinarily settles over Galena should be disturbed by such a sordid ordeal. Some citizens made preparations to leave town the day of the hanging while others tried to console themselves with the thought that the law had spoken and the mandate of the law must be carried out. After all, Galena nor Stone County was not to blame for the hanging. The crime was not committed here, neither the murdered man nor the murderer were residents of the county. Nor did the jury of Stone County men which found Jackson guilty of First Degree murder assess the penalty-that was done by Circuit Judge Robert L. Gideon, whose home is outside the boundaries of Stone County. So Stone County citizens feel they are victims of circumstance and were forced by the strong arm of the law to take a man's life.

Jackson was brought here late Thursday afternoon from the state penitentiary at Jefferson City where he had been in solitary confinement since December 12, 1934-more than 20 months.

Sheriff I.H. Coin, Deputy F.A. Moore, Sheriff Henry Simmons of Taney County and Highway Patrolman Harvey George went to Jefferson City last Thursday s for the prisoner, accompanied by several other officers. Jackson's first remark after walking outside the gate was that it was good to be out in the sunshine. It was the first time he had seen the sun in months, and the second time since he entered the cell there. On one other occasion, he was taken to the prison hospital to have a tooth pulled.

On the way to Galena, Jackson was quite talkative. He talked freely with officers about his condition, his philosophy of life, members of his family, but he would not discuss the man he murdered.

During the early hours of Thursday night officers from the surrounding territory gathered in Galena and cars filled with curious men and women drifted into Galena from nearby sections. Residents of Galena watched the crowds for a time, then retired to their homes to get some rest so they could get up early the next morning. There was considerable revelry in the town during the night, probably by outsiders, who sought to entertain themselves while waiting for the fatal hour.

By five o'clock Friday morning, most of the crowd had arrived. They pressed against the entrance to the enclosure surrounding the gallows, eager to be admitted. A few minutes before six o'clock, the door was opened and those who had passes surged into the enclosure packing it like sardines in a box.

Just how many were inside is not known, though it is thought the space would accommodate at least 400 people. Fully that many, and perhaps more, were outside waiting to get a glimpse of Jackson.

After the crowd had entered the enclosure, Sheriff Coin, dressed in a neat brown suit, mounted the gallows and asked for quiet. On the runway to the scaffold appeared Father Ahern, Jackson's spiritual advisor, followed by Jackson and numerous officers. Father Ahern was reading the rite of contrition and Jackson repeated the words after him. After mounting the steps to the gallows, and completing the rite, Jackson turned facing the crowd outside the enclosure and spoke through a window. "Folks, not everybody realizes what it takes to die. It's easy, if it comes accidental, but it's not so easy when it comes gradual."

He hesitated, turned back, and gazed straight ahead, his lips moving. Deputy Dale Davis strapped his legs.

The black hood was slipped over his head.

As if waiting for that signal, Jackson mumbled, "Well, be good, folks."

The noose was quickly slipped around his neck.

Sheriff I.H. Coin, looking straight ahead, pulled a lever.

Jackson's body shot downward 11 feet to stop with a thud as the rope jerked taut. Thus, Roscoe "Red" Jackson hitch-hiker-killer, had paid in full to civilization for destroying the life of a good man who had befriended him and who Jackson had repaid with death.

Stone County News-Oracle
Galena, MO
May 26, 1937

Chapter Fifteen

GOD'S CREATURES

LIVELY CHASE ON BROADWAY TODAY

Poplar Bluff, MO

An adolescent rooster, two sausage-shaped dogs, a crate of eggs and a mountainous man figured yesterday in a brief pandemonium at a local market.

The mountainous man had purchased a long-legged cockerel.   Using the wings of the bird for a handle, he lifted it out of a crate.

"Squawk!" said the bird.

The man stopped to bargain for a basket of peaches beside a display of dressed chickens.

At the sight of those unfortunate fowls, the cockerel said, "Squawk! Squawk!", gave a vicious kick, and then raced free down the sidewalk.   The owner of the bird was a close second.

Hard pushed, the bird flapped its wings and increased its squawks.

Two sausage-shaped dogs were napping in the shade.   The squawks shocked them into consciousness.

One of the dogs ran across the street.   The other sought refuge in a display in front of the store.   He knocked over a crate of eggs and spilled them all over the pavement.   The eggs "busted and run".

"You'll pay for those eggs," shouted their owner at the puffing poultry pursuer.

The man viewed the wreckage, and replied:

"I'll pay for no rotten eggs."

The chase had attracted the attention of the entire population that happened to be along the street.   Finally, the bird was stopped in a corner, and after he had established himself as a real fighter, he was captured.

The owner turned around, with a bird in one hand and mopping sweat with the other.   He was disgusted at seeing a reporter.

"Say," he said, "I'll give you the bird if you won't use my name in this fuss," and he held out the chicken.   The reporter had already seen enough of the chicken and emphatically refused to take it.

Therefore, names are omitted in this story and unless the squawking cockerel has escaped again, he is probably sizzling in the pan now.

The Daily Republican
Poplar Bluff, MO
June 30, 1926

ED ANGELO HAS KITTEN THAT PLAYS PIANO

Poplar Bluff, MO

This is a story about the "Kitten On the Keys."

The kitten is particular is owned by Ed Angelo. She is an unusual cat, full of fun, likes music and enjoys a friendly frolic with dogs. Yes, the cat is indeed peculiar in temperament.

Angelo wouldn't take a farm in Georgia for that cat, he says. She entertains the well-known caterer with an occasional piece on the piano and, while the music she makes is not the latest popular skits, still it is music to the ears of the kitten.

"The cat", says Angelo, pointing at the little kitten lying asleep in the corner, "Is a world beater. She likes music. She enjoys hearing the visitors play the piano, but when no one is around and the place is rather quiet, the kitten climbs upon the piano and walks back and forth over the keys."

Yes, she is a remarkable cat. Her history is something unusual, also. Her mother lived at Ed's place for a long time. Finally, about six months ago, the old cat came in carrying her little one by the neck. She dropped the kitten down carefully, talked to her in cat language, then turned around and walked out.

"I haven't seen the old cat since", said Ed. "It's pathetic. She thought the little one would have a good home here, so she brought her down and then left, probably to find a place to live somewhere else. She may have thought we wouldn't want town cats."

The kitten apparently enjoys the soothing effects of the piano music. She will walk from one end to the other, look around, and then walk back. Once in a great while she will hit a key twice, for effect.

Not only that, but the kitten is fond of dogs. She often goes visiting to Barnett's Music House and enjoys an hour capering with "Dinkey", the Barnett dog.

This morning Ed wanted the cat to perform, but she refused, saying "Meow".

Ed thinks he may be able to develop her musical nature so that someday she may be as much of an artist on the piano as she is at drinking milk and catching mice.

The Daily Republican
Poplar Bluff, MO
September 3, 1926

BEE TREE HUNTING

Poplar Bluff, MO

If you've never watched an experienced bee hunter scaling the cliffs, scanning the bluffs and racing through the woods in quest of a "rich" bee tree, you have missed a treat. If you've never helped to cut that tree when found, suffered a few stings from the infuriated bees as you robbed them of their honey, then known the wonderful amount of sweetness that comes from eating wild honey, fresh from the tree, you have missed even more.

Hunting wild bee trees is an old, old sport. It has been practiced a long time in the hills. The arts of the sport are handed down from father to son as time rolls on, and like all other American sports, there are experts at hunting bee trees.

Bee hunters use various methods of locating the trees. Whatever the methods employed, an investigation will reveal considerable art.

Bird-Like Eye

Probably the greatest requisite of a bee tree hunter is a bird-like eye. One that has been trained to see everything before it at a glance. Second to the apt eye is an alert body and a pair of willing limbs to convey that body swiftly when necessary.

Usually the bee hunter selects a spring or a small creek somewhere in the deep woods and as far as possible from any home. He does this, first, because he does not want to lose any precious time trailing a bee only to find it leads him to the apiary in some farm yard.

As he leisurely strolls along beside the stream of mountain water, he stops suddenly, for he spies a small ball of something feeding in the soft earth or in the water's edge—a bee!

With caution he stoops over the busy little fellow and dusts some flour or other white coloring on its back. The he steps back and waits for it to fly away and observes as it leaves the general direction it goes.

The bee rises into the air and disappears. It is not to be gone very long for soon it drops back to the same place behind the creek. The hunter then calculates the distance its home may be from the creek, by the time it took it to make the trip. If he concludes it is not too far away he then gets ready to go farther with his work.

An old bee hunter who has probably found as many "trees" as any other man in the hills said when a bee had what water it wanted, it would then rise, probably waver in its upward flight until it was well above the tops of the trees, and then it always took a direct course to its "hive."

Rises Into Air

This being the case we again return to the man beside the creek, who is watching the bee. It is now filled with water again and then rises into the air. The man is also on his toes, his hat is pulled down to shade his eyes, and a lot of eagerness is being displayed as he watches it rise into the uppermost sections of the towering trees and even on until it is "in the clear."

The white on its back helps some in keeping it located, furnishing white for the top of its back and wings. The under color being natural, there are two colors to be glimpsed.

111

If the hunter was successful in getting the direction the bee took, and if he knows about how far away the tree is (judging by the time required for it to make the round trip) he is then ready to do some more calculating.

He follows in the direction as that taken by the bee. If there are bluffs to be climbed, he climbs the, if there are other creeks to be waded he wades them, for he cannot afford to lose his course.

When he has traveled about as far as he thinks the bee went the first time, he located himself and begins investigating every tree and rock in the vicinity. Every tree with a hollow in it is a good place for bees, as is every large rock with an opening in it. Bees are found in both places but the first named is the most likely. Sometimes they go into a hollow stump, and trace a hollow root into the ground and store their honey there.

Bees are working at this time of year in the woods just like they are in the well-kept aviary. It is probable that when the tree is finally located there will be a large number of bees sticking to the tree near the entrance, and a few will be flying around as they do about the patent "guns."

Once the tree is located it is time for something else. Most bee tree hunters advise leaving the trees found this late in the season until next summer. This is because they say that to rob them now might cause them to die out this winter.

A few weeks earlier all trees found were cut. Sometimes the bees are put into a patent gum and taken home where they will be added to the long string of bee hives already there, or occasionally they are robbed of their honey and the bees given to someone else. Occasionally it is possible to rob a tree and not destroy the home of the bees, and then, if they care to do so, the hunters leave the bees where they are and will come back again when they have made more honey.

The American Republic
Poplar Bluff, MO
August 29, 1931

MAKING OF PAPER

Poplar Bluff, MO

From the wasp man learned how to create a great industry which is building plants all over the South and which, in the opinion of some informed men, will become as valuable to Dixie in the future as cotton has been in the past. This industry is the manufacture of paper from wood.

Wasps produced paper form wood to use for their nests long before man learned to write and had any thought or need of paper. Chewing up tiny slivers of wood, the wasp thus makes a kind of pulp and spreads it out in the shape desired till, bit by bit, the cone-shaped nest is finished-a home of paper.

Though man had often watched the wasp at this work, it wasn't till the middle of the last century that a German, Frederick Keller, thought of copying the little insect's method. He invested a machine for grinding wood into pulp-and the huge paper-from-wood industry was on the way.

Up to that time, rags had been the chief source of paper. A wise old Chinese scholar, Ts'ai Lun, discovered about 2,000 years ago, how to make paper from the bark of the mulberry tree. Later the Chinese learned to make paper from rags, and rags continued to supply most of the world's paper for hundreds of years.

Not Enough Rags

But there weren't enough rags for the purpose and paper remained high in price. The result was to limit all sorts of printing and hamper the spread of reading and knowledge. Then wood paper appeared, and printing was enormously increased. Newspapers, magazines, and books were turned out in a huge and growing volume, at prices almost everybody could afford.

At the same time, paper was put to a multitude of other uses-bags, packages, sanitary drinking cups, and the like-which have added much to the convenience and health of living.

Came Into South

Years ago the kraft paper industry started to come into the South, manufacturing dark wrapping paper and material for boxes. Then a Southern genius, the late Dr. Charles Herty, showed white paper – newsprint paper – could be made from Southern pine. Before that, it was believed only Northern spruce and fir was suitable – than pine had too much resin in it.

Now a plant to make newsprint paper is to be built at Lufkin, Texas. It is predicted that others will follow.

A vast market for newsprint paper from Southern pines exists in this country, for at present about 75 per cent of this kind of paper is imported largely from Canada. We paid Canada almost $110,000,000 for paper in 1937.

And so from the wasp man got an idea which already yields the South a substantial income and which may well dot its pine lands over with a humming, wealth-building industry.

The Daily American Republic
Poplar Bluff, MO
June 8, 1939

JACK, THE FIRE STATION DOG

Poplar Bluff, MO

WHERE'S THE FIRE!

If you don't know and can't find out just follow Jack, because Jack will always go there if the truck doesn't run off from him. He has been left only about a dozen times in four years.

Jack is a little fox-terrier who lives at the Poplar Bluff Fire Department. According to Fireman Cal Smith, Jack is five years of age, and has been a member of the fire department for four years. He has attended more fires in Poplar Bluff than any other dog – I am safe in saying that, because he has missed only about a dozen.

Back in 1937, Joe Graves decided he couldn't keep a fat little pup. The fire department took him over, lock, stock and barrel.

Jack never sees a stranger. In fact, when I met him for the first time a few weeks ago – he merely looked at me as if I were of the common run! But he made me feel at home, just the same, when he sat up for me.

There is some story behind all this sitting up business. No one has ever taught him; he just started sitting up when he wanted someone to notice him. If you don't notice him when he sits up, he will bark; and that means that he is irked in his own doggish way (he assumes an air of sophistication in his peevish spells).

Jack gets his food from the various eating placed in town. Some people will wrap up some bones, and Jack brings them to the fire station. He eats only at the station, if I know dogs, because he is afraid he'll miss a fire. When he misses one, he looks up all the stray shoes and boots he can find and carries them out in front of the station for a good "het up" shaking.

The boys played a dirty trick on him the other day. They switched trucks on him. Instead of using the small truck, they jumped in the big truck, while Jack ran to the small one. He was left, and was he unhappy.

He used to go to the Farrington Drug Store (then the Graham) and get magazines off the racks and brought them to the station for the boys to read. The drug store manager had to move the rack up out of his reach or else go out of the magazine business. The boys at the station said the only drawback was that Jack couldn't read and, therefore, did not know a comic from a Wild West Weekly. Reading is about the only thing Jack can't do.

He likes ice cream, but doesn't care for candy.

Jack doesn't like the idea of these new-fangled floor dressings. With the new dressing they have on the station floor now, he has a mighty hard time getting off on a quick start to mount the truck. He just slips and slides like a big dog on ice. If you yell fire, he is off like a bolt. Then if you have fooled him, he is disgusted and shows it. He pouts.

He rides to the fire on the seat, and then gets back on the ladder when the truck is stopped at a fire. About the only thing that can move him from that perch is heat. He will stay till it gets pretty hot. He goes back to the station on the ladder.

J.L. Swindle
The Daily American Republic
Poplar Bluff, MO
March 25, 1941

Chapter 16

HARD TIMES

OLD LAWS PROVIDED DRASTIC PUNISHMENT

Flogging and Imprisonment and Even the Pillory Was Used In Missouri on Gamblers, Horse Thieves, and Vagrants.

Poplar Bluff, MO

Forgotten laws of Missouri, show a strong contrast between the human values of the past and present, says an article appearing in the Missouri Historical Review.

"Some of the early laws sound ridiculous now, but there is no doubt that even the most ludicrous of the pioneers' laws served an evident purpose in its day," says the article.

"Missouri's state laws were first revises and compiled in 1825. Examination of this first state revision reveals some unusual laws that have been forgotten but deserve to be remembered.

The pillory was in use in pioneer Missouri, just as the lash was among the forms of punishment. The Sabbath was a day of no labor, and gamblers found life hard-at least there were laws touching on all these and numerous other subjects. Even the tramp, in his own way, could not be self-respecting, for on the one hand he was faced with being bound out for three months of work, and on the other he was threatened with twenty-five lashes on the back.

Among the strangest statutes are those relating to the treatment of prisoners. Adult vagrants were hired out to the highest bidder for a term not exceeding three months, the person hiring him having the same power over the unfortunate that a master had over a slave. If the vagrant was not thus bid into temporary slavery, he was lashed not to exceed over twenty-five times, and turned loose.

Early punishments were of three kinds. The first was the lash, to be applied on 'such offender's bare back and without favor of affection'. The second was standing in the pillory, and the last was imprisonment. Woman were not subjected to the first two punishments, but imprisonments was substituted for them.

Prisoners of means were required to furnish their own food while in jail, but a poor prisoner, if he swore he was unable to buy the subsistence for himself, was provided with 'necessary food'. Felons unable to pay their fines and costs could be sold into virtual slavery for a period not exceeding seven years. Laws provided that convicts were to be given a haircut once a month and half of their heads wee to be shaved, to provide easy detection in case of escape.

A sharp distinction was made between criminals and prisoners fined for debt. One statute made it unlawful for any sheriff or jailer to confine debtor could not pay for his maintenance while in jail, the plaintiff or person on whose charges the man was imprisoned would have to pay the maintenance charge at the rate of 37 and a half cents a day. And if the plaintiff did not pay the charge, the prisoner was released.

Laws pertaining to slaves were, in general, the same as those applying to white persons. Punishment and protection were both provided by law. Yet there were special laws to take care of special situations. Insurrection of slaves was punishable by death and riots, unlawful assemblies and seditious speeches were punishable by stripes. If a white person were found at an unlawful assembly of slaves he was liable to not more than twenty lashes on his bare back, well lain on. Ferrymen were forbidden to cross a slave over the Mississippi River unless the slave carried a permit signed by his master.

Working on Sunday was not countenanced. If a man worked on the Sabbath he could be fined one dollar for each offense, and if he made his slaves work also, he could be fined one dollar for each slave that performed labor.

Gamblers were suppressed with a diligence that rivaled Nevada's present compassion with them. A person found guilty of setting up or keeping a gambling table was not only subject to a fine of $500, but he was forced to stand in a pillory for one hour and receive between 10 and 39 lashes.

Horse thieves and hog thieves were frowned on. After a conviction as a horse thief, there was little left of worldly things to comfort a man. To a fine of not over $500 was added a maximum of 39 striped on his back, an assessment of double damages to the injured party, and the miscreant was disqualified from voting, giving evidence as a witness, serving as a juror, and holding any office in the state.

Miller were important men in early Missouri. Along with professors, students, ministers, and ironworkers, they were exempt from service in the state militia. All other able bodied men between 18 and 45 years of age, excepting public officers, had to be enrolled in the militia. The milling trade was strictly regulated. Among the provisions concerning the miller was the one that he would be fined $5 if he did not grind grain in 'due turn' as it was brought to him for grinding. There was not a chance to play favorite there."

The American Republic
Poplar Bluff, MO
July 22, 1931

CHICKEN HOUSE BECOMES HOME TO FAMILY OF SEVEN

Wright County, MO

In the early '30s, almost overnight, money went out of circulation. This left people to do the best they could with what they had on hand. Opportunely for us, my widowed mother had just paid $800 for 160 acres of land here in Wright County. It was all timbered, with no well or dwelling of any kind, but we had a plan.

The four older kids, myself included, were going to cut logs, have them sawed into lumber and hire someone to build a house, a barn, a chicken house and other buildings as needed. We were also going to hire someone to drill a well.

The bottom dropped out of our plan when the bottom dropped out of the stock market. The cash flow was gone. There was no money for a sex-penny nail, let alone money for the trees to be processed into lumber. At that point, we had just enough lumber to construct a 12-foot by 24-foot hut.

We kids set to work hammering and sawing, thinking in terms of "chicken house" so Mother could realize at least part of her dream. We ran out of nails before we could put up the door and all the wallboards.

When we showed Mother what we had done, she shouted praises to the Lord and we moved in the next day! My younger brother and sister loved it. My three brothers and I, who had built the shack, were in shock. For more than four years, the seven of us lived in that chicken house.

Eventually, we added the door and filled in the hole in the wall; but there were still cracks between those boards, and the cold Missouri winters were hard middle of the room, we had a wood heater we would huddle by. At night, we piled quilts…so high it would weigh us down.

Privacy was the biggest problem. To change clothes we'd get behind the door or under the quilts on the bed. Bathing was another story. We never did get the well drilled, so we had to carry the water from a source a half-mile away.

To do our wash, we kept a huge kettle by the spring. On washday, we would carry out dirty laundry, a bucket, washboard and what soap we could afford down to the spring. We set the iron kettle on three rocks, used the bucket to fill the kettle, built a fire and heated the water.

An awful drought came and we had to go farther for water. Because of the water shortage, we sold most of our cattle for a meager $5 to $18 a head.

My mother took the money, put it in a glass jar and buried it. Even though we had hope that the next day would bring better times, she had learned not to trust banks and not to spend money unless absolutely necessary.

We lived for weeks on gravy, bread and greens. The green were weeds (sour dock, wild mustard, slick thistle, plantain, dandelion, wild lettuce, polk and others), which my mother gathered. She knew an awful lot of weeds, which were good to eat, and how to mix them to make a delicious meal.

During the same time period, the man who was to become my life-mate had steady work in another part of the county. His days began at 4 a.m. in the barn. He milked 22 to 23 cows by hand, separated the milk from the cream and worked the fields all day until it was time to milk again.

He did this seven days a week and was paid $10 per month plus room and board.

There were no sick days, no overtime pay, and no 10-minute breaks. If he couldn't handle the work, there were others to fill his position. As a rule, his folks would come by on Saturdays and collect the $2.25 he had earned to buy groceries.

In 1936, we were married after knowing each other only six weeks. I worked for pennies a day, and he hired out to do farm work for $1 a day. We didn't realize how well off we were. Things got worse and times were hard, but in 1939 out luck changed.

We were out of work, penniless and living with my mother while we rented some land on the shares. That meant if we produced a certain amount of soybean, corn, etc., the government would reimburse us accordingly. We had rented the land with a promise of $125 rent for the year and, with hard work were able to produce enough crops to be reimbursed $80 by the government. Additionally, the government lent us $550.

With this money, we bought five Jersey cows, a team of horses, a brood sow, 200 baby chicks, a harness, plows, a harrow, a cream separator, an incubator, a pressure cooker, fruit jars and enough seed to plant. We began by selling cream for 19 cents a pound and lived on that until we could sell young chickens, and later we sold eggs for 12 cents a dozen. Then we sold out young bull calves, and times got better.

Opal Higby
Springfield News-Leader
Springfield, MO
December 1999

INTERESTING AND TRUE STORY TOLD OF PIONEER DAYS

Poplar Bluff, MO

On a beautiful spring day, in the year of 1818, while Missouri was still a territory, a covered wagon winded its way westward from North Carolina.

The oxen plodded slowly along over the rough roads of the sparsely settled country, farther and farther westward. The mother and younger children rode in the wagon under the great white cover or wagon sheet, most of the time; but the father Samuel Kittrell and his eldest son, Solomon, who was then eleven years old, usually plodded along beside the oxen.

Samuel was a man of middle age, strong and bronzed, a typical pioneer and woodsman, while young Solomon was as active as the squirrels and deer they saw scampering over the hills. The mother frequently begged them to stop near the settlements, but the proceeded on their way, until all roads, bridges and settlements were left far behind. The traveled on as best they could over the trackless forests.

One day after they had left the last settlement many miles behind them, and the poor mother and children were growing very weary, they came upon a beautiful valley where there was plenty of grass for the oxen, and a nice place to camp.

They Camped

There was a fine spring nearby, also a small creek near where the oxen could drink. The valley was surrounded by hills, which were covered with heavy timber of oak, pine, gum and other kinds. The dogwood and red bud were in bloom, also many wild flowers.

The woods abounded with game of all kinds, including deer and wild turkeys. Solomon unyoked the oxen while the younger children gathered firewood and the mother got her kettles and pans from the wagon and prepared their evening meal over the campfire. After looking around for a while, Samuel decided he would go no farther as he had found just the kind of place he was looking for to make a permanent home.

As the tired mother and children climbed into the wagon to sleep that night, they were very thankful they had found a home at last and could soon sleep in a real house.

It did not take long for the father and boys, Solomon and Lemuel, to clear a small patch of ground near the spring and build a log cabin with a fireplace, which was used for cooking as well as heating purposes. Cook stoves were then unknown and the people lived mostly on wild game and fish, with corn bread and hominy, also honey made by the wild bees. The oxen lived mostly on the wild grass, which grew abundantly in the woods. The winters are short in Southeast Missouri, and there was no underbrush then as there is now since the large timber has been cut. The family was soon established in their new home where they lived a life almost as primitive as the Indians.

They cleared a little land for corn and garden, planted a few fruit trees, also gathered wild fruits and berries. They dried the surplus fruit as they knew nothing of canning at that time.

Planned School

Thus the years passed, and the children grew up. A few more settlers had moved into the county. Solomon married and, as he was a keen businessman, he soon became the leading citizen of Butler County (or what was later Butler County). His father was just a "squatter" but Solomon homesteaded a great deal of land in the beautiful Cane Creek valley. The small creek near his father's cabin was called Goose Creek while the large creek was named Cane Creek because of the cane growing along its banks. He built a substantial log house about a quarter of a mile from his father's cabin. His brothers married and scattered and his father and mother went to live with him, and stayed there till the grim reaper called them.

Solomon had several slaves, and they did most of the farm work, as well as the cooking. The "Negro kitchen" as it was called was standing till a few years ago, with the fireplace made of rock, where the old Negro "mammys" did the cooking.

There were no cook stoves till years later, nor any sewing machine, nor even washboards. We would not know how to wash now without washboards or machines. This is how they did it: a bench was made of split board with four holes bored in it and four legs fitted into the holes. There were no nails then either. The clothes bench, large iron kettles to boil in and plenty of soft soap in gourds were taken to Goose Creek. The bench was placed in or new the creek. Then the clothes were wet and placed on the bench, plenty of soft soap rubbed on then they would beat them with a paddle made for the purpose. Then they were boiled in the kettles, rinsed in the creek and hung on the bushes to dry.

Used An Ash Hopper

On every farm there was an ash hopper, a V shaped box was built of boards with a trough at the bottom. The wood ashes were emptied into this during the winter. It was kept covered to keep it dry. In the spring, several buckets of water were poured into the hopper. Lye soon began to run out of the trough. It was caught in a vessel and put into a large kettle with grease usually cracklings saved from butchering. It was then boiled until it formed a soap.

All the clothing was made at home grown cotton and the wool from the sheep. The spinning wheel and the loom were always busy, and as all stockings, mittens, etc., had to be knitted, all the family from the little girls to grandma kept the knitting needs busy.

Solomon had a tan yard where hides of all kinds were made into leather and boots and shoes were all made at home by an old Negro. There was also an old Negro blacksmith who did all the repair work, also shod the oxen. Yes, the oxen had to be shod the same as horses do now, but not with the same kind of shoes. As an ox has a cloven hoof he needed 8 shoes instead of four, or perhaps I should say four pairs of shoes.

The old Negro also made bullets of lead which he procured almost in the pure state. He was the only one who knew where to find the lead-the Indians showed him. They often tried to follow him when he went for the lead, but never succeeded.

There was also a large grove of maple trees on the place from which sugar and syrup were made. The trees were tapped early in the spring, then the sweet water was boiled in large kettles.

Pine Knots For Light

Sometimes they had to work far into the night to finish a batch of syrup or sugar. They used pine knot torches for lights. The nearest market was Cape Girardeau, about eighty miles away. Usually several men would go together and, as it took several days to make the trip with the slow ox teams, they enjoyed many a campfire together. This was also a protection against Indians and thieves. However, the Indians were mostly friendly and were often a help to the white settlers. When they went to market they would take whatever they had to sell, which was mostly furs, and bring back what they could not raise on the farm, this consisted of powder and shot for their guns, flour, salt, sugar, hardware and other things.

As Solomon's children grew to school age and other settlers arrived, they decided they needed a school. There was a log house built about one hundred yards west of the spring near Samuel Kittrell's old cabin.

There was a log left out for a window and the door was hung with wooden hinges, the door facing put on with wooden pins fitted into holes bored into the logs. This was long before they ever had square nails to use.

The seats were of "puncheon" or boards split by hand with legs fitted into holes. The floor was a earth and a fireplace for warmth. There was usually three months of school and the teacher "boarded around" among the pupils. The teachers had a very limited education. The three R's (reading, riting and rithmetic), was all they were required to teach. The one who used the birch or hickory the most was usually considered the best teacher.

Had a Distillery

Solomon had a distillery where whiskey was made and sold for twenty-five cents a gallon. There was no government tax at that time. During the time the government opened a road through here for the purpose of transporting troops to the Mexican border. It is still in use and is called the "Old Military Road". It passed just in front of Solomon's house.

This county suffered greatly during the Civil War, being a "border" state. There were no regular battles fought in the county, but soldiers from both north and south marched through the county, and the "bushwhackers" robbed, pillaged and burned a great deal.

Butler County had been organized by this time and one time a cannon ball was fired through the courthouse, but no one was injured.

There were only a few people, about a dozen, in Poplar Bluff, the county seat them, but now it is a thriving city of about 12,000 inhabitants.

Solomon Kittrell died after a long and useful life and was laid to rest near his father, Samuel, in a little country graveyard about a mile from his home.

His son, affectionately known as "Uncle Lem" died a few years ago at the age of seventy-nine, and was laid beside his father. He told me most of this story of the life of his father and grandfather. I must also thank his sister, Mrs. Martha Kittrell Smith who is still living. We now own the farm that was settled by old Samuel Kittrell, the oldest farm in the county. We drink out of the same spring and wade in the same creek.

I often vision those far away days when you could shoot a deer or turkey from your back door, and see Indians more frequently than white neighbors. We have two pieces of money we found on the farm dated 1722 with Carlos III and other Spanish inscriptions and a half-dime dated 1853.

There is also an old apple tree o the farm, which is the oldest and largest in the county. It must be at least seventy-five years old as "Uncle Lem" said he ate apples off it when he was a little boy. It bore several bushels of apples last year but about the time they were ripe, a tornado struck and tore off about half of the limbs.

I have a good snapshot of it before it was spoiled and one of Solomon Kittrells house. Sorry I did not get one of the "Negro kitchen" before it was torn down.

This farm is situated about ten miles northwest of Poplar Bluff and some of the land along Cane Creek is still owned by descendants of old Samuel Kittrell, the Butler County pioneer.

Mrs. Cecil Burton
The Daily Republican
Poplar Bluff, MO
April 6, 1928

Chapter Seventeen

WESTWARD, HO!

THE TURBULENT LIFE OF "PRETTY BOY" FLOYD

Charles Arthur Floyd was born on February 3, 1904, in Georgia, but his parents, along with seven children, moved to a small farming community, Atkins, in Sequoyah County of Eastern Oklahoma, northwest of Fort Smith, Arkansas. The area was the Cherokee or Nation of Indian Territory. Atkins was names in honor of a former mail carrier, Robert Atkins.

Atkins is at the edge of the Cookson Hills of the Ozark Mountains, a rugged place once considered a den of wrongdoers. It became the home of "Pretty Boy" Floyd, an outlaw of the great depression era, who was once the top man on the FBI's "Most Wanted."

Floyd's father was farming and struggling to keep from being foreclosed because of droughts, dust storms and plagues, which brought farming to a standstill. Those were hard times during the depression. The family finally got into bootlegging whiskey.

Charles Arthur married 16 year old Ruby Hargrove. Money was extremely difficult to obtain. He left his home and went north looking for farm work. He spent many nights sleeping in hobo camps and was unable to find work. He was willing to work, but jobs weren't available.

Floyd eventually stopped looking for work and purchases his first gun. At the age of 18, he committed his first crime by holding up a post office, netting $350. His was easy money for him. His next robbery was a Kroger store in St. Louis, getting about $16,000. A lot of money was spent on new clothes and a new Ford. The robbery funds were soon consumed. Floyd's new clothing and car made him a prime suspect of the robbery. He was arrested, his home was searched and some of the money was discovered still in its wrappers.

Floyd was sentenced to five years in the Missouri State Penitentiary at Jefferson City, MO. During his incarceration, his wife gave birth to their son, Jack Dempsey Floyd, and she secured a divorce. After serving a term of three years, Floyd was released and he vowed never to be locked up a again.

On a visit to his parent's home, Floyd discovered his father had been shot to death in a family feud by J. Mills. The accused was acquitted of the crime. Charles Arthur Floyd took his father's rifle, went into the hills, and J. Mills was never seen again.

In the mid-twenties, Floyd lived and operated in the East Liverpool, Ohio, area as a hired gun for the rum-runners and bootleggers along the Steubenville, Ohio, and Midland, Pennsylvania stretch of the Ohio River.

He eventually left the East Liverpool area and headed west, becoming notorious in Kansas City, where the city was run by Tom Pendegast. The town had its share of hired guns, murderers and successful gangsters. Here is where Floyd learned the use of a machine gun and acquired the nickname, "Pretty Boy Floyd". It was given to him in a brothel, and he always hated the name.

During the next twelve years, Floyd robbed as many as thirty banks, killing some ten men. During his crime spree in Oklahoma, the bank insurance doubled. It was alleged he filed a notch in his pocket watch for everyone he killed. His first bank robbery occurred at the Farmers and Merchants Bank in Sylvania, Ohio. Floyd was arrested at his Akron, Ohio, hideout, was tried and convicted, but he escaped by jumping out of a train window near Kenton, Ohio while on his way to the Ohio Penitentiary.

The first man Floyd killed was a police officer, Ralph Castner, who stopped him from robbing a Bowling Green, Ohio bank on April 16, 1931. Floyd was in the company of William (Willis) Miller, known as "Billy the Killer" and two sisters from a house of ill-repute in a district in Kansas City. A clerk in a store recognized the two killers when they were purchasing dresses for the women. The clerk alerted the police, who arrived while the group was walking down the street. When the group was ordered to stop, Floyd and Miller opened fire, Castner was killed immediately; and Chief Carl Galliher dropped to the ground, opened fire, killing Miller and injuring Beulah Alezi. The other female, Rose, age 23, was captured, but Floyd escaped in a car.

On June 17, 1933, Floyd and an associate, Adam Richetti, were reported as the killers behind the "Union Station Massacre" in Kansas City, where five men, including FBI agent, Raymond Caffrey, were gunned down in an attempt to free Frank "Gentleman" Nash, a notorious outlaw. Floyd swore to his dying day he was never involved in the crime.

During the next seventeen months, Floyd and Richetti were hunted by many law enforcement officers across the country. After John Dillinger's death, Floyd was names as Public Enemy No. 1, with a reward of $23,000, dead or alive. Floyd's reign of terror took him back to East Liverpool, Ohio.

Floyd was recognized as a folk hero, a "sagebrush Robin Hood", stealing from the rich banks, giving to the poor to buy groceries and tearing up of mortgages during their robberies.

On October 19, 1934, Floyd was spotted by three men dressed as hunters. Floyd and Richetti were positively identified as two of the men who robbed the Tiltonville People's Bank of Ohio. Police and FBI were alerted throughout the state. The following day, after the robbery, a shootout occurred between two men and the Wellsville, Ohio, Police Department. Richetti was captured, but Floyd again eluded the police, kidnapping a Wellsville florist and stealing his car.

On October 22, 1934, the local police blocked all roads in the area where Floyd had been seen. Firearms were issued to every man. A patrolman, Chester Smith, refused a weapon and chose to keep his 32-20 Winchester rifle. Finally, the hunt ended at the Conkle farm on Sprucevale Road near Wellsville.

Floyd had knocked on the door of the Conkle farm, where Ellen Conkle welcomed him into her home, fed him a meal, and received one dollar for the food. After he had eaten, Ellen Conkle volunteered her brother to drive Floyd to the local station. Floyd was getting into the car when two police cars were spotted speeding along the narrow road to the Conkle home. Floyd jumped from the car to hide behind a corn crib.

As the policemen approached the farm, they spotted a man behind the crib. Chester Smith recognized the face of Floyd. Floyd started to flee. After being told to halt, he fled anyway. Smith fired a shot from his rifle, hitting Floyd in the arm. He dropped to the ground, dropped his gun and grabbed his right forearm. He jumped up and continued to run, darting for cover in a wooded area. Smith fired again, hitting Floyd in the back at his right shoulder. The Federal Agents and local police opened fire on Floyd. He fell to the ground and his gun was by his side. He was carried to the shade of an apple tree, still alive, and he had two Colt .45 automatics. He had never fired a shot from either. Within a few minutes, Floyd was dead.

Floyd's mother did not want her son's body viewed by the public, but before a wire reached Chief McDermott's office, more than 100,000 people had viewed the body of the notorious outlaw. The mob of people stormed the funeral home in the space of three hours. Shrubbery was trampled, the lawn was ruined and a porch railing was torn off.

Floyd's body was shipped in a baggage car back to his home turf in Atkins. On a Sunday, October 28, 1934, masses of people traveled the dusty, dirty roads to the grave site. The roads were crowded with old cars, new cars, horses, buggies and wagons. Poor people, rich people and famous people lined the roads to the graveyard.

There was swearing, shoving of people as they fought to get near the canopied grave to even get clods of dirt from the burial site for souvenirs. Some of the people wisecracked, ate peanuts and some brought their lunches and spread them on tombstones and ate as if they were tables.

Sheriff Bill Byrd tried, without much success, to keep the funeral orderly and occasionally seized a newsman's camera, something they had earlier barred from the cemetery. The people were in masses like nervous cattle ready to stampede. They did overrun all graves before them. Some 20,000 people attended Floyd's funeral.

Atkins was a descendant from "The Grapes of Wrath". The post office closed in 1943. A headstone has been desecrated by souvenir hunters. It is now a ghost town and a new headstone now marks the grave of the once notorious outlaw, Charles Arthur "Pretty Boy" Floyd.

Jay Mondy
Wappapello, MO
June 17, 2001

References:
Atkins-Pretty Boy's Funeral, 1934 by Jim Martin Etter
Ghost-town Tales of Oklahoma, New Forums Press, Inc., Stillwater, Oklahoma
Charles "Pretty Boy" Floyd, Public Enemy No. 1, GeoCities-internet – 1997

Akin, OK

PUBLICATION DESIGNED TO
SATISFY CONTINUED HIGH INTEREST

Coffeyville, KS

There is a twofold purposes for the assembling of this material on the Dalton Raid in one publication:

1. There remains, as this is written (June of 1954), wide-spread interest in the Raid, the personalities involved in it and the locale-Coffeyville, Montgomery County, Kansas.
2. The Dalton Raid is an essential part of the history of the great Southwest.   It is currently treated in novels and magazine articles. This publication is intended to prove an accurate guide for those who want to read of the Dalton Raid. Every effort has been made to present only authentic material in these pages.

It was on October 5, 1892, that the Plaza section of downtown Coffeyville echoed to the second of gunshots and running feet.

In 12 minutes of rifle, shotgun, and pistol fire eight men were killed, four men were wounded, and the name of Coffeyville was indelibly stamped upon the pioneer history of the great Southwest.

That was the Dalton Raid.

The men who fell in the raid, on the side of law and order, were just ordinary pioneer citizens who answered the age old call of man and the West-grab a Winchester to defend your home and property. None was a professional full-tome law enforcement officer.

While Charles T. Connelly, 46, was referred to as "marshal," and was carrying out the duties of that office, he was actually a school teacher. He was not even armed when the fight started.

The Journal of November 4, 1892 picked up for reprint this item from the Liberty Review: "Miss Maggie McCarty has been appointed principle of the West Side School in Coffeyville to fill the vacancy caused by the death of Prof. Connelly. Miss Maggie is an excellent lady and is working her way up to the front as an educator in this county."

Charles Brown, 59, was a shoemaker.

George B. Cubine, 36, was described by The Journal of the day only as "a mechanic."   Lucius M. Baldwin, 23, was a young clerk in Read Brothers store.

Baldwin was not the first man shot in the Raid. That dubious distinction went to Charles T. Gump who was wounded in the hand, but the young clerk was the first to be fatally wounded. He was felled by Bob Dalton in the alley in back of the First National Bank and died three hours after he had been hit.

Cubine and Brown died on almost the same spot – the front door of the Rammel Brothers' drug store. Cubine was shot down in the doorway as he started out to join the gun battle, and Brown was hit when he went to the rescue of his fallen friend.

Marshal Connelly was a victim of Grat Dalton's gun, shot in the back when he walked into the alley where the Dalton horses had been tied.

The other wounded defenders were Thomas G. Ayers, First National Bank cashier, who was shot under the eye, and T. Arthur Reynolds, a clerk in the Isham Brothers & Mansur Hardware Store. Reynolds was hit by a glancing bullet in the foot.

The fourth wounded survivor of the Raid was the bandit, Emmett Dalton. Emmett was shot off his horse by Casey Seamen when Emmett attempted to pull his fatally wounded brother, Bob, into the saddle with him in a final, futile getaway try.

Other Coffeyville citizens who took a shooting part in the short but bloody gun fight, as based upon the best available accounts of the Raid, were John J. Kloehr, later a Coffeyville peace officer but then a liveryman; Henry H. Isham, who also provided most of the guns and ammunition used in the Raid from his hardware stock; Lewis A. Dietz, an Isham-Mansur clerk; M.N. Anderson, a carpenter attracted to the scene of the battle by the gun fire; Charles K. Smith, son of a barber on the Plaza; Parker L. Williams, F.D. Benson, and C. S. Cox.

Kloehr stood out as the individual hero of the battle. He exposed himself to the bandit fire by maneuvering through the battle area and was credited with having finished off Bob and Grat Dalton. The other two bandits, Bill Powers and Dick (Texas Jack) Broadwell, were the victims of concentrated fire rather than of any individual defender.

After the Raid, Kloehr was given, among other awards, a special presentation rifle from Winchester Arms. The gun hangs on the fireplace in the Chuck Wagon room in the Condon Bank.

Col. D.S. Elliott, then editor of The Coffeyville Journal, wrote of Mr. Kloehr:

"John Joseph Kloehr was born in Aschachbad, Kissingen Bavaria, Germany, in the year 1858. He emigrated with his father and other members of the family, in 1871, and settled in Coffeyville where he has resided ever since. He has been engaged in the livery business for the past 10 years. He is a quiet, reserved and peaceable citizen. As a member of the local gun club, he has acquired some skill and considerable practice as a marksman. He deplores the circumstances which compelled him to use his rifle against his fellow man. He did it in defense of the rights of citizenship."

As did they all, those heroic Coffeyville Defenders of that long ago October.

Why did the Daltons try to rob the two Coffeyville banks?

There are two answers to this:

One (and the more logical) is that the job presented a challenge to them. They were familiar with Coffeyville and its bank setup, and they wanted to do something which could eclipse their cousins, the Younger Gang, and the James Boys.

The other version is they had incurred a small gambling debt and were on a $25 note to a Southeast Kansas bank. They were trying to get money to pay this off.

Why did the Raid fail?

Here are the two key reasons:

1. When one of the gang cased the banks he decided the horses should be tied on 8th street. But when the bandits rode into town for the Raid, they found the street torn up so they had to leave their horses in what became Death Alley. Defenders in the Isham Hardware Store had a clear view of that alley and fired into it from the protection of the store. Bob is supposed to have cased the bank in July of 1882 and was reported to have been back in Coffeyville the week before the Raid. That was an after-dark visit in search of whiskey.

2. Cashier C.M. Ball of the Condon Bank stalled the three bandits who came into that establishment-Grat Dalton, Bill Powers, and Dick Broadwell-by telling them the time mechanism on the vault had not released itself for the day. This delay gave the citizens time enough to arm themselves for the showdown fight which followed.

How much money was taken in the Raid?

Approximately $20,000 was secured in each of the banks and was in the possession of the bandits when they were shot down. At the end of that banking day, the Condon Bank was $20 short, but the First National Bank checked out with an average of $1.98.

Gene Sullivan
Coffeyville Kansas Journal
Coffeyville, Kansas
May 30, 1954

COWTOWN DAYS

Kansas' first cowtown celebrates
Without Kansas the cowboy as we know him would
Never have come into existence

The cattle were in Texas, but the cowtowns were in Kansas

Baxter Springs, KS

Rich with diverse history from the Native American heritage to the first settler, John Baxter staked his claim near Spring River in 1849.

Through the Civil War battles, including Quantrill and his guerrilla's bloody massacres in 1863, into the mining, farming, ranching era, and even Jesse James and friends reportedly robbing the local bank in 1876; to the famous Highway 66 winding its way through the community, to all events that bring notoriety to Baxter Springs and all important facets of the community's history, quite possibly the most defining segment in history for all of Baxter Springs families is that of the cattle drives and why the town proudly wears the badge of being the "First Cowtown in Kansas."

In the mid to late 1800's, Texas cattle ranchers began to avoid trouble with southwestern Missouri farmers who feared the cattle herds would trample their fields and spread dreaded livestock disease. Instead they began driving large numbers of longhorns at one time along the old Shawnee Trail and Texas Road.

The Shawnee Trail was the first major trail of the Old West to open in the 1840s, beginning in the southern most part of Texas at Brownsville extending north through Dallas, southeast Kansas, and northward to Kansas City.

Sedalia and St. Louis, the old Shawnee Trail, was closed because of the Civil War and a quarantine against fever-bearing longhorns.

But after the war, the cattle business was booming all over the place and, as settlers and railroads moved west, the old cattle trail opened up again. The Shawnee Trail through Baxter Springs offered the cattlemen the shortest distance from Texas to northern markets, as well as an abundance of rich grazing land and pure water. The natural mineral springs were well known among many Indian tribes for their medicinal value. Our town offered active stock yards and a drovers' association organized for buying and selling cattle.

Sturdy corrals were built to contain upwards of 20,000 head of cattle, removing the need for night herders.

The very best of the cattle boom days were from about 1868 to 1872, and Baxter Springs rapidly began to prosper and grow. We were a boom town by 1880 and became the first frontier town on what was then called the southern border.

Especially large cattle drives (upwards of 20,000 to 25,000 longhorn) came through in 1867 to 1868. When the railroad was built in 1870, Baxter Springs became a wide-open cowtown and a shipping point so crowded the townspeople of "the toughest town on earth" had to put up with gun totin' cowboys, cattlemen, gamblers, and ruffians.

During this time, everyone carried a gun for protection. Public hangings were a common event, and gun fights caused hardly a stir. Rough-housing saloons were numerous, and the town was in one continuous state of uproar night and day, especially during the cattle-driving season. Located in the southeastern corner of Kansas only six miles from the Missouri border and about one-and-a-half miles north of Indian Territory, Baxter Springs with its wild and wooly reputation was known far and wide. Cowboys along the trails at night would quietly sing favorite tunes to calm the large herds and prevent stampedes. A favorite trail song entitled "The Cowboy," author unknown, goes like this:

> All day long on the prairies I ride,
> Not even a dog to trot by my side;
> My fire I kindle with chips gathered round,
> My coffee I boiled without being ground.
> I was in a pool and wipe on a sack;
> I carry my wardrobe all on my back;
> For want of an oven I cook bread in a pot,
> And sleep on the ground for the want of a cot.
> My ceiling is the sky, my floor is the grass,
> My music is the lowing of herds as they pass;
> My books are the brooks, my sermons the stones,
> My parson is a wolf on his pulpit of bones.

Tony Coble
Baxter Springs News
Baxter Springs, KS
August, 2001

WYATT EARP – LAMAR LAWMAN

Lamar, MO

Nearly everyone has heard of western legend Wyatt Earp. Some may know he served briefly as a peace officer in the Kansas cowtowns of Wichita and Dodge City, and many more are aware he later gained fame as a deputy marshal in Arizona Territory after the celebrated shootout at the O.K. Corral. Fewer readers may realize, however, Earp actually got his start as a lawman right here in the Ozarks, serving as a town constable at Lamar, MO.

Twenty-one-year-old Wyatt moved to Lamar about 1869 along with his father, Nicholas Earp, and other members of the family. On January 3, 1870 he married a young woman named Urilla Sutherland, daughter of the local hotel owner. Earp's father, a justice of the peace in addition to running a grocery and bakery in Lamar, performed the ceremony.

Two months later Wyatt was appointed a constable in the small town. He and his father soon became embroiled with city leaders in a controversy over a proposed new ordinance prohibiting hogs from running free in the town. The Earps opposed the law and felt corralling pigs was not the fitting province of the town constable. Nicholas Earp ran for the Board of Trustees on a platform opposed to caging the porkers and won the election.

Wyatt Earp's only official law enforcement task as constable, that is recorded for posterity, was a run-in with three drunks on the evening of June 13, 1870, on the streets of Lamar. Earlier in the day a local man had received a visit from his out-of-town brother, and the two men went carousing around town. Taking with them "a good supply of "forty rod," according to The Southwest Missourian, the two men got rip-roaring drunk. Young Earp "found one of them upon the street incapable of taking care of himself and took him down to a stone building which he had appropriated for the use of such customers. As Mr. Earp was about turning the key upon his bird the other one came staggering up, enquiring for his lost brother. Mr. Earp opened the door and slid him in."

As Wyatt was leaving his makeshift jail and heading back toward the square, continues the town newspaper, "another hard case in the shape of a tramping butcher" came by and demanded Earp buy him a lead pencil to replace one he claimed the constable had borrowed from him some time earlier. Wyatt drew the newcomer butcher down to the calaboose on the pretext of finding him a pencil, "and, of course he shared the fate of the other two."

During the night "the three caged birds" escaped through a hole in the roof of the building, "and the stranger, not liking the reception he met with here, left for parts unknown." The other two men appeared before Wyatt's father and were fined five dollars and costs. "A few more examples," concluded the newspaper, "and the town will be better for it."

Wyatt announced his intention to run for election in November to his position as constable, and his main opponent turned out to be his older half-brother, Newton. Wyatt won by a vote of 137-108. The election apparently caused no lasting bitterness between the brothers because Newton later named a son after Wyatt.

About the time of the election, tragedy struck when Wyatt's wife, Urilla, died unexpectedly. The exact date is not known nor is the precise cause of death. One report says typhoid and another says she died from complications of giving birth to a stillborn baby. Equally sketchy are the circumstances of a fistfight that broke out in the streets of Lamar shortly afterwards between the Earp brothers and his brother-in-law, the two Sutherland brothers. Although the exact cause of the brawl has never been determined, the intimation had been the Sutherlands somehow blamed Wyatt for their sister's death. Both sides came out of the affray battered and bruised but with no serious injuries.

A couple of months late Wyatt left town under a cloud of suspicion. On March 14, 1871, Barton County filed a suit against Earp, alleging he had failed to turn over license fees he had collected as constable of Lamar, for the fees were supposed to go to the school fund. On the 31st of the same month, a man named James Cromwell filed a suit against Wyatt for falsifying court records and pocketed the $20 difference. When the court sent the new constable looking for Wyatt to bring him in for a hearing, he and his father had already sold their property and left town.

Wyatt drifted south into the Indian Nation (Oklahoma), where he got into another scrape with the law during the spring of 1871. He and another man were indicted at Ft. Smith Ark. for horse thievery. Earp posted bond and skipped the territory, but, when his co-defendant was found not guilty, the court apparently lost interest in pursuing the fugitive.

Wyatt Earp turned to a life of adventure over the next few years, trying his hand at buffalo hunting, among other pursuits, and making the acquaintance of a young lawman named Bat Masterson before landing in Wichita and Dodge City during the mid 1870's and finally moving on to Tombstone, Ariz., around 1879. Wyatt's uncle remained in Lamar, and in later years Earp descendants owned the birthplace of Harry S. Truman until shortly before the house became a state historic site in 1959.

Though famous for his associations as a lawman in towns further west, Wyatt Earp got his first experiences as a lawman in Missouri on the streets of Lamar.

> Larry Wood
> The Ozark Mountaineer
> Kirbyville, MO
> December 1991

SHOOTOUT, SPRINGFIELD, MISSOURI

Records of the United Stated War Department show that on October 30, 1861, James Butler "Wild Bill" Hickok was hired as a wagon master at Sedalia,

Missouri. His pay was $100 per month. Similar records from the office of the Provost Marshal General show Hickok served as a special policeman in the corps during March, 1864.

"The United State to William Hickok, March 10, 1864, for services rendered as special police under the direction of Lt. H.H. Burns, A Provost Marshal District, Southwest, Missouri, at Springfield, from March 1 to March 10, 1864, for 10 days at $60 a month, $20.

Near the end of the Civil War, Hickok wrote this letter, dated February 10, 1865, from Cassville, Missouri:

T Brigadier – General Sanborn:
I have been at Camp Walker and Spavinaw. There are not more than ten or twelve rebels in any squad in the southwest that I can hear of. If you want me to go to Neosho and west of there, notify me here.

> J.B. Hickok

General Sanborn replied from Headquarters District of Southwest Missouri, Springfield, Missouri, February 11, 1865:

> J.B. Hickok
> Cassville, Missouri

You may go to Yellville (Ark.) or the White River vicinity of Yellville and learn what Dobbin intends to do with his command now on Crowley's Ridge, and from there come to this place.

> John B. Sanborn
> Brigadier – General Commanding

It was in Springfield five months later Hickok shot and killed David Tutt of Yellville. The Springfield Missouri Weekly Patriot gave the killing scant notice in its "Locals" column. In her book, A Living History of the Ozarks, Phyllis Rossiter made and gives this account of the shooting:

"Apparently Hickok and Tutt had known and disliked each other for years. Both had been dating the same woman, and to retaliate for Tutt's moving in on his girl, Hickok began courting Tutt's sister. On at least one occasion, Tutt confronted Hickok and asked him to stop seeing her. A short time later, Hickok, Tutt, and others were playing poker and a dispute developed over Wild Bill's watch. In some versions, Hickok gave Tutt the watch to keep, in pledge, until he could raise the money to pay off his gambling losses, with Hickok warning Tutt only to hold the watch, not to wear it. By other accounts, Tutt took the watch off the poker table over Hickok's objection. But apparently the next day Tutt appeared on the street wearing Hickok's watch, to the latter's displeasure. Ozark's historian Phillip Steele adds this to the story:

On July 21, 1865, the confrontation finally came. Tutt's friends notified Hickok, Tutt would be crossing the square at 6:00 p.m., if he wanted to try to get his watch back. Hickok responded, "He can't take my watch across the square unless dead men can walk." As hundreds of Springfield citizens gathered in doors and alleys around the square and Wild Bill on the other. Hickok yelled a warning to Tutt. Once more ignoring Hickok's demands, Tutt started across the square. As he did, he drew his gun. Hickok responded quickly, both guns firing simultaneously. Tutt fell dead, a bullet through his heart.

Hickok reportedly turned himself in to the local sheriff and stood trial. He was tried August 5, 1865, and acquitted. The jury rendered its verdict in about 10 minutes.

"Wild Bill Hickok"
Douglas Mahnkey
Kirbyville, MO
The Ozark Mountaineer
December, 1998

AUTHOR'S NOTE:

James Butler "Wild Bill" Hickok met his fate in a poker game in a saloon, August 2, 1876, in Deadwood Gulch, Wyoming. The territory later became South Dakota. The Gulch name was eventually dropped. Hickok was shot from behind by Jack McCall, leaving behind his fateful cards. Since the day of Hickok's death, the cards, aces and eights, have been referred to as a "Dead Man's Hand!"

Edited by Jay Mondy
Wappapello, MO
December, 2000

JESSIE JAMES DIED 10 YEARS BEFORE DALTONS WERE KILLED

St. Joseph, MO

The death here of Jesse James, the American Robin Hood, was one of the important stories chronicled by the St. Joseph Evening News in 1882, less than three years after the paper was founded.

The story, carried by The Evening News, was reprinted in a number or American newspapers and in a number of volumes of American folklore.

The news story, relating the events of that day, April 3, 1882, when the city received world-wide publicity, follows:

"Between 8 and 9 o'clock this morning Jesse James, the Missouri outlaw, before whom the deeds of Frank Diavolo, Dick Turpin and Schinderhannes dwindled into insignificance, was instantly killed by a boy, 20 years old, named Robert Ford, at his temporary residence on the corner of 13th and Lafayette Streets, in this city.

In the light of all moral reasoning the shooting was unjustifiable; but the law is vindicated, and the $10,000 reward offered by the state for the body of the brigand will doubtless go to the man who had the courage to draw a revolver on the notorious outlaw even when his back was turned, as in this case.

There is little doubt the killing was the result of a premeditated plan formed by Robert and Charles Ford several months ago. Charles had been an accomplice of Jesse James since the 3rd of November and entirely possessed his confidence. Robert Ford, his brother, joined Jesse near Mrs. Samuel's (the mother of the James boys) last Friday a week ago, and accompanied Jesse and Charles to this city Sunday, March 23.

Jesse, his wife and two children, moved from Kansas – where they had lived several months, until they feared their whereabouts would be suspected – to this city, arriving her November 8, 1881, coming in a wagon and accompanied by Charles Ford. They rented a house on the corner of Lafayette and 21st Streets, where they stayed two months, when they secured the house No. 1381 on Lafayette Street, formerly the property of Councilman Aylesbury, paying $14 a month for it, and giving the name of Thomas Howard.

The house is a one-story cottage, painted white with green shutters, and is romantically situated on the brow of a lofty eminence east of the city commanding a fine view of the principal portion of the city, river, and railroads, and adapted by nature for the perilous and desperate calling of Jesse James. Just east of the house is a deep, gulchlike ravine, and beyond that a broad expanse of open country backed by a belt of timber. The house, except from the west side, can be seen for several miles. There is a large yard attached to the cottage and a stable were Jesse had been keeping two horses, which were found there this morning.

Charles and Robert Ford have been occupying one of the rooms in the rear of the dwelling, and have secretly had an understanding to kill Jesse ever since last Fall. Ever since the boys have been with Jesse they have watched for an opportunity to shoot him, but he was always so heavily armed that it was impossible to draw a weapon without James seeing it. They declared they had no idea of taking him alive, considering the undertaking suicidal.

The opportunity they had long wished for came this morning. Breakfast was over. Charlie Ford and Jesse James had been in the stable currying their horses preparatory to their night ride. On returning to the room were Robert Ford was, Jesse said:

"It's an awfully hot day."

He pulled off his coat and vest and tossed them on the bed. Then he said:

"I guess I'll take off my pistols, for fear somebody will see them if I walk in the yard."

He unbuckled his belt, in which he carried two .45 caliber revolvers, one a Smith & Wesson, and the other a Colt, and laid them on the bed with his coat and vest. He then picked up a dusting brush with the intention of dusting some pictures which hung on the wall. To do this he got on a chair. His back was now turned to the brothers, who silently stepped between Jesse and his revolvers.

At a motion from Charlie both drew their guns. Robert was the quicker to the two, and in one motion he had the long weapon to a level with his eye, and with the muzzle not more than four feet from the back of the outlaw's head.

Even in that motion, quick as a thought, there was something which did not escape the acute ears of the hunted man. He made a motion as if to turn his head to ascertain the cause of that suspicious sound, but too late. A nervous pressure on the trigger, a quick flash, a sharp report, and the well-directed ball crashed through the outlaw's skull.

There was no outcry just a swaying of the body and it fell heavily backward upon the carpet of the floor. The shot had been fatal, and all the bullets in the chambers of Charlie's revolver, still directed at Jesse's head, could not more effectually have decided the fate of the greatest bandit and freebooter that ever figured in the pages of the country's history.

The ball had entered the base of the skull and made its way out through the forehead, over the left eye. It had been fired out of a Colt .45, improved pattern, silver-mounted and pearl-handled pistol, presented by the dead man to his slayer only a few days ago.

Mrs. James was in the kitchen when the shooting was done, separated from the room in which the bloody tragedy occurred by the dining room. She heard the shot, and dropping her household duties ran into the front room. She saw her husband lying extended on his back, his slayers, each holding his revolver in his hand, making for the fence in the rear of the house. Robert had reached the enclosure and was in the act of scaling it when she stepped to the door and called to him: "Robert, you have done this!"

Robert answered, "I swear to God I didn't!"

They then turned to where she stood. Mrs. James ran to the side of her husband and lifted up his head. Life was not yet extinct, and when she asked him if he was hurt, it seemed to her he wanted to say something, but could not. She tried to wash the blood away that was coursing over his face from the hole in his forehead, but it seemed to her the blood would come faster than she could wipe it away, and in her hands Jesse James died.

Charles explained to Mrs. James that 'a pistol had accidentally gone off.' "Yes," said Mrs. James, "I guess it went off on purpose." Meanwhile Charlie had gone back in the house and brought out two hats, and the two boys left the house. They went to the telegraph office, sent a message to Sheriff Timberlake of Clay County, to Police Commissioner Craig of Kansas City, to Governor Crittenden and other officers, and then surrendered themselves to Marshal Craig.

When the Ford boys appeared at the police station they were told by an officer that Marshal Craig and a posse of officers had gone in the direction of the James residence, and they started after them and accompanied the officers to the house and returned in custody of the police to the marshal's headquarters, where they were furnished with dinner, and about 3 p.m. were removed to the old circuit courtroom, where the inquest was held in the presence of an immense crowd."

Gene Sullivan, Managing Editor
Coffeyville Journal, 1954
Coffeyville, Kansas

STORIES OF JESSE JAMES

Why Robert Ford Shot the Noted Desperado and the Case of John A. Hurbank's Gold Watch

Poplar Bluff, MO

The recent disinterment of the famous bandit and outlaw, Jesse James, has brought up quite a number of interesting recollections of the man, who for nearly 30 years, held the middle west in terror and fear. One of these stories which, by the way, happens to be singularly apropos as well as new, is now going the rounds concerning the true inwardness of his death at the hands of Robert Ford, it is said, had no thought whatever as to the reward at the time he killed Jesse James. It appears that for a long time previous to the killing of James the latter, for some unknown reason, had become suspicious of Ford, and had determined to kill him. This suspicion was, so the story runs, entirely unfounded, Ford having no notion of betraying James, who was living in St. Joseph, MO., under the alias of Howard, relates the Washington Post.

At all events, Ford subsequently learned of Jesse's misgivings, and tried his best to show the latter that his fears were groundless. This only made matters worse, the result being that Ford made up his mind to kill Jesse before the latter killed him. On the day, therefore, that Jesse met Ford on the street and invited him to his house, he did so, intending to kill him when he got him there, and the removal of his revolvers (for the first time in his life) was not, as some have supposed, through carelessness but an act premeditated and for the purpose of throwing Ford off his guard. But Ford had seen Jesse do tricks similar to this before and was not deceived, and when the former got up on a chair to hang some pictures he took the chance thus afforded of ridding himself of an enemy and the country of its most noted outlaw.

Another curious memory of the James boys career was the case of John A. Burbank's gold watch. It appears that some years after the Civil War the legislature of the then territory of Dakota presented Mr. John A. Burbank, a wealthy resident of Richmond, Ind., with a very handsome gold watch for some especially valuable and meritorious service he had rendered the commonwealth. Some time after this occurred Burbank happened to be on a stage coach en route from Malvern, MO, to Hot Springs, Ark., and, in crossing the border between the two states, the coach was held up and robbed by the James boys, who took Burbank's watch. The watch fell to Jesse's share of the spoil, and he took such a fancy to it that he wore it constantly until the day of his death, a period of 22 years. At the time he was killed the watch, after an absence from its owner of 22 years, was returned to Mr. Burbank, who probably has it today, if he is still living.

The Daily Republican
Poplar Bluff, Mo
August 25, 1902

THEY THOUGHT HE WAS JESSE'S BROTHER, FRANK

The late John James loved to tell about the time two Pinkerton detectives arrested his father, Randles James, for robbing the Iron Mountain train at Gads Hill. They were certain he was the noted outlaw, Frank James, brother of Jesse James.

It was Friday, February 13, 1874, just two weeks after the Gad's Hill robbery, when the two detectives drove their buggy to the Randles James' farm on Cane Creek. They called Mr. James to the door and asked if he had any hogs for sale. They said they were stock buyers and were traveling about the country buying stock for a large packing firm in St. Louis. Both men were dressed in flashy suits with heavy overcoats and derby hats. They looked like typical stock buyers of that day.

Mr. James said he had some hogs that had been running on the open range and he had penned them up the week before to feed out, and they were not ready to market yet. The bogus stock buyers insisted they be allowed to see the hogs, saying they would return in a month to purchase them.

At the hog pen, some 100 yards from the house, the detectives quickly drew revolvers from under their coats and told Mr. James he was under arrest. They handcuffed his hands behind his back, placed him between them in the buggy and started for Marble Hill, Missouri as fast as their horse could travel. Mr. James asked them to let him stop at his house so he could get a heavier coat and tell his family where he would be. The request was refused. The detectives thought they had the outlaw, Frank James, and were not about to take a chance of his being of his being rescued by members of his outlaw band.

It was after dark when they arrived at the sheriff's office in Marble Hill. The Pinkerton men awoke Sheriff Hopkins and informed him they had captured the notorious outlaw, Frank James.

They asked Sheriff Hopkins to hold their prisoner in the Marble Hill jail until train time the next morning saying one of them would stand guard all night to prevent his escape.

Sheriff Hopkins, after one look at their prisoner, informed the detectives they had made a mistake. "That is not Frank James," he said. "That is Randles James. I have known this man all my life. He is a good law-abiding citizen. This man has never broken the law in his life."

The Pinkerton men did not believe him. They produced a photograph. "Look sheriff, here is a picture of Frank James. You can see it's the same man. He may call himself Randles James, but he is Frank James alright."

At that late hour Sheriff Hopkins was in no mood to argue with the detectives. He made them release Mr. James and advised them to catch the first train out of Bollinger County. He also threatened to lock them both in the Marble Hill jail if they ever attempted to arrest a citizen of Bollinger County again.

Angered at their mistake and the sheriff's harsh warning to leave the county, the Pinkerton detectives left Mr. James in Marble Hill to walk the eight miles back to his home on Cane Creek. In later years, Randles James like to tell his children about the time he was arrested by detectives who thought he was Frank James, the outlaw.

Clyde F. Willis
The Bollinger Co. Historical Society
Echo Volume II, October 1959
Marble Hill, MO

135

FRANK JAMES TELLS STORY
OF CENTRALIA MASSACRE

The former Rough-Riding Outlaw Goes Over the Field of Battle and Describes the Action With Minuteness – An Incident of a Grandson "Yelling, shooting our pistols, upon them we went. Not a single man of the line escaped."

Centralia, MO

One of the most terrible conflicts of the Civil War occurred near Centralia, Boone County, MO, in the afternoon of Tuesday, September 27, 1864. Nearly 200 Federal soldiers, commanded by Major A. V. E. Johnson of the Thirty-ninth Missouri Infantry, riding out after guerrillas, met their Captains Bill Anderson and George Todd, with 225 men. Scarcely a dozen of the Federal soldiers escaped with their lives, while only two guerrillas were killed and one mortally wounded. There was nowhere in the history of the world record of a charge more destructive than that made on that September afternoon. Every man in the Federal line of battle perished, and only half a score of those left to hold the horses got away.

The conflict has been described by surviving Union soldiers and by persons who were near at the time of or after the fight. But not until now has one of the chief actors of the Confederate side given his version. On a recent Sunday morning, for the second time in his life, Frank James rode over the battlefield and for the first time, described the fight.

"There is the spot," said Frank James. "Two miles and more from Centralia, shortly before the main road was left for a broad lane which led to S.L. Garrad's home. Yonder on the rise near the hayrack was the line of the Federal troops. Just this side toward Centralia, stood the detachment which held their horses. On the edge of the wood beyond our men formed."

His memory served him well. He had not been to the field before nor since the day of the fight. No work had been spoken to indicate the locality. But he remembered accurately the entire surroundings. "I can go," he said, "to any battlefield where I was engaged and pick out almost instantly the locations. I guess it's the closeness to death that photographs the scene on one's memory."

A few moments later he came into the field itself. Corn was growing rank and a herd of cattle calmly feeding on the pasture land. Where the Federals stood was the golden yellow of a hayfield. There Mr. James wandered around for a few moments drinking in his surroundings with almost passionate eagerness. Then he told the story, quietly at first, but as he proceeded his face lighted up and there was a ring in his voice and his whole frame seemed ready for the fray again.

"The day before we had many a small skirmish down in Goslin's lane, between Columbia and Rockport. I don't know what day it was. We could scarcely keep account of the months at that time, much less days. We killed a dozen Federal soldiers in Goslin's Lane and captured a wagon train of provisions and stuff out in the Perche Hills that night when we joined forces with Bill Anderson. I was with Captain George Todd, one of the hardest fighters to ever have lived, but less desperate than Anderson."

James paused a moment – his conversation was in scraps all day and only here put in connected form – he paused a moment and continued: "Bill Anderson had much to make him merciless. You remember the treatment his father and sisters received at the hands of the Kansas Jayhawkers. That night we camped on one of the branches leading into Young's creek not far from the home of Colonel M. G. Singleton. There were about 235 men, all told, in our combined command. Funny, isn't it? I've met or heard of at least 10,000 men who claimed to be with Quantrell or his lieutenants during the war, when the truth is there were never more than 350 or 400 from one end of the line to the 0 other.

"In the morning Anderson took about thirty of his company and went into Centralia. I was not with him, nor was any of Todd's company. In Centralia Anderson captured a train, carried off a lot of stuff, shot down some soldiers who were on the train and did other things about which I know nothing save from hearsay and which Todd condemned when the boys returned. In the afternoon Captain Todd detailed a detachment of ten men under Dave Pool to go out and reconnoiter. We had heard there were some Yankee troops in the neighborhood. This squad was composed of Dave Pool, Wood and Tuck Hill, Jeff Kinder, Bill Stuart, John Pool, Payton Long, Zach Sutherland, and two others whose names I don't remember. They were to find out if there were any Federal around, how many, and, if possible, push them down toward our camp. Pool did his duty well. He found out the location of the Federals, rode close to them, and then galloped rapidly away, as if surprised to see them. The Federals followed. I have never found anybody who could tell how may there were of them. Pool reported to us there were 350 and he was usually very accurate. On they came out from Centralia. Pool and his men came on and reported. Todd called out, "Mount up, mount up!"

The sharp, piercing eyes of James flashed, "I don't care what your historic books say, they carried a black flag. It was apparently a black apron tied to a stick. We captured it in the battle that followed.

"We had no flag. We had no time to get one and no chance to carry it if we had one. The Yankees stopped near the rise of the hill. Both sides were in full view of each other, though nearly a half mile distant. The Yankees dismounted, gave their horses into charge of a detail of men and prepared to fight.

"John Koger, a funny fellow in out ranks, watched the Yankees get down from their horses, and said: "Why, the fools aren't going to fight us on foot!" And then added, in seriousness: "God help 'em."

"We dismounted to lighten the belts on the horses, and then, at the word of command, started on our charge. The ground, you will notice, rises sharply and we had to charge uphill. For a moment we moved slowly. Our line was nearly a quarter of a mile long, theirs much closer together. We were still some 600 yards away, our speed increasing and our ranks closing up, when they fired their first and only time. They nearly all fired over our heads. We were lying low on our horses, a trick that Comanche Indians practiced and which saved our lives many a time. Only two of our men were killed. Frank Shepherd and 'Hank' Williams. A third, Richard Kinney was shot and died three or four days afterward from lock-jaw. Shepherd and Kinney rode next to me on either side. Kinney was my closest friend. We had ridden together from Texas, fought side by side, slept together, and it hurt me when I heard him say, 'Frank, I am shot.' He kept on riding for a time and thought his wound wasn't serious.

"On we went up the hill. Almost in the twinkling of an eye we were on the Yankee line. They seemed terrorized. Hypnotized might be a better word, though I reckon nobody knew anything about hypnotism then, though George Todd, by the way, looked like Svengalli. Some of the Federals were at 'fix bayonets,' some were biting off their cartridges, preparing to reload.

"Yelling, shooting our pistols upon them we went. Not a single man of the line escaped. Everyone was shot through the head. The few who attempted to escape we followed into Centralia and on to Sturgeon. There a Federal blockhouse stopped further pursuit. All along the road we killed them. The last man and the first man was killed by Arch Clements. He had the best horse and got a little head start.

"That night we left this woods and this neighborhood and scattered. I recrossed the river near Glasgow and went southward."

"It has been reported that my brother, Jesse James, was not at the Centralia fight; that he was sick in Carroll County at the time. This is a mistake. Jesse was here. He killed the commander of the Federal troops, Major Johnson. The Younger boys were not at Centralia."

The plowshare had taken the place of the sword on the hillside. Frank James took an ear of corn from the battlefield. "I want some sort of a relic" he said, "and this is the most peaceful-looking I see." Later in the day, Adam Rodemyre of the Centralia Guard gave him a bullet found on the field.

After two hours on the battlefield a visit was made to the Pleasant Grove burying ground on the Silver farm, where Frank Shepherd and "Hank" Williams are buried. The burying ground is a typical country cemetery, lying in a secluded spot, away from the main-traveled road, some four miles from Centralia.

The living guerrilla stood with his black slouch hat in his hand at the side of the sunken graves of his dead comrades. "To this completion we must come at last." He said, looking down at the withered graves. "Our boys are scattered everywhere. You will find their graves in the hollows and on the hills by the gulf and on these prairies. Many have no monument. They don't need any. They made their monument while they lived. They left a record for daring courage that the world has not yet surpassed. They don't need any monument after they are dead. Their sleep is just as sweet here as it would be in the beautiful city cemetery." Frank James pinched a twig from the great, green pine tree and walked away. "The marvel to me," he said to me, "is that I am not sleeping in a place like this. What have I been spared for when so many of my comrades were taken? Two men shall be working in a field; one shall be taken and the other left. That's Scripture –you know my father was a Baptist preacher – a good man and a good preacher – It's Scripture, and it's life, too."

A brief stay was made at the farmhouse of William R. Jennings. Mr. Jennings helped bury the Federal dead the day after the battle. He could not remember the number, but there were several wagon loads. "I felt sorry for one poor boy, hardly more than 17 years old, who had almost reached the woods in an attempt to escape. All the Federals," continued Mr. Jennings, "had been shot in the head. So unerring was the marksmanship of the bushwhackers that frequently we would find no wound on the soldiers' bodies until we would turn back the eyelid or look into an ear, and there would be the single little hole that brought death." When the old man closed his story the party turned to go. "Well," said Mr. Jennings, "I hope we'll meet in a better world than this." "I hope so," said Mr. James, "where there is no fighting."

"When great, big, grown men, with full possession of all their faculties, refer to that battle as the Centralia Massacre, I think they are pleading the baby act. We did not duck the fight. Johnson foolishly came out in numbers and he found us. Then we killed him and the men. Wouldn't he have killed us if he had had a chance? What is war for if it isn't to kill people for a principle? The Yankee soldiers tried to kill every one of the Southern soldiers and the soldiers for the South tried to kill all the Yanks, and that's all there is to it.

"We were just out there in the bush, not molesting anybody when Johnson and his men came out after us. We never took prisoners. We couldn't do it. How could we carry them around with us? We either killed them or turned them loose. As for the Centralia night, it reminds me of Macbeth, 'Never shake thy glory locks at me; Thou canst not say I did it.'

"We didn't make war on women and children. They are the only people whom I sympathize with during war. Men ought to be in the fight on one side or the other. Nor did we fight the citizens, except when they played the informer. I understand one citizen was killed in Centralia in a drunken row. That ought not to have been done. The Yankees killed many more noncombatants than we did."

When the old soldier spoke of the mistreatment of the South there was a grim, sad look about his mouth and a cold glitter in his eyes. "Bushwhackers did some bad things but they never devastated and ruined the country."

"There was order No. 11 – Ewing's. I am glad General Brigham put that on immortal canvas. That is a picture that talks. That order simply ruined hundreds of peaceful homes in Western Missouri. I know one man up in Jackson County who made a fortune going around picking up cattle that had been abandoned. A high-toned cattle thief."

"I think I know all the trees and shrubs in Missouri and what they are good for. I have had to use them for food and medicine sometimes, you know. Occasionally they fool me in Shaw's Garden, in St. Louis with the trees and plants from other countries, but with nothing from Missouri."

A bright-looking boy, about 12 years of age, shook hands with Mr. James, "My name," he said, "is Marquette Richards. My grandfather, John Marquette, was the man kicked in the fight." James looked kindly at the manly little fellow. "Well, son, you may be proud of your grandfather. He was about the bravest of Johnson's command. He fought all the way. Arch Clements shot him near Sturgeon. He rode a dun horse." No contrast of the day was more striking than that of Frank James and the mite of a boy.

"The stories about guerrillas riding with the reins of the horses between their teeth and firing with pistols in both hands is simply dime novel stuff. There was never any such thing. We always held our horses with one hand and the pistol with the other. It was an important to hold the horse as it was to hold the pistol.

"Anderson always made us keep our horses in good condition. If a man did not keep a good horse and good pistols he sent him to the infantry. I rode a horse named 'Little George' at Centralia.

"At night and when we were in camp, we played like schoolboys. Some of our play was as rough as football. The truth was we were nothing but great big boys, anyhow.

"If you ever want to pick a company to do desperate work or to lead a forlorn hope, select young men from 15 to 18 years old. They will go anywhere in the world you will lead them. As men grow older they grow more cautious, but at that age they are regular daredevils. Take our company, and there has never been a more reckless lot of men. Only one or two were over 25. Most of them were under 21. Scarcely a dozen boasted a mustache. Wasn't it Bacon who said when a man had wife and children he had given hostages to fortune?

"Arch Clements, who was the real brains of Anderson's command, was only 20. He, Payton Long and myself, followed the Federals nearly to Sturgeon. He was first Lieutenant. Clements came from Kingsville, Johnson County. He was killed at Lexington.

"There were only two of the guerrillas who would fight in a battle in a personal difficulty, George Todd and Dick Kinney. They would get mad in a battle just like in a fist fight.

"Very few of our men went through the war without wounds of some kind. Quite a number of the guerrillas are still living." Mr. James mentioned a number of men who were at the Centralia fight.

Henry Noland, William Noland, First Lieutenant James Little, Second Lieutenant Clark Renick, Orderly Sergeant John Baker, Payton Long, Foss Key, Jim Gibson, Clark Hockensmith, Dick Glasscock, and William Bassham were killed in Kentucky. Jim Evans and George Robinson were captured and hanged at Lexington, KY. Captain William Anderson was killed near Albany, Mo. Jim Anderson was killed in Texas after the war. Captain William H. Summit after the war. George Todd was killed near Independence on Price's last raid. Dick Burnes was killed in Jackson County after the war. William Hulse of Jackson County died after the war and Daniel Pent died in Kentucky.

"The greatest raid made by the guerrillas was the one in September 1864. We were north of the Missouri River only about two weeks. We had with us never to exceeded 250 men. We averaged a battle a day and we killed over 1,000 Federal soldiers, besides destroying much Yankee property. The only battles in the world's history to surpass Centralia are Thermopylae and the Alamo. Next to the Centralia fight is the skirmish at Baxter Springs, KS, where we killed 130 of General Blunt's body guards."

"We never met many Federal soldiers who would fight us on equal terms. They would either want to outnumber us or they would run away.

"I believe the saddest thing I know connected with the war," said Mr. James, and the man of blood and iron showed much feeling as he told the story, "occurred in the battle of Franklin, Tenn. Young Theodore Carter was fighting there. But a few yards away was his old home with his mother standing at the window, watching the battle and waiting for him. He fought bravely that day. Almost within a stone's throw of his mother's door, within steps of the yard where he had played as a boy, he was shot down and died.

James Clark, engineer of the Wabash Branch Railroad is the same man who took the ill-fated Wabash train into Centralia on the fatal September morning. As with Frank James the snow of years has drifted on his head and he is an old man now.

St. Louis Republic
St. Louis, MO
Sunday, August 5, 1900

INSCRIPTIONS ON WESTERN TOMBSTONES

He is young,
He was fair,
But the Injuns
Raised his hair!

Bill Blake
Was Hanged by Mistake!

Here lies a man named Zeke,
Second fastest gun in Cripple Creek.

Here lies the body of Thomas Kemp,
Who lived by wool
And died by hemp!

Here lies Slip McVey,
He would be here today,
But bad whiskey and a fast gun
Put him away.

Here lies Butch,
We planted him raw.
He was quick on the trigger,
But slow on the draw!

Grim death took me,
Without any warning,
I was well at night,
And dead in the morning!

Here lies Lester Moore,
Four slugs from a .44.
No Les, no more.

Chapter Eighteen

100 AND CLIMBING

TIME MARCHES ON

On West Fifth Street in Mountain Grove, Missouri, is an old, well preserved, two-story, frame home, home of Fred and Cecile Leach. Recently, the couple moved to The Autumn Oaks Nursing Home in Mountain Grove. Mrs. Leach has arthritis and difficulty in hearing. Mr. Leach has a pacemaker. Otherwise, both appear in relatively good health. Neither has a formula for longevity. Yet, a visitor can easily detect that each lovingly pokes fun at the other. Too, each has maintained a good sense of humor over the years. Religion and Politics offer fodder for kidding. She is a Democrat. He is a Republican. Fred stated, "She kills my vote!"

"He goes to one church and I go to another," said Cecile. She's Methodist. He's Episcopalian. "Fred Leach was born in Republic, MO., November 15, 1897. His family lived several years in Springfield, where he worked as a "Skate Boy" for a time at the roller rink at the old White City Park, where the Assemblies of God Headquarters now stands.

Fred's father, Wiley Leach, died in 1911, and his mother, Mary Ellen, moved the family, including Fred and his brother and two sisters to Mountain Grove, where she had relatives.

Cecile Leach, a member of the Wheeler family, was born January 4, 1898, in Houston. The family moved to Mountain Grove in 1904, and her father started a real estate business.

Fred and Cecile met at the Mountain Grove High School. "Cecile was a great basketball player," said Fred. The girls played in bloomers in those days.

"I don't see how we ever got around in those," states Cecile. "If my mother could see how they dress today, she would never let me play basketball!"

The Leaches have seen electricity arrive and automobiles become plentiful. They knew Civil War Veterans. They made it through two world wars and the Great Depression. "We starved like everybody else, "Fred said of those dark days in the 1930's.

Yet, they do not dwell on the past. They prefer to keep up with current affairs by reading newspapers and watching TV and public television shows.

Fred served a stint in the military during World War I, although he was not sent overseas. He later worked 12 years as an elevator builder in St. Louis. In the 1930's, he took a job as an insurance company elevator inspector in Detroit.

Moving back to Mountain Grove in the late 1940's, the Leaches ran a flower shop just off the square. Fred would up his working years following in the footsteps of his father and grandfather. He leased and ran the a wheat grinding operation for a dozen years, into the early 1960's at Hodgson Mill on Bryant Creek in Ozark County. During that time, Cecile owned beef cattle – Angus. She raised the cows on her family's Wheeler Arch Farm, just south of Mountain Grove.

In their free hours over the years, the Leaches camped, fished together and got away to their cabin in Canada. They belonged to archery and gun clubs, with Cecile winning a number of competitions. Fred did wood working; Cecile knitted.

They remain extremely independent and see little point in looking back on their lives and rehashing the events of the century. They have survived and they stay away from words of wisdom. They simply consider themselves fortunate to have made a good living and remained healthy.

Cecile and Fred are each 102 years old. Each has gone through one century totally and a small portion of two other centuries. They were married May 1, 1920 and had no children.

When it was time for me to depart from the Leaches and the nursing home, I stated, "Mr. Leach, you were a handsome man in your youthful years."

Mr. Leach asked, "Do you mean I was only handsome when I was young?" He gave me a nice friendly smile.

Jokingly, I asked, "Mrs. Leach, what are your plans for the future?"

She replied, "You can bet I don't want to live another 100 years!"

Jay Mondy
Nursing Home Visit
Rewritten From:
"Simple Folks, Living Well"
Springfield News Leader
July 8, 2000

Fred and Cecile Leach
Bagnell Dam-1932

UNCLE BEN HODGE, AGED 111, DOES ALL HIS FARM WORK AND LIVES BY HIMSELF

Oldest Man in State Does His Own Farm Work and Is Strong as Man Third That Age

LIVES ON FARM IN NORTH PART OF COUNTY

Is Clearing up Farm So When He Gets Old He Can Rent Place and Live Off the Proceeds

Hendrickson, MO

"I'm good for twenty years yet."

So says Benjamin F. Hodge, age 111, and believed to be the oldest resident in Missouri. "I'm going to live till I'm 130 and then I am ready to quit this world."

"Uncle Ben" lives on a farm in the woods about five miles east of Hendrickson. He is "pretty sure" he is 111 years old, but if there is any mistake in this figure, he knows he is at least 109. He doesn't remember clearly whether his relatives told him years ago he was born in 1815 or 1817.

And Uncle Ben is hale and hearty. He can outwork any man one-third his age and he really enjoys his friends he is still a "real man." Only recently "Uncle Ben" sought to obtain a job on the highway construction gang.

Worked on Road

"They told me they didn't want me because I was too old," he says. "I then told them that I would work for $1 a day, and if I didn't turn out more work than anyone else on the force, I would work free. Even with that assurance they wouldn't take me. Later I got a job with another foreman, and he told me later that I did more work than any two other men."

Working on his little farm from the early hours of morning until late at night, Uncle Ben says he is thankful that he is healthy and can go to bed at night and sleep soundly. He lives in a little one room log hut which he built on the forty-acre farm he purchased about four years ago. It is home to the old bachelor, and he spends his time on that farm, seldom leaving except to go to Hendrickson for provisions.

Looks to Future

"When I bought this farm," he says, "it was in the woods. Not a foot of it was cleared. I have cleared seventeen acres and have it in cultivation. I want to get a few more acres cleared before I get old so I can rent the place out and get enough rent from it to live on." And he meant it. He plans to retire in a few years and then live with some of his relatives. They are well along in years, too.

The Daily Republican
Poplar Bluff, MO
June 25, 1920

NEGRO 107 YEARS OLD ATTENDS FAIR

Enters His Twenty-third Consecutive Exhibit of Garden Produce

Sedalia, MO

Old Uncle Jacob Hunter, a Sedalia darkey of 107 years, rambled into the State Fair offices recently to enter his twenty-third consecutive exhibit of garden produce in the Agricultural Department of the exposition, which opens next Saturday.

Uncle Jacob has been an exhibitor every year since the establishment of the State Fair in 1901 and has never failed to take a prize.

Hunter raises corn, vegetables and tobacco on five vacant lots on East Ham Street; and his products have gained him no little reputation as a truck gardener. In 1921, at the Centennial State Fair, he took first prize in the competitive exhibits of tobacco; and last year he place second. His entries for the approaching fair include tobacco, beans, pumpkins, tomatoes and beets.

The old Negro is very proud of his collection of prize ribbons won at the State Fair, which includes about thirty altogether. Five of these are blue ribbons, the highest ward.

Born in South Carolina a 1817, the ancient darkey remembers little of his native state. Missouri has been his home since early childhood, for a change of masters brought him to a farm five miles east of Versailles, in Morgan County, where he spent most of his life. He has lived in Sedalia for the last thirty five years.

The Daily Republican
Poplar Bluff, MO
August 14, 1923

MAN 119, WILL BE GUEST OF AMERICAN REPUBLIC

Poplar Bluff, MO

Thomas N. "Uncle Tommy" Kemp, Missouri's oldest citizen, will celebrate his 119th birthday tomorrow.

To this patriarch September 10 will be "just another day" inasmuch as he had planned no particular observance of the occasion.

Last night, however, "Uncle Tommy" agreed to visit the American Republic office from 2 until 4 Thursday afternoon, during which time he will welcome anyone wishing to see him.

Welcome Visitors

"I'll be glad to meet anyone wishing to visit me tomorrow while I am at the American Republic office," says Kemp. "I wish to see how a newspaper is run, and I will be around the office from 3 until 4."

Those desiring to bring or send him a birthday greeting or remembrance of any kind may do it with the assurance the aged man will appreciate any such gift.

Seventy years ago Mr. Kemp, then 49, was "too old" to take part in the Civil War, even though his physical condition would have justified.

Born in 1812

Quite hale and active, although suffering for the past year from rheumatism, Mr. Kemp looks forward to many more birthdays and, in fact, there is a possibility he might set the age of the venerable Turk, Zaro Agha, 157, as his goal.

The American born citizen says September 10, 1812, was the date of his birth, and his relatives and acquaintances generally accept this claim.

He says he remembers the presidential election in 1820 and every campaign since. Outside of being partially deaf, and having occasional attacks of rheumatism, Kemp says he is "as well as a man reasonably can expect to be when he is near 120 years old." His memory is good and his eyesight fair.

Kemp still gets enjoyment out of working on his farm. He often recalls incidents 50 to 75 years ago on the farm, since farming has been his vocation most of his life.

Parents Died When He Was Young

"I was born in Huntingdon, Tenn.," says Kemp, "My parents, Aaron and Tabitha Kemp, died when I was young. I was working regularly when I was eight."

Kemp's first regular job was rider on a pony express and mail. He was married in Kentucky in 1836 and his first wife died five years later. Two children were born to them. In 1841 he was married again, this time to the sister of his first wife. She died 40 years later. They were the parents of seven children, six of whom are dead. He resides with the one daughter, Mrs. Amanda Rudicile, 59.

The American Republic
Poplar Bluff, MO
September 11, 1931

AT 109, ARKANSAS MAN HAS SEEN LIFES CHANGES

Mountain Home, Ark.

Mark Holland, 109 years old on May 17, has seen the country develop from the primitive to the ultra-modern and believes the old days were the best because "People were happier then."

They lived simpler in the days when Uncle Mark was a boy, he says, and took care of themselves. He thinks the people "got along all right without all the new things like cars, radios and other modern conveniences."

This Confederate veteran, who probably is the oldest in Arkansas, speaks of modern modes of travel "in the know". He has ridden in everything from the ox cart to the airplane, choosing the latter at the age of 94, when everyone else here appeared somewhat timid at traveling in the first plane to land in this section.

"I'm 94 years old and haven't much more time to live anyway," said Uncle Mark concerning his initial plane jaunt. "If you will make up the $10 to pay for the ride I'll take the first trip."

The crowd gathered at the little airport and accepted his proposition.

Uncle Mark Holland is feeble but can get around by himself most of the time. He was born in Kentucky in 1826, but cannot remember the exact place of his birth. The family went from Kentucky to Texas before coming to Baxter County, Ark., where he has resided for the past 63 years.

The veteran says he served in a Kentucky regiment during the Civil War. He believes it was the Second Kentucky Regiment, but Uncle Mark does not remember which company exactly. He is the father of four sons.

The Associated Press
Daily American Republic
Poplar Bluff, MO
June 21, 1935

SHE'S 112 AND HAS SEEN THREE WARS THUS FAR

Sapulpa, Okla.

Aunt Lizzie Devers has lived through four wars and is looking forward to the end of her fifth conflict.

Mrs. Devers, who will celebrate her 112th birthday tomorrow, has seen the Mexican, Civil, Spanish-American, and first World War open and close. Wars, she says, are due to pure cussedness.

Aunt Lizzie, who has outlived nine husbands, makes her home near the edge of Sapulpa with her "boy". Her son, Sam Pinkham, is a mere youngster of some 70-odd years, though.

She still walks to Sapulpa business district, almost a mile away, and works her vegetable garden.

Daily American Republic
Poplar Bluff, MO
April 30, 1943

SYLVIA SCHMIDT HASN'T MISSED
AN ELECTION SINCE 1920

Puxico, MO

People will remember the 2000-2001 election for years to come. Voters have been waiting for days to find out who will become the next president of the United States.

Sylvia Schmidt, who turned 101 this year, remembers many elections of the past including when the 19th Amendment was ratified in 1920 giving her, and other women, the right to vote.

"We were jubilant, glad we could take part," said Schmidt.

She has exercised her right to vote ever since. She has not missed a single election nor has she cast an absentee ballot.

"I'm an old woman able to vote," said Schmidt. "I've been voting all my life. I've never missed."

The first presidential candidate Schmidt voted for was Democrat William G. MaAdoo. He ran against Republican Warren G. Harding who became the 29th president. From this election in 1920 to the election in 2000, Schmidt has voted a straight Democratic ticket.

Another memory of Schmidt's was during the civil rights movement which organized both blacks and whites to end policies and practices of segregation. Rosa Parks, a black woman, refused to give up her seat in the front of a Montgomery, Ala., bus. For her refusal, she was forced off the bus.

"The blacks are no different than us," said Schmidt.

Schmidt wore a "I'm still with Mel" button on election day to support Mel Carnahan's campaign.

"That's my boy. I believe that Carnahan would of got it," said Schmidt of Carnahan winning the election for U.S. Senator of Missouri. "To be sure, they are putting her (Jean Carnahan) in his place because she was the one that was close to him and she knew his wants and desires."

Schmidt strongly believes that everyone needs to exercise their right to vote.

"If I didn't love my country I would not have gone down there (to the polls) today," said Schmidt.

Schmidt also believes that being able to vote is a privilege and an honor that a lot of people in other countries do not have. "I'm so sorry for the Palestinian people. They are fighting for their own rights and country."

When asked if she would stay up election night to watch the returns come in Schmidt replied, "You bet I am!"

Sandy Hale
Puxico Press
Puxico, MO
November 15, 2000

114-YEAR-OLD EX-SAILOR STILL "ROLLS HIS OWN"

Van Buren, Ark.

With only a few relatives and a group of old friends present, James McCann, "Uncle Jimmie" as he is known to thousands of people in this section, celebrated his 114ᵗʰ birthday a few days ago at his little home in Dora, five miles west of here. With his wife, Sarah Elizabeth, to care for and comfort him, "Uncle Jimmie," ex-sailor and soldier of fortune, expects to spend the remaining years of his life at Dora. He is believed to be Arkansas' oldest man.

Born June 24, 1813, under the shadow of the Rock of Gibraltar, at Algeciras, North Africa, the aged man has lived a varied and interesting life and his story of 114 years is a narrative filled with interest. He is of Irish descent and has been an American citizen since 1857, when he took out his papers on board the U.S.S. Powhatan, on which he had shipped.

Of the thrilling stories he tells of his many experiences, his favorite ones are those which took place during his 53 years at sea. He retired from active sea life more that 45 years ago, and spent a few years at sea. He retired from active sea life more than 45 years ago, and spent a few years as a cook on coasting vessels and in restaurants, moving to Arkansas in the early eighties after marrying his present wife at Carthage, MO. She is his third and has borne him four children.

Drove a Mule Car

"Uncle Jimmie" begins his story with his boyhood days around Algeciras and the Rock of Gibraltar, across the narrow straits, telling of the death of his mother when he was five years old, of sailing with his father for American when he was nine years old, of how his father fell overboard and was drowned on the trip across the Atlantic, of how he was cared for by the captain of the ship, for whom he served as cabin boy "until I thought I was a man, and left him." The story goes on, how he visited dozens of ports and received hundreds of smiles from many lassies. One of them, a girl in Key West, Fla., was his first wife.

After leaving the sea life at Galveston, Texas and moving north, Jimmie and his present wife settled in Fort Smith, Ark., where he worked several years as a driver for a mule car. When the cars were put out by modern invention, he and his family moved to Long Bell, an addition to Van Buren, where he worked several years in a mill. Although old, he was strong and able to work. His next efforts were in operating a restaurant here. This he sold a number of years ago and moved to Logtown addition, where he resided until moving to his present home. He was unusually active until a few years ago, when he fell from a high porch and suffered a broken leg and other injuries.

Spoke Nine Languages

When Uncle Jimmie finishes his story he calls for his tobacco and makes a cigarette, to show his company he still can "roll his own," though almost totally blind. He talks of his son, Gene, named for the ship "Eugenia," on which he sailed for a few years following the Civil War. During the war, and for a few years prior, the old sailor was in the United States Navy and now draws a pension from the American government. Identification of several tattoo marks on his body obtained the pension for the aged man, as his discharge papers had been lost.

Before losing his eyesight, Uncle Jimmie claimed to read and write nine languages, including Spanish, Greek, Portuguese, French, English and Arabic. He still is able to write his name in a clear, legible hand.

He has been in battle, was overboard on a plank three days and nights when his ship sank, was shipwrecked three times, one ship burning. He spent some time in the Holy Land, which he visited as a sailor, and has been in practically every large in the world.

The aged man believes that God and hard work have caused him to live so long. When asked what he thinks about as he lies on his bed, hour after hour, or puffs away on his cigarette in the cane-bottom chair, Uncle Jimmie usually answers, "I'm thinking – all the time – I wish I was there again. The happiest days of my life were those when I was sailing the seas."

He is optimistic of present-day conditions and says that he is ready to die and thankful that God has permitted him to live to well beyond the century mark.

The Daily Republican
Poplar Bluff, MO
June 28, 1927

Chapter Nineteen

UNUSUAL STORIES

CRUEL FATHER PUTS CHILDREN TO PLOW

Little Ones Bruised, Emaciated, Starved

Six of Everett King's Offspring Taken From Him By Juvenile Court, He's To Be Tried Friday For Attempted Attack Upon Hunger-Weakened Daughter—Tots Wrapped in Chains, Clubbed and Then Hung Up in Loft By Fiendish Parent—Four Months Old Infant Beaten Until It Suffers Spasms—Wife Driven From Home.

Poplar Bluff, MO

Everett King, brute, was stripped of the guardianship of his six small children this afternoon after Juvenile Judge D.B. Deem heard endless testimony of his barbarous cruelty. Then he was sent back to jail to await a preliminary hearing Friday afternoon at 1 o'clock before Justice Henderson, at which time he will answer to a charge that he attempted to ruin his hunger-weakened daughter, nine years old.

Mutterings and threats of lynch law were heard in the courtroom during the trial this morning and afternoon. Men and women stood aghast before the evidence which was heaped against King, who did not dispute it except in a few instances. Emaciated, starved, bruised and limping children— his own offspring—apparently fearing him more than death itself, told their tales of pitiful suffering after being encouraged and assured fo protection from their fiendish father.

Indisputable testimony was adduced that King had HITCHED HIS LITTLE CHILDREN, TWO ABREAST, TO A PLOW AND HAD DRIVEN THEM LIKE HORSES IN THE FIELD FOR A FULL HALF DAY! The oldest of the six children is ten years of age. THEY PLOWED ROWS A QUARTER MILE LONG! His defense was that he had been behind the plow and had PUSHED!

He beat his oldest child, Mike, across the face until it was gashed and torn and blood streamed from it. He threw the child face down on the floor, sat on the boy and rubbed his face upon rough boards!

He hammered a smaller boy on the face with a club that had a nail in it. The child's temple and eye were discolored today and the scar of the nail shoed in the flesh.

He forced one child to sleep out one cold night with a woodpile for a bed. The boy was afraid to enter the house and stayed out in the woods alone all the next night.

King, it was alleged, asserted that his daughter and son, aged 9 and 7 years, had been intimate. Declaring they were guilty, he is accused of having stripped them of clothing, wrapped then in chains, beat them with clubs and hung them up naked in a loft so that their toes barely touched the floor. He left them hanging for a half hour, it was alleged.

Testimony was brought out that he had whipped his 4-month-old baby until it had spasms.

King starved the little ones, it was alleged, putting them on dry bread diets for weeks at a time. They were repeatedly beaten, savagely beaten, the merciless father apparently taking delight in smashing their flesh and crunching their bones.

His wife testified that when she protested she, too, was driven from her home, and that the older the children grew the more inhuman became King's treatment of them.

One little girl, whose illness showed in her dull eyes and faded, thin cheeks, sat with hands listlessly folded and listened to the evidence. Testimony was given that this child's illness had been laughed at by the father, who beat her and declared her laziness and meanness alone were responsible for her appearance. Her body is emaciated. She has not had sufficient nourishment. A hopeless look is in her eyes.

The King children, after they had been guaranteed the protection of the court and freed forever from the power of their father, became more cheerful, and limped about, chatting with the kindly folk who crowded the courtroom.

Judge Deem declared openly that never had he heard of such pitiless inhumanity. He demanded to know why neighbors had permitted it to continue so long, and learned that while sentiment was bitter against King, yet one had waited upon another for definite action until they could no longer stand it. They then reported to Probation Officer Hubert Powell, who arrested King, and, with former Constable Tidwell, provided for the children.

Judge Deem removed the six children from the father's guardianship and turned them over to the protectorate. Their mother and grandmother assert that with the father out of the way, with his barbarous cruelties eliminated, they can provide for the little fold and give them comfortable homes, four going to one lace and two to the other, and Powell will look after them also.

King is a farmer, 37 years of age. He made practically no defense other than occasionally to make some ridiculously absurd explanation of how a child happened to be cut or bruised or welted. His trial on a charge of attempted incest is coming up Friday afternoon and, it is reported, that many neighbors would testify against him. He is now in jail.

The Daily Republican
Poplar Bluff, MO
November 4, 1913

MILLER COUNTY WHITE MAN SOLD AT AUCTION IN 1859

Miller Co, Mo

On September 11, 1859, a charge of vagrancy was brought against a man in Miller County named William Williams, filed by Constable Barnabas Reed of Glaize Township. The warrant was presented to John K. Hall, a justice of the peace who lived in the vicinity. The Sheriff of Miller County in 1859 was Samuel T. Harrison.

A vagrant was a rover, vagabond, tramp or beggar who wandered around without a regular job and made it a way of life. By law, a vagrant back then could be arrested and jailed.

So, three days later, on September 14, 1859, Williams (about 25 years of age) was found at the home of Samuel Ash in Glaize Township. Constable Reed put him under arrest. Samuel Ash was Williams' father-in-law. His young wife was Mary Ann Ash, age about 19 years. They had married in Miller County on March 2, 1856. William and Mary had a young son named, Jeremiah, who was approximately one year old when his father was arrested in 1859.

According to the testimony of Samuel Ash, Reed came to the Ash home "in the middle of the night" demanding Williams to surrender. Ash talked William Williams into giving himself over to the constable; and the two of them (Reed and Ash) escorted Williams to the home of John Hall, the Justice of the Peace.

Even though it was after midnight, Justice Hall immediately summoned six jurors to come to his home. They arrived in a short while and, without much pomp or ceremony, they found him guilty of vagrancy. One of the jurors, was named Andrew Ulman. He insisted that Williams be untied during his trip to jail. By the next morning, probably only a few hours, Williams was incarcerated in the county jail at Tuscumbia.

For three days, a notice was hand-posted on the courthouse door advertising that a "vagrant" would be hired out for a cash payment for a period of six months to the highest bidder.

On the morning of the fourth day, the Sheriff (Samuel T. Harrison) of Tuscumbia sold William Williams for cash at the auction.

Mary Ann (Ash) Williams began the bidding at a dime and she continued to raise the bid at one cent until she acquired her husband's freedom. The bid reach $2.55 when Sheriff Harrison yelled, "Going, going, gone, to Mrs. Mary Ann Williams for $2.55."

In 1860, William, Mary Ann, and their two-year-old son, Jeremiah, were still living in Glaize Township near others mentioned in this article. After the 1860 census, they appeared no more in Miller County census records. The Civil War scattered many families in many directions. I do not know what happened to the William Williams family.

Peggy Smith Hake
Miller County Historian
Window site: Out of the Past
www.members.tripod.com/
dever8/
Old Settlers' Gazette
KJPW Radio
Waynesville, MO
July 28, 2001

THORN IN FINGER

Sportsman Saved From Fangs of Big Copperhead Snake By Lesser Campfire Mishap

Gridley, Ark.

Col. E.H. Weber and a party of friends recently spent a few days on White River in Arkansas fishing and hunting. One night after the evening log heap had been put in trim, Colonel Weber retreated some distance from the fire for some nearby driftwood with which to replenish the fire when need be. He stooped in the dark and accidentally dropped a large calabash pipe form his mouth.

In the twilight, the color of the pipe and that of the sand blended, and he was unable to locate the pipe. He searched in his pockets for matches but found, to his displeasure, he had none. He then stooped on his knees and searched about in the sparsely scattered grass for his friend. A moment later the Colonel was running to the light of the fire with a thorn sticking securely in his index finger. He had left the pipe behind.

With the thorn removed he returned to the search of his pipe with a flashlight. In an instant he had located the lost pipe and, to his dismay, something much more unpleasant. Not quite two feet from where the pipe lay, there was a large copperhead snake coiled and ready to strike. Colonel Weber shot the snake with an automatic pistol and it measured nearly 5 feet.

After the snake lay dead before the big, open fire, Colonel Weber sighed as if very much relieved and said, as he stood looking down upon the reptile: "Well, I suppose that thorn was a lucky accident. It probably saved my life."

Poplar Bluff American
Poplar Bluff, MO
August 6, 1919

MYSTEEERIOUS BELL RAT DISTURBS HOTEL GUESTS

Tinkling Rodent Eludes Its Pursuers.

Elusive as Tam O'Shanter's Ghost Patrols Streets at Night

Poplar Bluff, MO

Elusive as Tam O'Shanter's ghost, a large gray rat, with a tiny tinkling bell strapped around its neck, patrols that streets of the downtown district at night and disturbs the slumbers of persons at rest at the hotels.

The mystery surrounding the roaming rat and its silver bell seems as dark and enveloped with as much gloom as the most intricate case with which Sherlock Holmes ever had to combat.

Guests at the Wright and Quinn hotels are thinking of making up a purse to get a Pinkerton here to solve the mystery.

The office boy at The Daily Republican office, however, has suggested that either Nick Carter or "Old Broadbrim" be employed, although he says that "old King Brady" is the better detective, but would charge too high a fee.

Who belled the rat?

Recently there was a story in Everybody's Magazine about a belled rat, and, it is believed, some Poplar Bluff citizen became enthused with the idea, caught a rat and tied the bell on it.

Several shots have been taken at the rodent, but the bullets sped wide of their mark. The rodent has been seen speeding across streets, but always managed to dodge rocks and bricks.

Drummers have decided to give the "Raffles" rat a run for its life tonight, and will be out to look for it.

The Daily Republican
Poplar Bluff, MO
June 6, 1919

MAN DROPPED OUT OF SIGHT AT QUICKSAND BOG

Gayle Day, Age Twenty-Five Years, Met With a Peculiar Circumstance-Believed Under Earth

Advance, MO

The Gayle Day, a young man, twenty-five years old, was swallowed up alive Saturday afternoon between 3 and 4 o'clock about six miles northeast of Advance, seems to be the cause of the mysterious disappearance of the young man, who has not been heard of since that time.

Day, with two companions, was hunting in the section mentioned. He informed his associates that he would go across a bog and scare ducks over toward them. He left them and has never been seen since.

The bog mentioned is underlain by quicksand, and it is believed that the earth's surface broke with him and he was swallowed up.

The bog is a great mystery and is feared and avoided by those familiar with it, but as the young man was a new resident in the county, he probably was not acquainted with the danger that lurked beneath the earth's surface. It is believed that prior to the New Madrid earthquake in 1811, that section was a lake, and that the disturbance changed the topography, leaving the quicksand bottom of the lake as the surface of the earth.

The Daily Republican
Poplar Bluff, MO
January 17, 1911

Chapter Twenty

HORSE THIEVES

PREACHER OUT MULE; ANXIOUS

Aged Stranger Comes Along and "Borrows" Animal; Fails to Return the Beast

James Brannum, Baptist Minister of Agee and David Rudielle Wait for Property

Agee, MO

James Brannum, a Baptist minister of the Agee neighborhood, and David Rudielle, of the same neighborhood, are anxiously awaiting the return of an aged man who "borrowed" a mule and saddle from them a few days ago, promising to return them Sunday. He hasn't come back.

A correspondent has expressed the opinion that hope is dying within the sympathetic breast of the lenders and they are fearful, lest their kindly charity was bestowed upon an imposter whose decrepit body, they are beginning to believe, became charged with great energy once his legs were astride the mule and he had vanished from their sight.

A few days ago a man, weighted by years, appeared at the Brannum home. He was in much distress because his legs were weak and he was trying, he said, to get to Neelyville to get his little daughter. If he only had some sort of conveyance he could make the journey in a jiffy and return quickly and happily.

The Rev. Mr. Brannum's heart went out in sympathy, so he loaned the visitor a mule upon which to travel the great distance. But an old man cannot well ride bareback, so Mr. Rudielle, whose heart also was touched, loaned a saddle which was strapped securely upon the animal's back and the old man boosted upon it.

From that moment until late yesterday, neither Mr. Brannum nor Mr. Rudielle had heard even the echo of a word of gratitude from the wayfarer – and they are beginning to doubt the wisdom of their loan. If the traveler does not send back some sort of report shortly, it is said, officers will be made acquainted with the facts and his apprehension attempted.

The Daily Republican
Poplar Bluff, MO
March 26, 1914

KEARBEY GETS HORSE THIEF

Sheriff Captures W.R. Sievers, ex-soldier, Near Idalia

HAD CHAPMAN'S HORSE AT TIME OF ARREST

Sievers at Supper Table When Officer Appeared –Says He was Drunk At Time

Idalia, MO

Sheriff Kearbey late last night arrested W.R. Sievers, the man who last Wednesday night stole a horse and buggy belonging to L.W. Chapman. The arrest was made near Idalia, Stoddard County. Sievers was eating supper at a farm house when Sheriff Kearbey and Stoddard County officers appeared and, after being closely questioned, Sievers admitted his guilt and agreed to return to this city. At the time of his arrest the horse was in Sievers' possession, and the buggy was located near Dexter.

When the officers approached him Sievers stated that he purchased the horse from a Stoddard County farmer, but finally admitted that while under the influence of drink he took the horse and drove away.

Sievers was arraigned this morning before Justice Davidson on the charge of grand larceny and demanded a preliminary trial. The case was set for hearing May 13, and the prisoner in default of bond was placed in jail.

On arriving in the city this morning Sievers was taken to the office of Prosecuting Attorney Ing and questioned about the matter. He maintained that he was drunk when he stole the animal and stated that, at no time, did he try to sell him, but said that he was on his return trip to Poplar Bluff at the time of his arrest. He said that he intended to return the horse to its owner.

Sievers was dressed in a soldier's uniform and said that he had lately been discharged from the service and was on his way home. Stopping off here he picked up a chance acquaintanceship of a woman whom he too, for a short ride on the evening of the theft. Sievers stated that he and the woman drove about the city for several hours after the theft and that he left her at the county bridge.

The Daily Republican
Poplar Bluff, MO
May 9, 1914

ANOTHER HORSE BORROWED BY NICE OLD MAN

Horse Bates of East of City Tells Sheriff of
"Loaning" Animal September 4

Broseley, MO

Horace Bates, of near Broseley, in the Ash Hill Neighborhood, was in the city Monday and told Sheriff C.E. Robinson of loaning a good horse and saddle, the property of his son, George, to an old "gentleman" with a crooked index finger on his right hand, on September 4th, to make a trip to Puxico, who, to date, has never returned. Upon hearing the story Sheriff Robinson called to mind several similar stories in which the leading character has always been this nice old man who "borrows" a horse wherever he stops, but never returns.

Several months ago a horse was missed in a nearby Arkansas town under the same circumstances, and the sheriff this morning stated that the clever horse thief has been operating in Southern Missouri and Northern Arkansas for the past several years.

The man came to the Bates place a few weeks ago and told a story of how he had been living with people in the Fisk neighborhood and they, having returned to their former home, left him homeless. He expressed a desire to make his home with the Bates family. After staying a few days he evidently decided to go to Puxico after his clothes. A few years ago a man, presumed to be the same, came to a farm home on the county farm road and gave a similar story. He borrowed a horse to attend church, Sheriff Robinson said, and the services are not yet over.

The Sheriff urges that farmers of the county keep a lookout for this man and notify his office.

Poplar Bluff American
Poplar Bluff, MO
September 16, 1919

CHAFFEE MAN LATEST VICTIM

Chaffee, MO

E.A. Ozee of Chaffee is the latest victim of the crooked finger horse thief. Sheriff C.E. Robinson today received a circular from Ozee telling of the loss of a brown mare, 16 ¼ hands high, that the thief disappeared with on March 18. The description that Mr. Ozee gave of the man compared identically with that of the descriptions that have been given for the past fifteen years by victims of his operations.

Newspapers have published accounts of his thieveries for the past ten years and still the crafty old thief is at large. Mr. Ozee's description of the man who stole his horse was that he was near 70 years of age, smooth shaven, very much gray and nearly bald and the predominating identification was that the index finger of his right hand was withered and turned under toward the palm and was practically useless. The man gave his name as Frank Fowler.

The crooked finger horse thief is one of the most crafty and diplomatic old scoundrels ever experienced in Southeast Missouri and Northern Arkansas, as is proven by the fact that his thieveries have been running unhampered for the past fifteen years. He is still at large, having never at any time been within the grasp of the law.

His operations, as has been stated on numerous occasions, are always directly under the eyes of his victims and never by stealth. He ordinarily gives his victim a hard luck story and then, while the sympathy of the victim is aroused, he asks to borrow a horse to take a few miles away to pull the wagon of his beloved child or some other fictitious relative that is being carried to the grave, or that someone is sick and must be gotten to a doctor, etc., and he somehow seems to get away with it, although his "Hue" has been advertised and broadcasted for these many years.

His operations are contained strictly to the country and farmers are consequently warned to be on the lookout for him. Numerous rewards have been offered for his capture and someone who is lucky enough to capture the old fox will not only be doing the country a good turn, but will realize a little cash for their own efforts.

The Poplar Bluff American
Poplar Bluff, MO
March 24, 1920

CROOKED FINGER HORSE THIEF IS NABBED AT LAST

Eluded Capture for 14 Years;
One of Smoothest Crooks Ever Encountered

Sikeston, MO

After eluding the law for 14 years, the crooked finger horse thief has at last been captured. For 14 years he has escaped capture, although, newspapers have published his description aboard, handbills by the tens of thousands advertising him have been distributed over the whole of Southern Missouri and Northern Arkansas and rewards amounting to hundreds of dollars have been offered for his capture. The credit for the capture of the old thief is shared equally between Sheriff C.E. Robinson of Butler County and a brother-in-law of Ed Tune, a farmer residing on the Frisco Railroad, thirty miles northeast of Sikeston.

The old man had been living with Mr. Tune for a number of weeks and had gone to. of one hand that was crooked under and was lying useless on the palm of his hand.

This invariable mark and the fact that each time he had given a different name, soon gained for him the name of The Crooked Finger Horse Thief or "Old Crooked Finger."

When interviewed this morning by Mr. Bates, he acknowledged the theft of his horse and stated he was sorry he had not regained it, since it was his understanding that he had.

Sheriff Robinson considers this the biggest accomplishment of his administration. He was so much bent upon the capture of the old miscreant that he had offered person rewards for his capture.

Marlin's preliminary hearing will come up in Justice O.A. McKinney's court Friday afternoon.

The Poplar Bluff American
Poplar Bluff, MO
April 15, 1920

Sheriff Bennett Captured Horse Thief

Butler County, MO

Old fashioned horse thievery seems to be staging a comeback together with the current back to the farm movement.

For the first time in years, a self-confessed horse thief was captured this afternoon in the northern part of Butler County by Sheriff Frank Bennett of Greenville.

Claude Joplin of Greenville became suspicious when a would-be trader offered a horse for sale this morning. He called the sheriff, and the chase was on.

Confessed Theft

It terminated in the upper part of Butler County, where Arthur Gatlin, 30, confessed, according to the officers, that he stole the horse some time ago in or near West Plains. According to Butler County officers, the opinion persists that the horse originally came from the near counties of Wayne, Stoddard, Ripley, Butler or perhaps Madison.

The horse was described as black, blaze faced, weighing 800 to 900 pounds, possibly 10 to 11 years old, and having no shoes.

Gatlin got into trouble last year when he issued a fraudulent check payable to Jim Pool of Fisk in payment for a load of hogs which he later sold on the St. Louis market. He was sentenced from Butler County.

Daily American Republic
Poplar Bluff, MO
June 28, 1934

Chapter Twenty-One

MR. PRESIDENT

Harry S. Truman Library and Museum, Independence, MO.

HARRY WAS HERE

Monett, MO

On Wednesday, September 29, 1948, at around 9 p.m., a special train pulling 17 cars steamed into Monett's Frisco station. It was greeted by a large, friendly crowd. On board the Presidential Car, the Ferdinand Magellan, was Harry S. Truman, the 33rd president of the United Stated, accompanied by his wife, Bess, and daughter, Margaret.

Harry Truman had become president upon Franklin Roosevelt's death in April 1945, only three months after he had taken office as vice president. Prior to that, he had served in the U.S. Senate from Missouri and had held a variety of local offices in Jackson County. He was now fighting for his political life.

That past July, Truman had been nominated in his own right for the Presidency by a split and dispirited Democratic Convention, and just a few days before, on September 17th, he had set out on what would go down in history as the famous 1948 Whistlestop Campaign, which would earn him the title of "Give 'em Hell Harry" for his blunt and vigorous attack on his Republican opponents and on the "Do-nothing 80th Congress" they controlled.

As Truman put it that night in Monett, he was now engaged "in a crusade in the interest of the people" – which boiled down to a battle to preserve and expand the New Deal and Fair Deal social and economic reforms in post World War II America. His opponents were, as he described them, the "special interests," represented by their minion, the Republican Party, and its candidate, Thomas E. Dewey, who was said by some unkind folk to resemble the little man on top of the wedding cake.

In Truman's eyes, these "gluttons of privilege" sought to turn back the clock by dismantling the hard-won reforms enacted on behalf of the working man, the farmer, and the small business man, as well as to block future progressive actions. Harry Truman had come to Monett with this message, to warn its citizens, such as its many unionized railway workers, of this threat to their well-being, and to ask for their votes on election day for himself and his fellow Democrat candidates.

From the day he became president, Harry Truman had faced a steady stream of complex domestic and international problems arising from post World War II demobilization at home and reconstruction abroad, and from the deterioration in our relationship with the Soviet Union, our former wartime ally. He was called upon daily to make decisions affecting the lives not only of his fellow Americans, but also of millions of men and women around the world.

The world itself was becoming a tense and dangerous place. The very day Truman spoke in Monett, Russian fighters had buzzed U.S. air transport planes bringing in relief supplies to a beleaguered Berlin. His decisions would shape the future of the post-war world unto this very day.

Few presidents have faced an environment so demanding and so hostile. One in which the stakes were so high and the risks so great and, like the ill-starred Andrew Johnson, Truman had come to the Presidency un-elected and following the death of a beloved popular leader.

Eleanor Roosevelt had understood this. When, after his April 1945 swearing-in, Truman had asked Mrs. Roosevelt, "Is there anything I can do for you?", who had shaken her head and said, "Harry, is there anything we can do for you? For you are the one in trouble now."

In the judgment of those who consider such matters – historians, political scientists, and the like – Harry Truman, the son of a Missouri farmer, whose education had gone no further than high school, generally met the great challenges of the post-war world boldly, effectively, and correctly. But in doing so, his actions were often unpopular and sometimes aroused intense controversy and debate, creating a situation favorable to his political opponents.

Compounding this problem were his plain speech, combativeness, stubbornness, and his occasional pettiness in trivial matters, all of which made him appear to lack Presidential stature, especially when compared to his predecessor, Franklin Roosevelt. His image, moreover, was not helped by his past ties with the Pendergast political machine and his appointments of political cronies.

As a result of all this, by 1948 public opinion had soured on Harry Truman. He was generally held in low regard, even within his own party. There were calls from some Democrats for him to step aside for a candidate who could win at the polls.

To make matters worse, at the Democratic convention the party split. The liberal Henry A. Wallace and the conservative Strom Thurmond formed their own third party tickets, the Progressive and State Rights, respectively, threatening to take a sizable number of traditional Democratic votes on election day.

The Republicans, who had regained control of the Congress in 1946 for the first time since Hoover's day, had nominated Thomas E. Dewey, the popular liberal and internationalist governor of New York State, who had also run against Franklin Roosevelt in 1944. His running mate was Earl Warren, then governor of California. They made a powerful political team, one that could, with a progressive platform on which to run, easily appeal to working and middle class Americans who were ready to vote for a change.

As the campaign began, Dewey and his fellow Republicans had every reason to be optimistic of victory. Not only did most influential political pundits think Truman's candidacy hopeless, but so did many Democratic leaders, including some of Truman's own advisors. The Republicans came to the election in a strong position, controlling the Congress and equal in number with the Democrats in governorships.

Thomas Dewey's election seemed a foregone conclusion to everyone-except to Harry Truman, who, it is said, even had doubts himself at the outset. As the campaign got underway, Truman and his close advisers put together a simple and direct campaign strategy: One that would carry his message to "every whistle stop," as Truman put it.

This strategy would turn the situation around by election day – but, for that "miracle" to happen, Truman himself had to battle every step of the way, for few shared his belief in victory. For instance, the very night before his Monett appearance, Truman was informed there was no money available to get the train out of the Oklahoma City station. It was only through the efforts of Governor Roy J. Turner of Oklahoma that sufficient funds were raised to send the train on its way into Missouri.

The speech Truman gave to Monettans that late September evening from the platform of the Ferdinand Magellan was short and to the point: a plea to the voters to remember on election day who truly cared for the interest of the working man, the farmer, the small businessman – that is, Harry Truman and the Democratic Party – and give them their votes.

The country would then be safe, he said. If they did not, if they should instead turn the government over to the "special privilege boys," whose aim it was to dismantle the reforms enacted on their behalf, they would be sorry. More to the point, they would have only themselves to blame! Truman's speech echoed in its rhetoric the sentiments of William Jennings Bryan, who had also spoken in Monett during his turn-of-the-century Presidential campaign.

This was Truman's standard stump speech. He had already given 14 variations of it that September day, beginning with a 7:35 a.m. speech at Shawnee, Oklahoma. Less than an hour before, he had addressed the citizens of Neosho and, after Monett, he would go on to speak at 10 p.m. to a very large, enthusiastic crowd gathered at the depot in Springfield.

Finally, at 11 p.m. in Marshfield, he concluded the day with speech number 16. This was the largest number of speeches Harry Truman was to deliver on any day of his 35-day 1948 campaign, the average being about 10 speeches a day.

In all, during the Whistlestop Campaign, Truman traveled about 31,700 miles, speaking on 356 occasions to 12 to 15 million people in cities and small towns across the country. Hard work, no doubt, but then Harry Truman thrived on a good fight and meeting the people.

He was to record later in his memoirs that he actually gained weight during this ordeal. And as he looked out into those crowds and saw how the people came to see him and hear his message, he sensed that victory was his, and when it came, he would not be surprised.

On November 2, 1948, the American people handed our fellow Missourian the greatest political upset of this century. In the end, all the great pundits of the day, most notably the pollsters, were wrong in their predictions. Some could hardly bring themselves to believe it.

President Truman received 24,105,695 votes (49 percent) to Governor Dewey's 21,969,170 votes (45 percent). Strom Thurmond and Henry A. Wallace polled 1,169,021 (two percent) and 1,156,103 (two percent) respectively. President Truman had carried 28 states, with a total of 303 electoral votes. The defeated Dewey carried 16, with 189 votes. Thurmond carried four, with 39 votes, and Wallace carried none. Notably, Truman had carried all 13 of the country's biggest cities and the seven largest agricultural states.

Yet these returns can be misleading. For the first time since 1916, a Presidential winner had failed to receive a majority of all votes cast. The race was also closer than it appeared. The key states were Ohio and California, and the contest was tight in both, fluctuating throughout election night. In the end, Truman carried Ohio with only 7,000 votes and California with about 18,000.

If Dewey had won these two states, Truman would have had only 254 electoral voted, 12 less that the required 266 for election, and the House of Representatives would have had to decide the outcome. As it was, Governor Dewey did not concede the election until 10:14 a.m. on November 3, after it was clear the Ohio, Illinois, and Iowa had gone to his opponent.

To what did Truman owe his victory? As in all elections, there were many factors involved, with each contributing in its own way and all coming together to produce the final results. Two principle reasons, however, may be cited for the outcome.

First, Truman ran a strong campaign, with a clear, simple, and well-directed message, reminding voters of what they had won in social and economic reforms under the New Deal. Those gains, he stressed, achieved with so much difficulty, could now be easily lost to the special interests. This message had a particular appeal to labor and the farmer, as well as minority groups, who were to provide Truman with solid support on election day.

Second, Dewey ran an un-energetic campaign, one in which he was hesitant to take a strong, specific stand on the issues but rather talked of "unity". He was reluctant to assert his leadership over the party by bringing its reactionary element into line, and was unwilling to attack or debate his opponent in his usual vigorous style.

Because of its over-confidence, the Dewey-Warren team acted as if they were already elected. They forgot they had to win the election. In the end, Dewey failed to convince the American people that he, as president, could lead the Republican Party down a moderate and progressive path, rather than one leading back to 1932.

So it was that come election day, the American people – with their memories still fresh of the Great Depression and its great hardships, and of the many economic and social reforms enacted in its wake – were not yet ready to entrust the nation to the party of Herbert Hoover. That would not come until four years later, in 1952, after the fall of China, after Korea, after Joe McCarthy and communist spies, after the firing of General McArthur – with the election of Dwight D. Eisenhower.

To compliment Truman's great victory, the Democratic party also recaptured control of both houses of the U.S. Congress. Again, it was an upset. The thinking had been there was a chance that the Democrats might perhaps regain the Senate, but little expectation they would take the House. The Democrats also gained a majority of governorships, including several important ones that had been in Republican hands.

The 1948 election shoes how a determined, fiery candidate, with a clear simple, and convincing message and a well thought out strategy for its public delivery, can overcome great odds and win, especially when aided by a complacent opponent lacking an effective, energetic campaign.

Jerry Wallace
The Monett Times
Monett, MO
September 29, 1998

PRESIDENTIAL BEGINNINGS

Harry S. Truman Birthplace State Historic Site

Lamar, MO

Even with the most humble of beginnings, true greatness shines through. In the rural Missouri town of Lamar, the 33rd President of the United States was born. Harry S. Truman endeared himself to the citizens of the state through his genuine country manners and his down-to earth sensibility. His character and will to fight the odds were instilled in Harry at a young age in the "Show Me State."

Harry Truman's roots were firmly in Missouri. Both sets of his grandparents moved to a place called Westport Landing – later renamed Kansas City – in the 1840's. His parents, John Anderson Truman and Martha Ellen Young, were both born on farms in that area. After John Anderson and Martha Ellen were married in 1881, they moved to Lamar where John continued farming and dealing with livestock.

According to the official deed, in 1882 the Trumans purchased a 20 by 28 foot house for $685. On May 8, Harry S. Truman was born in the downstairs southwest bedroom of the one and one-half story house. On that day, to celebrate the birth of his first child, John Anderson proudly planted an Australian pine tree at the southeast corner of the house, where it thrives today.

When Harry was 11 months old, the Truman family moved from Lamar and, over the next six years, lived in Harrisonville, Belton and Grandview. In 1890, the family settled in Independence, where Harry started his formal education. He graduated from high school in 1901 but never went to college. He entered the work force so his brother and sister could complete their education.

The long, hard, tedious hours of farm work that Harry put in as a young boy helped shape his character and stuck with him the rest of his life. He was employed as a timekeeper for a railroad contractor in the mailing room of the Kansas City Star and worked in two banks. Returning to his rural roots, he left the cosmopolitan life in 1906 to help manage the family farm near Grandview.

Truman seemed content as a farmer during this period of his life. If it hadn't been for the major turmoil in Europe and America's entrance into the war, he might have remained a farmer for life. Instead, in 1917, Truman joined the U.S. Army to fight in World War I. He was shipped to France and it was there, under the most trying of circumstances, that he displayed his extraordinary leadership ability. He was promoted to Commander of Battery D, 1296th Field Artillery. His detachment was engaged in some of the fiercest combat action of the entire war in the Battle of Meuse-Argonne.

After his discharge from the Army, he married his childhood sweetheart, Elizabeth "Bess" Wallace, on June 28, 1919 in Independence. Trying his hand in the business world once again, he and a partner opened a men's clothing store in Kansas City. The business initially showed moderate success but eventually failed. Truman's values and character stayed intact, however, and he spent the next decade paying off every dollar of his debt.

His list of White House accomplishments and controversies is legendary. He ended World War II with the atomic bomb. He enlisted General Douglas MacArthur, a World War II hero, to "police" Korea during the Korean War and then fired him for his aggression. He integrated the U.S. military at a time when segregation ruled the land. While dealing with Senator Joseph McCarthy's anticommunist witch hunt, he prevented a railroad and steel mill strike by threatening to nationalize their operations. Truman's last controversial presidential act was his announcement that he would not seek a second full term as president in 1952.

In 1953 Truman and his wife returned to Independence. There were two dedications in his post-presidential life. This first was the dedication of the Harry S. Truman Library and Museum in September, 1957. The second was the April 19, 1959 dedication of his birthplace in Lamar as the Harry S. Truman Birthplace State Historic Site. Truman was there for the festivities.

Missouri Department of
Natural Resources
September 2001

Web site: www.mostateparks.com

MR. TRUMAN

Harry S. Truman Birthplace State Historic Site

Lamar, MO

Visit the birthplace home of the only Missourian ever elected President of the United States – Harry S. Truman. Born May 8, 1884, in a downstairs bedroom of a small frame house in Lamar. Harry S. Truman was the son of John Anderson and Martha Ellen (Young) Truman. The Truman birthplace, which the family occupied until Harry was 11 months old, was built between 1880 and 1882. The Trumans purchased the 20 by 28 foot house as newlyweds in 1882 for $685.

Visitors today can view its four downstairs rooms and two upstairs rooms as well as the smokehouse, well and outhouse located in the back. The modest furnishings inside the house and the surrounding landscaping accurately represent a typical home of its style during the time the Trumans resided in Lamar. It has neither electricity nor indoor plumbing.

The United Auto Workers donated the home to the state in 1959 for preservation as a state historic site. President Truman himself attended the dedication on April 19, 1959. The house is listed on the National Register of Historic Places. Like Truman's trademark country mannerisms and down-to-earth sensibility, the small home possesses an essence of Missouri hospitality that seems to welcome every visitor with open arms.

U.S. Department of Natural
Resources
September 2001

Chapter Twenty-Two

SHOW ME PEOPLE

THE BOYS FROM BIRCH TREE: CARNAHAN AND HOLDEN

Birch Tree, MO

Sandy-haired Melvin trotted along a dirt road to the schoolhouse gym, eager to watch the older boys play basketball, wishing he were tall enough to join them. A generation later on that same court a skinny, dark-eyed teen named Bobby showed hustle, playing both guard and forward. The small-town scenes aren't unusual. But for those two boys from Birch Tree, the future would be anything but typical.

Mel Carnahan rose to become governor. Bob Holden, 16 years Carnahan's junior, become state treasurer and hopes to follow his fellow Democrat into the chief executive's office.

The St. Louis area has given Missouri a dozen governors since statehood, but its population base is more than 1 million. With fewer than 600 residents, Birch Tree's status as birthplace of one governor and hometown of his possible successor could make a statistician stagger with disbelief. "It is a remarkable coincidence," Carnahan mused as he joined Holden in greeting most of Birch Tree's population on a recent Sunday afternoon for a potluck luncheon and political rally in the old gym.

"This community has produced one favorite son and is about to produce a second favorite son," said Travis Morrison, emcee at the homecoming. He declared that the tiny town would stand by both men. "Old friends are like a tube of toothpaste: they come through for you in a tight squeeze."

The country was edging out of the Depression but the work hadn't quite reached Birch Tree by February 1934 when Carnahan was born in a rock house just south of U.S. 60.

Driving slowly on the overcast homecoming afternoon, Carnahan did his best to locate the birthplace. He pointed to one likely structure, but said the house may have been next door, now a vacant lot.

Carnahan, 66, relies on family stories for this bit of history, as there is no distinguishing birthplace plaque or marker; who would have thought the second son of rural educators A.S.J. and Mary K. Schupp Carnahan could someday be governor?

So the Birch Tree homecoming yielded flashes of long-ago memories; of his piano teacher (a staunch Republican); of his babysitter, whose son was a basketball star; of a brief return residency during the sixth grade, when his mother served as Birch Tree's superintendent while his father ran for, and won, a seat in Congress, eventually serving for 14 years.

167

Keith Bowden, 64, calls himself Mel Carnahan's oldest friend. They were next-door neighbors as boys, holding up umbrellas as make-believe parachutes while hopping from atop an old shed. "In a town this small, this rural, there is nowhere to go but up. Politics looks pretty good when you're coming from a poverty area like this," Bowden said. "Mel's father made it in politics. And Mel made it in politics. Made it big." But the son started humbly enough at the rock house, then his family moved to "old Catlett place," a two-story white frame house where Carnahan's parents raised chickens and a garden while running Birch Tree's schools.

The governor-to-be lived in the house until he was 4. He hadn't been back inside for more than 60 years, until the current resident, City Marshal John Lee Holden and his bride Wanda arrived at their new house, illuminated inside by a single bare bulb. Lee's father once used it for grain storage. Raised in Kansas City, Wanda Holden wondered what she had gotten herself into and what kind of life the struggling couple could provide in such isolation for Robert Lee Holden II, born in August 1949 at St. Luke's Hospital in Kansas City.

But the farm represented the Holden's future after the Kansas City cattle company, where Lee Holden worked, was hit by flooding in the early 1950s. Three more children – Calvin, Steve and Cindy – would grow up in the house. The Holden's added rooms here and there, and eventually a second floor, but indoor plumbing wasn't installed until Cindy's birth; an oversized photo displayed at the homecoming showed Bob Holden bathing outdoors in a washtub. "I had brought a real bath tub from Kansas City and just decided that with a little girl in the house, it was time to put it in," recalled Wando Holden, 72. Holden's parents still live in the house, which today has such amenities as a satellite television dish.

Leading a tour, Holden rattled open the door to Corinth School, where grade one through eight shared a classroom. It is where his formal education began, after learning the facts of life helping his father raise cattle. He attended another one-room school for second grade, and then attended Birch Tree schools until 1967, when Holden was part of a graduation class of 25. "Bob Holden was the only person I ever went to school with who never made fun of me because I wore patches on my clothes," said classmate Dale Smotherman, 52. "I ain't proud of being poor, but we were all pretty poor. That's the way it was in the Ozarks."

The Corinth schoolhouse is now used for farm storage by Holden's uncle. The windows are boarded, dirt dauber nests dot the tin ceiling and there is much pungent evidence of visits from curious cattle. Holden stepped inside the classroom, dark except for a few slanting shards of sunlight across dist-covered blackboards. "Seeing this is a good way to hold on to your bearings and keep your feet on the ground," said Holden, 50. "It was just a different world."

Folks in Birch Tree seem amused when asked how such a small place could lay claim to a governor and a man who wants to be governor. "I assume it's just a matter of people from a small town wanting to better themselves and their communities," suggested David Ramey, 25, who moved from San Antonio to Birch Tree, where he owns a computer company, "because of the slower pace." "When those two gentlemen were young, they had to dream big to go beyond Birch Tree," he said.

Walter "Bill" Reed, who knows Carnahan and whose children grew up with Holden, said rural living shaped both men. "Everybody knows everybody else. I think small towns teach people to care," said Reed, 74, a barber in Birch Tree for 48 years and still selling $4 shaves with a straight razor.

Ambition, of course, knows no geographic boundaries. "I remember when Bob and I were both 16, we went to Missouri Boys State, and Bob came back saying that someday he was going to be governor," said Gary Reed, 50, son of the barber. "He just set that goal and stayed with it."

Daily American Republic
Poplar Bluff, MO
April 9, 2000

REV. JESSE PRATT: PASTOR AND SOLDIER

Ironton, MO

Jesse Pratt was both in Tennessee on January 13, 1804. Little is known about his parents or his exact place of birth. He was married twice: first to Frankie Fox, who died in 1842 or 1843 in Missouri, and second to Elizabeth Gibson. Jesse died in Warm Springs, Arkansas on August 18, 1888.

Jesse Pratt was, first and foremost, a pioneer. He was a religious man with a true spirit of adventure. He enlisted in Captain Dunn's Company, 2nd Regiment, 1st Brigade, Illinois Mounted Volunteers as First Sergeant in June 16, 1832 in Randolph County, Illinois for service in the Blackhawk Indian War. He was discharged at Dixon's Ferry, Illinois on August 12, 1832. His brother, Matthew Young Pratt, was in the same company. Specific actions of this unit are unknown, but Captain Dunn was seriously wounded by one of his own sentries in an accidental shooting. Captain Dunn survived the war and signed Jesse Pratt's discharge.

Pratt moved to Missouri sometime after the Blackhawk War, probably in 1837-38. He settled in what was then Washington County, but is now part of Reynolds County near present-day Black, Missouri. According to Hames Bell, author of "History of Black Missouri", Jesse became minister of the Black River Church in the late 1830s and early 1840s, attracting some of the great ministers in Southeast Missouri. He wrote that people came and camped all over the river bottoms near the church, often staying two or three weeks. Jesse served the Black River Baptist Church from 1838 until 1842 and from 1851 to 1858. He became the first minister of the newly-formed Baptist Church in Ironton in 1858, serving there until the beginning of the Civil War.

Jesse Pratt, probably because of his Southern birth, joined the Confederate Army. No exact date of his enlistment has been found, but it is known he was on active duty very early in the war.

Ironton was the southern terminus of the Iron Mountain railroad out of St. Louis, so the Union Army occupied Ironton very early in the war. General Grant was promoted to General in Ironton in 1861. He was only here for a couple of weeks, but he may have written an order for Jesse's arrest. He stated in this order that "a preacher from this place has been taking information to the enemy camp and I have ordered his arrest upon his return." Jesse is the only minister from Ironton found to have served in the Confederate Army. It is assumed General Grant was writing about him.

Jesse was a leader of a squad of "irregulars" in the Ironton area and they harassed Union forces in the Ironton area. At some point, Jesse became Captain of Company N, 15th Missouri Cavalry, which was made up on mostly Reynolds County residents. His son, Robert Gibson Pratt, was 1st Lt. of the same company, and his grandson, Jesse Gibson, was also in the same company.

Jesse's Company is believed to have captured and burned the Reynolds County Courthouse on December 22, 1863. They also took the entire Union garrison prisoner with no loss of life. The prisoners were taken to Ripley County, closely followed by Major James Wilson of the Union 3rd Missouri Militia. When Jesse and his company arrived in Ripley County, the entire 15th Regiment was camped for a Christmas holiday with their wives and children. Colonel Timothy Reeves was the Regimental Commander and himself a Baptist, minister from Ripley County.

While dinner and religious services were being conducted, Major Wilson attacked and killed or wounded over 100 people, many of them women and children. This became known as the "Wilson Massacre." Later, during the Missouri Campaign of 1864, Major Wilson was captured during the Battle of Pilot Knob. He, along with six of his troopers, was tried, convicted, and then executed by members of the 15th Missouri Cavalry.

Jesse Pratt remained active until the end of the war. Several mentions of him by Union officers in official correspondence are in evidence. Jesse surrendered, along with the rest of the 15th Missouri on May 11, 1865. He was paroled at Jacksonport, Arkansas on June 5, 1865. He remained in Arkansas, in the Warm Springs area, until his death in 1888.

(Ron Warren is the great, great, great, grandson of Rev. Jesse Pratt.)

Ron Warren
The Mountain Echo
Ironton, MO
February 25, 1998

THE AUSTIN YEARS

Potosi, Mo

A Connecticut Yankee who was to become "Missouri's First Industrialist" and the "Grandfather of Texas" was Moses Austin, a major figure in the early history of Potosi.

Born in Durham, Connecticut in 1761, he was the owner of a dry goods and importing firm in Philadelphia, later moving with the business to Richmond, Virginia. There he also became a pewter manufacturer and a lead and zinc miner.

In 1797, learning of the rich lead deposits in Missouri, he visited Missouri and obtained a grant from the Spanish officials, including a large part of Azor's grant at Mine A Breton. He brought his family here is September 1798, and the next year he settled in his magnificent home, Durham Hall.

Here, the hard-driving entrepreneur transformed lead mining and smelting into Missouri's first major industry. Here he sank the first reverbatory furnace west of the Mississippi. He built a store, sawmill, flour mill, blacksmith shop, bridges and roads, and a shot tower, turning out the first lead shot and cannonballs made is Missouri.

By 1802 he was smelting all the lead for the district and, in 1804, as his business prospered, he was named presiding judge of the Ste. Genevieve District. Moving north, he founded Herculaneum in 1809 as a shipping point for his lead and for spot production.

In 1816, with other prominent citizens of Missouri, he sponsored the Bank of St. Louis. Failure of the bank, along with other financial reverses, left him financially ruined in 1819.

Seeking to retrieve his fortune, he set out on horseback for San Antonio in November 1820 to obtain permission from the Spanish government in Mexico to settle 300 families in the province of Texas.

He was first ordered to leave Texas, however, with the help of Baron de Bastrop, whom he had known in Missouri, his petition was forwarded to Monterey.

As Austin returned to Missouri the hardships and exposure of the journey undermined his health and he died at the home of his daughter in Hazel Run on June 10, 1821, a few weeks after his colonization plan was accepted.

He was at first buried at Hazel Run, and later the bodies of Austin and his wife, Maria, were re-buried in the Old Presbyterian Cemetery in Potosi.

The Independent Journal
Potosi, MO
Reprint Edition, 1997

Chapter Twenty-Three

SO IT WAS

PROMINENT FARMER DISAPPOINTS UNDERTAKER

Case Pronounced Marvelous

Body Was Recovered From Gasconade River With Grappling Hooks

Gasconade, MO

Pronounced dead after all efforts toward resuscitation had failed to produce the slightest sign of animation, laid out upon a board death slab awaiting the arrival of an undertaker, Peter Frey, a prominent young farmer whose limp body was taken from the Gasconade River yesterday afternoon, rose to a sitting position and asked for four hours after the apparently fatal ordeal. Frey is little worse for his terrifying battle with death. Physicians pronounce his case a marvel in the history of the medical profession.

Frey, with a dozen neighbors, was seining in the Gasconade yesterday afternoon. He became entangled in the ropes and his cries for assistance brought William Kerr to his side. Failing to untangle Frey, and himself almost exhausted by the swift current, Kerr was forced to abandon his efforts toward a rescue.

J.P. Tacket, Frey's father-in-law, ran for a boat but reached the scene fully ten minutes after Frey sank from view for the last time. A grappling hook was brought into service and, with the assistance of strong swimmers, Frey's body was recovered. The common methods of first aid to the drowning were applied, without avail. Believing the case hopeless, Frey's body was carried to his home.

Four hours later, despite the purple discoloration of flesh common after death in the water, Frey showed slight signs of life. The grief-stricken family immediately resumed their efforts toward revival. His subsequent recovery is looked upon as almost a miracle in this community.

The Daily Republican
Poplar Bluff, MO
July 15, 1908

Jay Mondy

BLACK COMMUNITY STRIVES FOR NEW SECCESSES

Fresh ideas are emerging to speed recovery
From the 1906 exodus

Springfield, MO

At the turn of the last century, Springfield had a thriving black community. African-Americans practiced medicine and law. Black citizens served on the school board and City Council. The town's largest grocery store was owned by a black family. A black man, Walter Majors, built the first automobile in Springfield.

And then, on Easter weekend 1906, a mob lynched three innocent black men. While white Springfieldians celebrated redemption, black residents streamed out of town in a modern exodus. That story has been told many times in the past decade. Too often, though, that's where the retelling of Springfield's black history stops.

"We make a lot of 1906. It is important," said Mark Dixon, one of three steering committee members for the African American Agenda Collaborative. "So much is said about the fact that people left. So little is said about the folks who stayed, raised a family, went to work, did whatever they had to do to survive, even thrive, in the face of blatant discrimination."

"That is a marvelous thing to me and something to be proud of."

He and others list names that particularly stand out: the Woods brothers, the first black officers on the city police force; Franklin Greene, co-owner of Republic Ford; a long list of educators, pre- and post-segregation; Chester Shipps, who owns one of the oldest electric firms in town; men and women who went to work every day, persevering even when they were denied opportunities for advancement.

And there is Charlotte Hardin, who served on the school board from 1990 to '96, making her the only African-American to win a Springfield election since 1906. "I wish that wasn't so," she said. "I wish there were more."

But she believes her election still holds lessons. What really motivated her to run, she said, were the people who told her she couldn't do it. "What I try to tell people is, whether they want to start their own business, get a master's degree or run a particular office, they can do it. Resiliency is a good term. It's obtainable."

This historic sense of resiliency motivates the African American Agenda Collaborative. A retreat open to the city's black residents a year ago settled on four agenda points: wealth creation and preservation, black leadership development and board participation, parental skill development and support, and constructive youth activities. Dixon, Hardin and Samuel Knox, managing editor of United Magazine, serve as the steering committee. About 30 people are involved in four work groups.

"It's important for black people to realize self-determination in their lives," Dixon said. "That's not always been the fact for black people in this community and nation. This agenda was created for black people, by black people, to address the needs important to them and to improve the quality of life."

It's already had some early success. Knox said five African-Americans have been appointed to local community and governmental boards in the past year. The agenda project has been endorsed by The Good Community Committee and other civic leaders.

Initial steps toward wealth creation have come from partnering with the Small Business Administration and gathering information from workshops. "We want better involvement of the black community with opportunities and resources that already exist," Dixon said.

Knox said he would like to see this agenda lead, in the next 10 years, to a radio station with an urban format. A specialized "welcome wagon" to greet new black residents and professionals, orienting them to what is available and how to what is available and how to get involved. A larger black business community is needed.

Hardin hopes work on the agenda will lead to greater satisfaction with Springfield among African-Americans. "I hear so many who say they want to be elsewhere," she said. "I hope that changes."

Roger Leger
Springfield News-Leader
Springfield, MO
December 1999

MANY HAPPY RETURNS TO WHITE RIVER

Trips Pick Up Speed

Taney County, MO

I was fortunate to be born into a family that had long demonstrated a love affair with the natural beauties surrounding the White River as it made its way through Taney County.

I made my inaugural trip in the summer of 1911, traveling in a covered wagon. My dad was fascinated by the new dam being constructed at Powersite, so he and his brother hired Joe Worrell, who owned a team and wagon, to haul two families to Forsyth for a week's encampment. Of course, I didn't actually remember the trip, but family recounted over the years has created an enduring legend.

Travel time required two full days. One of the horses, old Blackie, had a mind of his own; when he became tired, he would lie down in his tracks and rest until the spirit moved him. With such interruptions, that meant one night spent by the side of the road, somewhere in the hills of Christian County. Mothers and children slept in the wagon and the men used folding cots out under the stars.

A picture of my dad fishing below the partially completed dam, including the scaffolding, has been lost but he had a rope tied around his waist, and at the other end it bound his 9-month-old son playing on the gravel bar, though not too close to the water. This was the beginning of my many trips to Taney County.

By 1916, both Dad and Uncle Albert had touring cars – one Studebaker and one Dodge Brothers. Regular trips were made to the White River, traveling south from Ozark by way of the Brown Bridge over Bull Creek and the favorite Bull Creek S Curve hill. We children were fascinated at seeing our car traveling one direction while directly downhill from us was the other car going to the opposite direction. Yet both were headed for the same destination.

For our July Fourth week's camping outing in 1918, however, we headed for Kissee Mills, traveling from Ozark to Chadwick, down Bilyeu Creek valley to Swan P.O., where we always stopped for cheese and crackers at Burger's Beaver Creek from the mill. A war was on, so we had to forgo our usual fireworks. Instead, each child was issued one box of regular kitchen matches.

In the evening we sat on a high bank, struck our matches and dropped them into Beaver Creek below. In 1920 we spent our vacation at Ozark Beach Resort, just above Powersite Dam. The highlight of this trip was a boat excursion on the Sammy Lane to Branson. This was my first visit to Branson, but only the beginning.

The next summer my older brother and I were allowed to travel alone on the Missouri Pacific Train to Branson via Crane where we camped for a week on the shore of Lake Taneycomo within what is now the city limits of Branson.

It was 1925 before we actually drove to the Branson-Hollister area. This road followed the hilltops south from Ozark through Highlandville, Spokane, Windy City, Reeds Spring Junction and into Branson over what is now Highway 248.

It was on this trip to the Young People's Conference at the Y Camp in Hollister, traveling in our Oldsmobile touring car, that we rounded one of the many curves and came upon an elephant in the middle of the road. This was a shock, but by traveling a little farther we caught up with the rest of the circus traveling over land toward Branson. For this trip to White River we got travel time down to four hours.

Finally, the new U.S. 67 was built, reducing travel time to less than an hour. One Saturday afternoon in 1983 my son's family decided to take me to Shadow Rock for an afternoon of swimming and trying out his new ski horse. That afternoon, in one-half day, we accomplished almost as much fun as required for a full week back in 1911.

Richard T. Garner
Springfield News-Leader
Springfield, MO
December 1999

CITY HONORS GABBY STREET

Pays Respects At Series of Events

Joplin, MO

Many dignitaries in the world of baseball came to Joplin to join local citizens in honoring one of the city's most famous residents at a day of special events in January 1950.

The day included dedication of a boulevard in his honor, a parade, two special events for school children, dedication of a youth basketball park in his name and a climatic banquet that night. Austin Harrison was general chairman of the ceremonies, sponsored by the Joplin Chamber of Commerce and various civic organizations.

In its major story covering the events, The Globe stated:

"Honors were heaped upon the broad shoulders of Charles (Gabby) Street here yesterday in a day set aside in his tribute, and he was knee-deep in compliments at the finish, an honor banquet at the Holiday Inn last night when the venerable man of almost 50 years in baseball said simply and clearly: "This has been the greatest day of my whole baseball career."

650 Attend Banquet

"Undoubtedly it was, from the time things started at 8:30 o'clock yesterday morning until the final tributes were paid at the banquet with more than 650 persons in attendance, including visiting baseball players, sports writers and announcers and Gabby's greatest boosters of them all—the baseball followers."

"And since it was Gabby's party, he had a perfect right to beam as his family, Lieutenant Charles E. Street II and Mrs. Owen Hull, his daughter Sally, were introduced, and it is probably that Mrs. Street, sitting by Gabby with a corsage of roses, had a right to wipe her eyes as 4-year-old Charles E. Street III was held up for inspection applause.

Sampling of Praise

Speaker after speaker took the platform.

Here is what a few said:

William Markwardt: "The biggest thing in 50 years in Joplin is Gabby Street;" Joe Becker: "Gabby fought his way up, he reached the top and I'd like to pay tribute to Mrs. Street as well as Gabby;" Joe Garagiola: "I hope I may someday be one-tenth the catcher Gabby Street was and one sixty-forth the man he is;" Red Schoendiest: "I have found no place quite like Joplin. Now I understand why Gabby Street chose Joplin for his home;" Stan Musial: "This response to Gabby, make me feel proud that I once played baseball in Joplin myself—even though I was on an opposing team;" Fred Saigh: "For fifty years Gabby Street has been an important part of baseball." (Musial played for the Springfield Cardinals as an opponent of the Joplin Miners in the Western Association.)

"Dr. Otto C. Seymour, pastor of the First Presbyterian church, delivered the benediction, and the Rev. Father Arthur M. Tighe, pastor of St. Peter's Catholic church, responded with the invocation.

"A day-long schedule of events got off to a fine start shortly after 9 o'clock in the morning with the arrival of a special Pullman with a large contingent of baseball dignitaries from St. Louis. Approximately 100 overcoat-clad admirers were at the Frisco station (6th and Main Streets) to meet the train.

"Gabby, his topcoat collar turned up and wearing a muffler as protection against the chill air, was at the steps of the Pullman car to greet his friends. His son, Charles E. Street, Jr., a first lieutenant in the marine air corps, also was on hand.

"Fred Saigh, Jr., president of the St. Louis Cardinals, was first to step off the train.

"Three of the regular Cardinal players were on the train. Stan Musial, the Redbirds' slugging outfielder, had arrived Tuesday night.

"Players on the train were Albert (Red) Schoendiest, the red-thatched second baseman; Enos (Country) Slaughter, hard-driving left fielder who last season enjoyed one of his many star years with the Cardinals, and Joe Garagiola, the young catcher who rates very high with Gabby, who was himself one of the star receivers of the game.

"Harry Carey, Street's partner in baseball broadcasting, also was in the delegation."

Street and visiting dignitaries attended assembly at Joplin High School, 8th Street and Wall Avenue, then went to 26th Street between Main Street and Maiden Lane.

They were luncheon guests of the Joplin Rotary Club, then greeted hundreds of school children at Memorial Hall at a special matinee.

It was a field day for autograph collectors wherever the visiting dignitaries went. There were baseballs, notebooks, pieces of scratch paper and other articles thrust into the hands of the visitors for signatures.

After the parade that followed the matinee, a new baseball park for the Gabby Street Youth Baseball League was dedicated, with the banquet closing the ceremonies.

Charles E. Gibbons
Angling in the Archives, 2000
Joplin, MO

Chapter Twenty-Four

AWE, SHUCKS

ALTON'S GENTLE GIANT

Robert Pershing Wadlow was born, educated and buried in Alton, Illinois. His height of 8' 11.1" qualifies him as the tallest person in history, as recorded in the Guinness Book of Records. At the time of his death he weighed 490 pounds.

Robert was born on February 22, 1918, and weighed a normal eight pounds, six ounces. He drew attention to himself when, at six months old, he weighed 30 pounds. A year later at 18 months, he weighed 62 pounds. He continued to grow at an astounding rate, reaching six feet, two inches and 195 pounds by the time he was eight years old.

His middle name, Pershing, was in honor of the World War I General Pershing, then commanding officer of the European conflict.

Robert was the first born of Addie and Harold Wadlow. Later the Wadlow family grew with the addition of two sisters, Helen and Betty, and two brothers, Eugene and Harold Jr. Despite Robert's size, all of his family members were of normal height and weight.

Footnote: Robert Pershing Wadlow once appeared in Sikeston and Poplar Bluff, Missouri. His unusual growth was due to an abnormal pituitary gland located at the base of the skull. His height and weight when walking caused blisters to form on both feet. He developed an infection in one foot and died July 15, 1940 at the age of 22 years and four months. When Wadlow died, he wore a size 37 shoe.

Jay Mondy

Robert Pershing Wadlow

THE ALTON BOY GIANT

Sikeston, Mo

The biggest member of the Seventy-Five Million Club will be one of the special attractions at the International Shoe Exhibit Saturday, May 6.

Robert Pershing Wadlow of Alton, IL, is 15 years old, 7 feet 8 and one-half inches high, weighs 360 pounds and wears a size 34 shoe made especially to order by the International Shoe Company.

Doctors say he will probably grow for another ten years. He is a regular boy in every way; belongs to the Boys Scouts, attends school everyday, plays with boys his own age, and is interested in everything that appeals to the average American lad.

Doctors associate this unusual growth to over-activity of the pituitary gland located at the base of the skull, which controls normality, and abnormality of growth and stature.

The shoes made for Robert are believed to be the largest shoes made for any human foot.

The American Republic
Poplar Bluff, MO
April 28, 1933

SHOES STOLEN OFF HIS FEET

Three Men Arrested at Hilliard on Charge of Taking Sleeper's Footgear

Brought To This City And Locked Up In Jail

Lucion Keeler and Louis Williams Make Arrests, Claiming They Have Evidence to Convict

Hilliard, MO

J.B. Pondexter, J.J. Cona and William Albert were arrested late yesterday at Hilliard on a charge of stealing the shoes from a man's feet.

The trio were brought here and locked up in the country jail pending a hearing. They were arrested by Lucion Keeler and Louis Williams, who are alleged to have sufficient evidence to hold the prisoners.

It is claimed the three men found a man sleeping in the waiting room of Hilliard's depot and they proceeded to rob him of his shoes taking them from his feet and attempting to make away with them.

Keeler and Williams investigated the matter and arrested the defendants.

The Daily Republican
Poplar Bluff, MO
August 16, 1912

CHARGED WITH CARRYING A CONCEALED WEAPON

Broseley, Mo

A dead man was charged in circuit court yesterday with carrying concealed weapons, specifically a blackjack.

Actually, of course, the charge placed against the name of the late Norman Whoberry will be dismissed when the case is called on the docket on the first day of the next regular term. Court attaches explain the procedures as one necessary to clear the record.

Whoberry, an 18-year-old Butler County lad, was shot and killed last Monday during a family altercation involving his mother and uncle, Bob Miller, from Broseley. On July 23, however, Whoberry was picked up and arraigned before Justice of the Peace Claude Graham on a concealed weapons charge. He was carrying a homemade blackjack. Whoberry waived preliminary hearing and was bound over to circuit court under $500 bond. The transcript of the case was not filed until yesterday.

The Whoberry-Miller fight came to an unexpected climax Monday evening, August 6, when Miller met his nephew at the home of Martha Walker near Broseley. Miller, when arraigned before Justice Fred Gray yesterday morning, stated he shot Norman when the youth grabbed an axe and made a motion as if to strike him. He was released under $3,000 bond for appearance in circuit court to answer a charge of second-degree murder.

Daily American Republic
Poplar Bluff, MO
August 14, 1934

AGED MAN JUST CUTTING HIS TEETH

A.H. Hatley of Maynard Can Masticate Right Now

Arkansas Has Molars Extracted and Later
All Grow in Nicely – Well Developed Chewers

Maynard, Ark.

Information from Maynard, Ark., states that A.H. Hatley, a resident of that place, 80 years of age, has broken the record in that part of the country for cutting teeth. It would be unbelievable if it were not an evident fact that anybody can witness.

Hatley is still cutting teeth. He had some extracted about six years ago and only a short while ago he developed all the symptoms of teething. He did not dream of any such thing but the first thing he knew a tooth had broken through the gums.

The process continued until now Mr. Hatley has a set of well developed chewers in the place of those extracted.

The Daily Republican
Poplar Bluff, MO
June 22, 1912

40 CENT CASE HEARD HERE

Smallest Judgment Ever Filed in Court of Appeals

Case to be Docketed for Hearing at
October Term of Court in Poplar Bluff

Springfield, MO

The smallest judgment that has been involved in any case filed with the Springfield Court of Appeals was awarded J.W. Sewell and Al Lasater of Ripley County against J.M. Stencil. The two men were given a judgment for 40 cents and are named as respondents in the case filed today with the Appellate Court.

The case will be docketed for hearing at the October term of the Court at Poplar Bluff.

The Daily Republican
Poplar Bluff, MO
July 23, 1914

FREAK CALF WAS BORN TO DR. JIM SMITH

Monstrosity Undergoes Successful
Operation at Hands of Dr. Seiple

Water Bag Over Head, Nostrils Far Apart

Indications That The Calf, Born Yesterday,
Will Live and Be Healthy Animal

Poplar Bluff, MO

This morning there was a curiosity in an animal way at Frank's livery stable – a calf, which those that like to use words of many syllables, call a monstrosity. The calf is owned by Dr. J.M. Smith and was born yesterday. It was a weird looking object at first, but by the time Dr. J. Seiple, the veterinary surgeon got through with the operation, every indication was the calf would get along all right and develop into a perfectly healthy animal.

The calf had a water bag over the upper part of its head, which concealed the nose.

The Daily Republican
Poplar Bluff, MO
July 15, 1914

DISAPPOINTED IN FIANCE SHE DECLARES WAR

Woman at Kennett Don't Like Looks of
New Papa and Fires Cupid

Kennett, MO

Mrs. Frances Wilson, giving her home address as Chicago, arrived in Kennett last Monday to meet an appointment to marry George Sutliff, with whom she had been in correspondence for some time and whom she says represented himself as being quite well-to-do, the owner of a large plantation and other property, claimed he was 38 years of age, and mailed her a photograph of a fairly good looking man of that age, claiming it was a likeness of himself.

Those acquainted with Sutliff can imagine the lady's surprise when she met her prospective husband, and the lady was not backward in expressing her feelings in the matter, nor in denouncing the would-be-gay, but thoroughly cowed lothario.

She said she saw Sutliff's advertisement in a matrimonial journal, and being a widow with two young sons, and needing a home, she was attracted by the proposition he outlined in his advertisement, and answered it. The correspondence was kept up for a month or two. They became engaged and he sent her money to pay the way of herself and two sons, George and Walter, ages 12 and 8, respectively, to Kennett.

The lady was in no way of the buxom clinging vine type, but was a veritable virago and was fully equal to the occasion when it came to denouncing the duplicity of her would-be-husband. She threatened to prosecute him for his misrepresentation and for the use he made of the U.S. mail, and so impressed him with the advantage she had of him and the sincerity of her intention to use it, he coughed up $20.00 in addition to what he sent, making a total of $80 he was out in the deal, and they agreed to call it square, and she left at 7:00 p.m. Tuesday with her sons, saying she was going to Memphis.

Sutliff says she first wrote him from Kansas City and later from Rockford, Ill., but claimed her home was in California. He says the misrepresentation was not wholly on his side of the deal; but there is no doubt they would have been married, had the lady been willing.

From Daily Dunkin Democrat
Poplar Bluff American
Poplar Bluff, MO
June 17, 1920

CHICK WITH FOUR LEGS AND WINGS IS PRODIGY HERE

Poplar Bluff, MO

An animal prodigy was brought into the American office this morning by Mrs. J.D. Brown, mother of Orville Brown, one of the American carrier boys, living in the Ashcroft addition, south of this city. The freak was a newly hatched chicken having two pair of wings and four legs on a single body, which from all appearances was otherwise normal. The chick lived for a few minutes after the shell was cracked. The egg the chick was in was slow in hatching and Mrs. Brown, to see if the egg contained a live chick, broke the shell. The shell should not have been broken for a day or two under the circumstances. Mrs. Brown believes the chick would have lived. Its death was caused, she believes, from premature exposure.

Poplar Bluff American
Poplar Bluff, MO
May 5, 1921

BARBER TRIMS CHIN WHISKERS OF HIS GOATS

Fredericktown, MO

Trust Barber T.R. Henline to advertise his profession even when he tends his prize Toggenberg goats.

He doesn't believe in goats wearing beards, so frequently he gets out his shears and clips off the chin whiskers.

"I'd rather have my goats clean-shaven," he said.

For 15 years Henline has been raising his beardless goats, dividing his time between his shop and the half-acre "ranch" on the outskirts of Fredericktown, her in the Ozark Mountains. He said he has supplied breeding stock for farmers as far away as Massachusetts. Goats, by the way, need something besides the tin cans, rags and paper for which their appetites are notorious, Henline claimed.

"True, they are great rustlers and will make the most of anything," he admitted. "It's almost impossible to starve them to death, but they should have a grain ration along with some hay and pasture for the best milk production."

Henline suggested: "Right here in the Ozarks, many people overlook a great opportunity. Goats are easy to handle, require little attention, and will produce more per dollar of investment than the average dairy herd."

The Daily American Republic
Poplar Bluff, MO
September 25, 1937

Chapter Twenty-Five

DO YOU REMEMBER

THE GEORGE WASHINGTON CARVER STORY

Neosho, Mo

The man who rose from a child born into slavery, and who grew into a heritage of racial repression and destitution, only to reach the very pinnacle of fame and respect of all races, is one of the most cherished stories in the pages of Newton County history.

And the story of that man – George Washington Carver – has done much to weld together a unity of thinking in inter-racial relationships in the area and in Missouri in general.

The story of this great Negro man, told and retold so many times, continues to be a guiding light and an inspiration to generation after generation.

George Washington Carver was not only a brilliant scientist, but a great man as well. He had a broad understanding of life, and developed a philosophy that could have been destroyed during the period of repression and destitution which faced his race during the entire period of his life.

His understanding of life was based upon an unswerving spiritual faith and a life-long and untiring search for knowledge. That he became one of the greatest scientists of all time is related closely to the fact that he had an untiring desire to gain more and more knowledge.

It was on June 12, 1952, that the National Park Service finally established the old farm site of the Carver family, located a few miles from Neosho, near Diamond, and a National Monument. The monument was dedicated in his honor about eight years following his death, which occurred on January 5, 1943.

Through the years Dr. Carver became known internationally as a world famous scientist, philosopher and humanitarian. Many of the minute details of this great man's life are still being whittled out of the past in order that those details of life may be preserved for posterity. Much of this work has fallen to Robert P. Fuller, historian for the Carver Memorial, and many painstaking hours have been spent in attempting to locate every detail of Dr. Carver's life.

Dr. Carver was a self-made man of the first order, yet his entire total character and his work was a reflection of unselfish contribution to society.

George Washington Carver's life is seen through the public's eye, most generally, as the man who made 300 discoveries of products derived from the peanut, revolutionized the economic position of the peanut, and increased hit value many, many times.

His first experiments with products derived from the peanut came following his appointment to the post of Director of Agriculture Research at Tuskegee Institute, Alabama, in 1896, an appointment made by Booker T. Washington.

The amazing number of products derived from the more or less useless little peanut included coffee, pickles, shaving lotion, milk, butter, flour, cheese, breakfast food, ink, soap and cosmetics, to name a few.

Dr. Carver was so enthusiastic about the possibility of the peanut he once said, "Why, if one knows the peanut, he can find food and shelter; he can produce medicine out of the same peanut. Washing powders are made, face bleach, candy and boards used in the walls of home. God, what is a peanut, and why did You make it? Ye shall know science and science shall make you free." From this statement was an interpretation of Dr. Carver's philosophy of life.

But his talents were not confined to the laboratory of this scientist. During his lifetime, painting was a major interest of George Washington Carver. He was talented to the extent that several of his paintings attracted considerable attention at one of the World's Fair exhibitions. He was accomplished in weaving and many beautiful rugs and other items were produced from his loom. At one time he toured the Midwest as a concert pianist, and showed extreme talent in that art.

His philosophy, too, was inscribed in a statement he made at one time to his students: "When you do the common things of life in an uncommon way, you will command the attention of the world."

In the scientific field, although peanuts were his prime interest, his accomplishments in the development of other products were many and varied. Experiments with the sweet potato resulted in a total of 118 useful products. Among those products were starch, vinegar, library paste, candy and shoe-blacking.

He developed dyes from clay, dandelions, onions, beans, tomato vines, and trees. And out of one of his dyes, he is believed to be the scientist who rediscovered the lost purple used by the Egyptians.

Dr. Carver's paints were made from clay, peanuts, and – cattle manure. From common wood shavings he was able to make synthetic marble, still in wide usage today.

And, it is believed that Dr. Carver never bought a tie or cravat. He made them himself.

The impact on the South from his discoveries of new products from peanuts was far reaching. Being the principle crop, new markets for both white and colored growers were established, and a brighter future in agriculture was developed.

But what about his man who became such an outstanding scientist, notable painter, inspiring musician, great philosopher and teacher – what about his early life?

His early life was a chapter of the history of Southwest Missouri at that time – a chapter of the final years of slavery, and of the conflict and brutality of the Civil War.

As near as can be ascertained through the probing of the Carver Memorial Historian, the Carver family in Newton County points back to 1838 when Moses Carver, a farmer, homesteaded some land near Diamond Grove. He came from Illinois with his wife and a young slave girl, apparently his only slave. On his 100 acre homestead, Carver built a log cabin which was the home. Moses Carver became a successful farmer over the years. In 1858, the slave woman on the farm gave birth to a son, which would be an older brother of George Washington Carver. This son, James, is thought to have died in Seneca later of smallpox.

A second baby was born to the slave woman in 1860. Although the exact date of his birth is not known, evidence has indicated that is was in late summer of 1860 and it was established by Congress as July 12, 1860.

The identity of the father is not known, but it is thought that he was a Negro slave from a neighboring plantation, who was accidentally killed while the children were quite young.

About six months after the child was born, night raiders rode to the Carver farm and kidnapped the mother and child, taking them into Arkansas. This was the practice at that time, reselling the slaves to other owners.

Moses Carver reportedly sent a friend by the name of Bentley to recover the mother and child, but he succeeded only in recovering the child.

George Washington Carver, given the name later because of his honesty, was then adopted by Moses Carver and his wife, Suzanne, and was reared on the Carver farm.

Moses Carver realized early that the child had amazing talent, and was able to secure some schooling for him.

At the age of 14, or about that, he went to Neosho where he fell in with kindly Negro residents, and it is thought they were responsible for his early formal education.

From that point, he made his was to Minneapolis, Kansas, where he worked his way through high school, then continued and in 1894, was graduated from Iowa State College, where he received his Master's Degree two years later. In 1928, Simpson College at Indianola, Iowa, conferred the then famous scientist the honorary degree of Doctor of Science.

His fabulous career moved onward, gathering honor after honor. On August 1, 1935, he was appointed collaborator in the Bureau of Plant Industry of the U.S. Department of Agriculture, Division of Mycology and Disease Survey.

In June 1937, during the commencement exercises at Tuskegee, a bronze bust of Dr. Carver, paid for by his admirers, both white and colored, was unveiled. He was awarded a membership in the Royal Society of Arts in London in 1917; the Springarn Medal in 1923; the Roosevelt Medal in 1939.

In 1951, the George Washington Carver National Monument near Diamond was established, and the present hope is that a museum will be added during the coming years.

Details of the amazing and talented career of this man are still being brought to light and are being compiled by the staff of the Carver National Monument.

Inevitably, the birthplace of this remarkable man was destined to become an object of great popular interest. Unfortunately, the small log cabin where he was born was long since destroyed, and it is not known precisely where it was located.

However, a site was established after a long study which is thought to be very near the exact site of the place where the genius was born.

At the dedication on July 13, 1953, a cast-stone bust of George Washington Carver was unveiled. It was donated by the George Washington Carver Memorial Institute. A bronze plaque was donated by the George Washington Carver National Monument Foundation containing the following inscription: "George Washington Carver Memorial is the only National Monument honoring a man for scientific attainment."

Although there were many persons responsible for accomplishing the realization of the national memorial, it was Richard Pilant of Granby who was able to promote the idea sufficiently to get Congress to act. George Washington Carver died on January 5, 1943, and on July 14th of that same year, Congress passed a bill authorizing the creation of the George Washington Carver Nation Monument. Because of difficulty in acquiring the private lands on which the site was located, it was not until June 12, 1952 that the lands were purchased. The letter date is actually the official date of the establishment of the George Washington Carver National Monument.

Neosho Daily News
Neosho, MO
July 2, 1958

THE ROY ON THE MOVE

The Roy navigated 1,797 miles over four rivers to reach Poplar Bluff

Puxico, MO

In the old days, the several timber workers in our area along and near the St. Francis River stored up their logs in anticipation of the rainy season to float them downstream to mills and markets.

It was a millennium scene we can only invoke in our minds today, but it was surely quite a grand and impressive portrait. Log after log after log, bumping together, moving along. A good part of the logs likely ended up downstream at Poplin, a sawmilling center with steamboat docking capabilities that was established on the east bank in Stoddard County, across the river from the land where Fisk, MO is situated in Butler County.

No doubt, the storied steamboat whistle blasts filled the Poplin air above a constant roar from nearby sawmills while the boat captains and their men told fascinating tales about life on the river.

So far as I can learn, the year in which Poplin is skimpy at best, but local histories say it was abandoned when Fisk was platted in 1899. Everyone moved across the river. There likely is a good story to explain Poplin's abandonment, but it apparently was never recorded. A former Fisk resident tells me, however, he has heard it said a levee was erected along the Butler County side of the river to protect the land there from flooding. The levee achieved its goal but caused great flooding of the Stoddard County land where Poplin was situated. According to this account, it was not long before the Poplin residents moved their homes and sawmills across the river and subsequently helped to organize the town of Fisk. The move was surely facilitated by a ferry, which was in operation there in the days before a highway bridge was erected in 1910, or shortly thereafter.

That may, or may not, have been precisely the way it happened, since, as with Poplin's founding, it's not known with certainty in which year its residents moved across the river. Neither is it recorded whether the new community continued on as Poplin or adopted its new name, Fisk, at that time but a St. Louis Post-Dispatch story dated July 24, 1898, stated Poplin was in Butler County. If the newspaper had it right Poplin, at one time, was in Stoddard, at another time in Butler, and still later became Fisk.

In any case, steamboats were a big part of life at Poplin, since the St. Francis at that time and in that locality, and on south, was a navigable river, a much appreciated resource in primitive times. The rivers carried practically all commerce and travel before the railroad arrived in our area. Indeed, save for pack animals and oxen drawn vehicles, the rivers carried everything.

Very few details are known about the steamboat traffic at Poplin, but we do know a draw-bridge was built by the Iron Mountain Railroad at the site in 1896 or earlier to allow steamers to pass upstream, which indicated the river traffic was substantial at the time. The draw-bridge was still in operation in 1910, but the meager information available suggests the steamboat traffic began to wane in the very early 1900's.

That's about all we'd know about Poplin and its steamboats were it not for that 1898 issue of the St. Louis Post-Dispatch, which carried a story about the community and one of its steamers, the Roy of Memphis built in 1896 for G.W. Fisk for use in his lumber business. It was described as 75 feet long with a 15-foot beam and 21 feet across its guards.

The newspaper reported George Huff of Poplar Bluff, on the Black River, purchased the Roy from Mr. Fisk's estate at Poplin, 11 miles away on the St. Francis, and employed Capt. Charles R. Miles and a crew of 11 to bring it home to him. It took them twenty five and one half days to get her there. In the meantime the craft traveled 1,797 miles, navigated four rivers – St. Francis, Mississippi, White and Black – and passed by or through four states – Missouri, Tennessee, Mississippi and Arkansas.

Within 30 Minutes after reaching Poplar Bluff, Capt. Miles had boarded the Iron Mountain and was at home again at Poplin, "after completing one of the most remarkable voyages on record."

Of Poplin, the newspaper said its "entire population is dependent upon its sawmills," adding: "On the bosom of the St. Francis, great rafts of logs are brought to the mills by small steamers, commonly called towboats, built specially for the purpose, being light of draught and of great power in proportion to their size. Such a streamer was the Roy."

The story, illustrated with art work, was discovered on microfilm by Puxico Press subscriber Frank Hoggard of Springfield, MO who passed a photocopy on to me. Having the opinion the reader would enjoy as much as Frank and me the account of the Roy's perilous voyage from Poplin to Poplar Bluff, I pass it along, as follows:

"Capt. Miles and his men started south on the St. Francis on the morning of May 23, 1898. Their first stop was at the town of St. Francis, 128 miles from Poplin, and a few miles from the famous sunken lands of southeast Missouri, caused by the earthquake of 1811.

Then their troubles commenced. The great chain of lakes formed by that gigantic upheaval vary in width from 300 yards to four miles. In that part of its course the St. Francis is nothing more than a series of lakes, with no regular channel. Navigation is almost impossible. The water is full of logs and the task of shoving them aside with boathooks was exhausting to the crew. In many places the logs where wedged so tightly between the banks they had to be sawed in two. They created a jam, and more than once the mariners were compelled to fell trees in front of the great masses to prevent them rushing down and demolishing the boat.

They finally reached Lake City, Ark., 328 miles from the starting point, without serious mishap and in fair condition, but from there on their journey was one of incessant toil. The men suffered severely, both from overexertion and the heat. During that part of the journey they hired seven different guides, as each was able only to take them through the immediate section in which he lived. Some of them could not even do that. Two or three of the guides became lost in the maze of false channels and the boat was dragged hither and thither until the right channel was struck or a more intelligent guide found.

Imagine a vast stretch of water as thick for purposes of navigation as so much mush; water lying in an almost endless depression in the earth, overgrown and impregnated in every part with heavy, clinging moss and smartweeds 20 feet high and almost as thick as saplings.

These huge islands of vegetable matter, when run into by the steamer, would stop her dead still, even with a head of steam of 150 pounds. Progress was slow and tortuous and exasperating. To add to the discomforts of the men their ice and water gave out and they were continually harassed by mosquitoes, which Capt. Miles solemnly asserts 'were big enough to shoot'.

The lake water was sickening to drink, but there was no other relief from thirst. The gigantic smartweeds, which will sting the body when crushed, gave the water a nauseating flavor and when the sun beat down upon them, the stench they gave forth was well nigh unbearable.

In fact, the lakes in that vicinity are little more than marshes. A few years ago they were opened and there was a fair channel, but recently they have become choked with weeds and willows and it is feared that the current will be shut off entirely and the chain of lakes degenerate into one extensive morass.

Fifty miles south of Lake City is Marked Tree. There, two members of the crew deserted. The vicissitudes of the voyage were too much for them.

From Marked Tree to the mouth of the St. Francis River, which empties into the Mississippi, is 239 miles. The channel is good and the voyage was made in good shape. Soon after turning out of the St. Francis they passed Helena, Ark., and steamed gaily by Friar's Point, Modoc, Knowlton and other villages to the mouth of the White River, 130 miles away.

But even while going down the Mississippi, the little boat was not without trouble. The firebox of the Roy is only 42 inches long. The only wood procurable was in lengths of 48 inches and all hands had to pitch in and cut it off. Most of them said something, but all sawed wood.

In the meantime, the party had passed St. Charles, Crockett's Bluff, Mt. Adams, Keevil and Clarendon, but they did not stop until they had cleared the region of sandbars.

After a short rest at Duvall's Bluff they again moved northward, stopping at Des Arc, Dry Oak, Peach Orchard and Augusta, finally arriving at Newport.

Twelve miles from there, at Jacksonport, they left the White River, which sweeps down from the northwest, and started northeast along the channel of the Black River, which rises in Missouri and which flows for a long distance within three miles of the banks of the St. Francis River, north of Poplar Bluff.

One peculiar fact noted by Capt. Miles is that while it is 12 miles from Newport to Jacksonport by water it is only three by land.

The first stop they made along the Black River was at Strawberry, Ark., 65 miles north. From there they proceeded by easy stages to Black Rock, 65 miles further; to Pocahontas, 45 miles; to Corning, Ark., 120 miles more and thence to Poplar Bluff, MO., 110 miles away.

Their unprecedented voyage was at an end and the men were all in good health. Nearly a month had elapsed since their departure from Poplin, 11 miles away, yet within 30 minutes, traveling by rail, Capt. Miles was at home receiving the congratulations of his friends.

The Roy was built for Mr. Fist by one James Smith, who was accidentally crushed to death between the wheel and the cabin during the boat's maiden trip.

Cletis Ellinghouse
Puxico Press
Puxico, MO
June 9, 1999

The sketch of the Roy of Memphis, a steamer, docked at Poplin, MO., appeared in the St. Louis Post-Dispatch Issue of July 24, 1889.

THE BURNT MILL

One of the most interesting and beautiful ruins of Perry County is an old mill located on the bank of the mighty Saline Creek near an old ford. The location of this mill is about four miles northwest of Brewer and eight miles southwest of St. Mary's, and only three miles from my old home where I was born and reared.

This old ford by the mill was used as a crossing over which many tons of Galena lead ore were hauled from the lead mines of Mine La Motte to St. Mary's landing from the 1840's to the Civil War period. The distance was about 40 miles, and the road which the lead was hauled was called the "Old Mine Road."

Soon after making the crossing going west toward Mine La Motte, the road begins to elevate up a very steep hill. About two miles from the crossing, where the top of the hill is reached, there is a section of the "Old Mine Road" which is called the "Narrows." (Those living in the vicinity of this road pronounce it as the NARS). The reason for this is the road follows along the tip of the hill for about a mile where it is only wide enough for a road, and for a distance of several yards it is only wide enough for one car to travel over. The hill drops off very straight and steep on each side. I remember as a child, I was always afraid to travel over this road for fear of meeting another car.

My great grandfather, Elliott Boyd, hauled lead ore over this road and made the crossing by the mill. He often camped alone the way overnight. There were many wolves in this area, and they would come close to the camping place at night searching for food.

The mill was constructed by Rozier and Valle in the early 1850's. The mill and mill race were soon destroyed by a great cloudburst which overflowed the might Saline. They then were determined to build a mill which would defy the might Saline. They used great care and skill in making a strong building and even boasted it couldn't be destroyed. When the mill race was completed, its completion was celebrated with a barrel of whiskey, which at that time sold for $0.375 per gallon. That same night a terrific storm swept the mill race down the Saline.

My Grandfather, Nicholas Rimboch, a native of Germany, was employed at the mill at the time of the burning and had been working there for two years. He locked the mill and went home on the evening of October 12, 1866, and that night the mill burned. He started to work the next morning and, as he was going along the "Narrows", he set someone who told him the mill had burned. He could hardly believe it and went to see for himself. A Mr. Thomas Brady was operating the mill at the time it burned.

Several myths have been told concerning the burning of the mill. One of them was the insurance policy stated several barrels of water should be kept on each floor of the mill at all times. Mr. Brady did not have the barrels of water on the floors until a week before the mill burned.

Another myth was that Mr. Brady sent his son over to the East to secure insurance on the mill, and the son got drunk and came back without taking out the insurance and without telling his father. The father then set fire to the mill to collect the insurance. These are simply myths and no one seems to know whether or not any insurance was collected.

The old walls were left standing and made a beautiful landmark. They show some of the most wonderful stone work that can be seen anywhere. In about 1900 one corner of the ruins fell into the creek. Today it stands with only three corners and one of those has been cracked for several years and look as if it could tumble anytime.

Several trees have grown up on the inside of the walls, and one tree has grown out one of the windows and up the outside wall. The old road passed just behind the mill so closely one corner of the mill could be touched by just the reaching of the hand from a car window. Recently the road has been changed to pass in front of the mill. The grounds near the mill have always been a favorite place for many people to use for recreational purposes.

Note: The old mill has badly deteriorated since this story was written

Naomi Hudson Lee
Perry Co. Historical Society, 1950
Perryville, MO
(now lives in Cape Girardeau, MO)

Chapter Twenty-Six

MATRIMONY PROBLEMS

MEN TRADE WIVES AND WIVES "SWAP" HUSBANDS

Unusual Condition Brought About by Cupid Results in Two Couples Landing in Bloomfield County Jail to Await Trial on Serious Charge at the Next Term of Court

Bloomfield, MO

A most remarkable love tangle – one in which two couples and five children are involved – has been uncovered here with the arrest of Mr. and Mrs. Curt Wallace and Mr. and Mrs. Otis Cravens, farmers of Stoddard County. They are held in the county jail pending trial in the circuit court on charges of adultery.

The fire of love that first burned so brightly in both families and which rekindled with the birth of children, had suddenly died out. Two happy homes have become the opposite through the peculiar activities of Cupid. In fact, conditions became such the two farmers actually traded wives.

Curt Wallace, age 27, and his wife Cora, 24, were married seven years ago. They have three children, Bertha, Owen and Loren, ranging in age from 6 to 2 years. Otis Cravens, ago 30, and his wife, Nellie, age 22, have been married for 8 years and have two children, Marie, 5, and Lee, 3.

Was Happy Till –

Cravens has lived in the vicinity of Bloomfield for many years. His married life was believed to be a success until he and his wife became acquainted with Mr. and Mrs. Curt Wallace about a year ago. Likewise, the married life of Mr. and Mrs. Wallace was happy until they met the Cravens. That was about a year ago. As they became acquainted with each other, the women becoming close friends and the men real "buddies", the conditions suddenly changed.

"We just lost our hearts for each other," Cravens declared. "I fell in love with Cora and Curt found he loved Nellie. The two women decided their love for the "other's man had developed and they no longer cared for their real husbands."

Conditions went along for several months, gradually becoming worse and worse. Both husband and wife became more and more dissatisfied. They couldn't agree on anything and they began to realize the great mistake they had apparently made.

Just Mismated

We were just mismated," they declared today.

As the two men and two women peered between the bars at the Stoddard County Jail today and related their marital difficulties, all seemed to be highly enthusiastic over the possibilities of correction the mistake when they are released. The related, at times with faltering voiced, how their love had charged.

"Do you still have the same respect for one another you had before your love tangle?" they were asked.

"Yes," they all replied quickly. "We don't blame each other for the mistakes. We are good friends and hold no grudge whatsoever. We intended to get a divorce and start our lives again, but the officers caught us before we had gone very far with our plans."

Traded Wives

The decision to "swap" wives was decided on Monday, February 2, they said. They really didn't think it was anybody's business but their own. They were merely doing as their conscience directed them, and say they believed that was the right course.

Wallace sent his three children to stay with their grandmother, Mrs. Ida L. Wallace of Greenbrier, and Cravens sent his two children to live with their grandparents at Cline's Island. That left the stage clear for the trade and the young farmers then proceeded to live with their new wives.

Wallace's mother did not think so well of the proposition and, immediately, notified the officers. State's warrants were issued and the strong arm of the law broke up the two new love nests.

"Yes, my mother had me arrested," Wallace said. "She couldn't understand and, if she had let us alone for awhile, we would have had our divorces and been remarried."

"I love Curt more than I did Otis," Mrs. Cravens declared. "I think it is wrong for the law to keep us from correcting a bad mistake of marrying the wrong person."

"And I love Otis the most," Mrs. Wallace insisted.

"Our love for our wives changed quickly," Wallace said, speaking for himself and Cravens, the latter nodding his assent.

Are Undecided

The two couples had not completed arrangements for the future of their children, they said in reply to the question. "My wife wants to keep one of ours," Wallace said, "and I guess my next wife and I will keep the other two. We will likely keep one of the Cravens' children, too," he said. They admitted the problem would have to be solved at a later time.

When the two couples were lined up before the camera after a Deputy Sheriff had taken them out of their cells, they disliked standing by their "real husband or wife."

"We don't look good this way," Mrs. Cravens declared when she was asked to stand beside her "real" husband. "I would rather stand by him," she continued, pointing to Wallace.

It is the most remarkable case in the annals of Stoddard County history, the officers here declared. To have the love of four people turn suddenly to the others has never been known in this section before. The four persons declare they are not ashamed of the situation. In fact, they tell of their experiences proudly.

Typical Farmers

Cravens and Wallace are typical farmers. Their wives are typical farm wives. All four are apparently above the average in intelligence.

Residents of Bloomfield consider the matter only lightly. But for the two mismated couples, it is different. The case is a serious one in their belief, affecting the lives of not only themselves, but of their five children.

The four people, whom Cupid had mistreated, will plead guilty when they are taken before the Circuit Judge, they admitted.

"We will take the penalty, and pay it," they admit.

And after their term is served –

"We intend to divorce our wives and get married again, marrying the other fellow's wife, in accordance with the law," they insist. "Our love is too great to disregard," Cravens said. "We can't live together this way, and we are going to correct the mistake." The women smiled, expectantly.

So after justice has been served, Cupid will enter into the field again and adjust the matrimonial error to suit the present conditions. They the two couples will return to their farms, the wives exchanging positions and assisting their new husbands in their efforts to provide a good living by tilling the soil.

The Daily Republican
Poplar Bluff, MO
March 6, 1925

PLEADED GUILTY

Bigamist Prefers Penitentiary To A Father's Vengeance

Butler County, MO

Ephriam Yates, wanted in Butler County for bigamy and in Jackson County, Arkansas for abduction, was arrested at Charlie Kittridge's place, near Hilliard, yesterday afternoon by Sheriff Hogg. He was at once taken before Judge Fort, when he pleaded guilty to bigamy and was sentenced to two years in the penitentiary. Yates was exceedingly glad to take his punishment in Missouri, stating that he was not all desirous of going back to Arkansas. He had a reason for this.

Yates was a tenant on the farm of a man named Nicholson, living near Swifton, Ark., He had a wife and four children, but this did not prevent him from making love to the young daughter of Nicholson, named Dovie, and of the tender age of 15 years. By persuasion, he finally got her to run away with him. On the night of June 5, they walked the fourteen miles from Swifton to Hoxie, where they took a train and came to Poplar Bluff. Here they walked five miles to the Kittridge place, where the girl secured work as a cook and Yates as a farm hand. Then they walked back to town, secured a license to marry, Miss Nicholson making affidavit to being 18 years of age, and a few minutes later were married by Judge Deem.

197

Yates said on being arrested that he would plead guilty if he did not have to go back to Arkansas, or if a plea of guilty would save him from that trip. He seemed to have a wholesome fear of coming within gunshot of the deceived girl's father. He also said the woman who is passing in Arkansas for his wife is a bigamist, she having had a living and un-divorced husband at the time of her marriage. At first he thought this fact would get him out of the present muddle, as he felt she would be afraid to prosecute, but thoughts of Nicholson made him prefer the Missouri penitentiary to anything. The girl was not arrested but will be returned to her parents.

The Daily Republican
Poplar Bluff, MO
June 11, 1904

MAN CHARGED WITH HAVING SURPLUS WIVES

West Plains, MO

One of the most interesting cases set for hearing in the February term of Howell County Circuit Court in West Plains is that of the state against Thomas J. Robbins, postmaster and merchant of Howard's Ridge in Ozark County, who is facing a charge of bigamy, and who, if guilty of the charge, has not only one extra wife, but two wives in excess of his legal quota.

Incidentally, Robbins seems to be facing a rather uphill technical legal battle as a result of a recent decision of the Springfield Court of Appeals, in which the appeal judges quashed a writ of certiorari through which Robbins' attorney, G.W. Rogers of Gainesville, had sought to have set aside an order made by Judge Robert L. Gideon of Forsythe, in May, 1933, when Gideon set aside a divorce decree which he had granted to Robbins from his second wife, Mrs. Grace Carter Robbins.

Mrs. Grace Carter Robbins, whose home is at South Fork and who is a former Howell county school teacher, was married to Robbins in February, 1930. In a petition for divorce, which she filed in the Howell County Circuit Court in December, 1933 shortly before she filed the bigamy charge against Robbins, she alleges that in May, 1933, he drove her from his home and, under duress and threats, compelled her to sign a waiver of service in a divorce suit which he had filed against her before Judge Gideon in the Taney County Circuit Court.

She says he then went to Forsythe and appeared before Judge Gideon, who granted him a divorce.

A few days later, according to Mrs. Robbins' charge, she employed an attorney and went before Judge Gideon, asking he set aside the divorce decree on the grounds that Robbins had obtained the waiver of service under threats. Upon reconsideration, Judge Gideon set the decree aside.

Less than three months after the Taney County divorce hearing and, at which time Mrs. Grace Carter Robbins says she was still the wife of the Howard's Ridge postmaster, she alleges that he was bigamously married to Miss Francis Johnson of West Plains.

Robbins was given a preliminary hearing on the bigamy charge in the court of Justice George Halstead in West Plains in January, 1934, and was bound over to the February term of circuit court here. However, his case was continued pending the decision of the Springfield Court of Appeals on the writ of certiorari.

In the meantime, however, Robbins had secured a divorce in Ozark Count from the Johnson woman, and had immediately married Miss Hazel Hammond, an 18-year-old Ozark County girl. Robbins is about 40 years old.

Robbins' attorney, in the preliminary hearing here last January, declared that following the setting aside of the divorce in Taney County Robbins returned to Forsythe and Judge Gideon set aside the order granted Mrs. Robbins setting aside the divorce, which left the divorce decree in force.

Mrs. Grace Carter Robbins has one child, a small son, by Robbins. In her divorce she is seeking custody of the child and also alimony in a lump sum.

Daily Quill
West Plains, MO
January 25, 1935

MAN 85, AND WIFE 81, MARRIED 65 YEARS, ASK FOR A DIVORCE

Ripley County, MO

This is a story of the case of McNabb vs. McNabb

Tottering up the aisle of the Ripley County Circuit courtroom yesterday

Afternoon came Sarah Jane McNabb. Slowly, painfully, she took her seat in the witness box and, from dimmed eyes, cast her gaze over the few straggling spectators that at that late hour remained. The wisdom of the ages was written on her face, but her glance was troubled.

"So you want a divorce Aunt Sarah?" inquired Judge Cope.

"I guess I do, jedge," she replied.

"How old are you?" he asked

"Eighty one years, jedge."

"And you have been married how long?"

"Sixty five years."

Judge Cope pondered.

"How did the trouble between you and your husband start?" he finally asked.

"Well, I'll just tell you jedge," said aunt Sarah. "It must have been the Old Boy. We jest ain't been worshipin' our Lord like we ought to. I don't want no divorce. I love that man, but it jest looks like it's the only thing to do. We can't git along."

Husband Listens

From his seat in the witness box, L.C. McNabb, gray haired, gray bearded, cast a belligerent eye in the general direction of Aunt Sarah.

"How old are you, Mr. McNabb?" asked Judge Cope.

"Eighty five, jedge."

"Do you want a divorce?"

"I can't say as I do," the old man scowled.

"Just what is the trouble between you and your wife?" inquired Judge Cope kindly.

"She went to Ok-ly-ho-my" quavered the defendant, his voice rising. "I writ her and told her if she would quit arunnin' around with other men and come back home it would be all right." Then, apologetically, "I don't mean by thet jedge that she was a'doin' nothing' wrong."

Judge Cope pondered again.

Shamed Them

Finally Judge Cope said: "Mr. McNabb – Mrs. McNabb – you have been privileged to live together far past the count of years allotted to the average man and woman. You have raised a family, you have fought hardships together, you have stood side by side in sickness, in death, and you have enjoyed together the pleasures and good fortune the Lord has seen fit to bestow on you. You have a record of which you should be proud. You have been married longer, I believe, than other couple in Ripley County. You have only a few years left to live. Do you not think you could live together in peace and happiness during these declining years and forget your past differences?"

Husband and wife bristled

"It ain't no use jedge," they chorused "We've tried it too many times."

Judge Cope waxed stern.

Asked for Support

"Mr. McNabb," he interrogated, "are you willing to help support your wife?"

"Oh" said the old man debonairly, "She'll git along."

"Let the record show" intoned the judge, "That the court takes the case of McNabb vs. McNabb under advisement and the defendant L.C. McNabb is ordered to pay to the plaintiff the sum of $10 a month for her support until a final decision is handed down."

"Now jedge" inquired the old man fidgeting in his seat, "how long will that be?"

"Unless I change my mind" said the judge "I'll never render a decision. You two don't want or need a divorce. You both go on home and look out for each other."

McNabb looked at his wife. Aunt Sarah looked at her husband. Slowly with feeble steps, they left the courthouse – together.

The Daily American
Poplar Bluff, MO
June 21, 1935

11ᵀᴴ WIFE IS LIVING WITH B.C. FARMER

W.L. Tillman, 88 years, Relates Matrimonial Story –So Many Wives He Cannot Recall Names

Poplar Bluff, MO

A man with a matrimonial history that exceeds anything heard of in the State of Missouri has been located in Butler County. The man is W.L. Tillman, living three miles from Wilby settlement and 15 miles north of Poplar Bluff. He is 88 years of age, in the best of health, shoeing none of the decrepitudes of old age and is living contentedly in a two-room cottage with his eleventh wife. The present wife, to whom he had been married for two years, is two years his junior.

In relating his matrimonial career, he labored over the names of 10 former wives, since so many were hard to remember, but on one of the numbers he stumbled; he "just couldn't, for the world, think of that woman's name" although she had lived with him a number of years. His mind is as clear as that of a man of 50 years, and he reads without glasses. Consequently, old age could not be blamed for his failure to remember the name of that spouse who had sat at his fireside 10 or 12 years ago.

Yes, he did forget something else. He said, upon first being interviewed that he had only nine wives to his recollection, but neighbors came to his rescue and told him he was checking short on two and after several heads and as many groups of fingers were put together, he was convinced there were, after all, the half score and one.

Nine of the wives have been divorces, another dead, while the eleventh is living with him and the pair are just as happy as turtle doves. Despite the array of matrimonial scalps hanging at his belt, he does not seem to be an eccentric and his present wife holds him not to blame for the disruptions in the ten affairs, before she became the favored one. He is of an even temper, apparently, and has accumulated enough in his four score years to make himself a man of substantial means in this community.

A representative of a big news syndicate made a visit to the Tillman homestead a few days ago, obtained the story of the old man's matrimonial totem pole and took a picture of the pair. The story of his career and his pictures are scheduled to appear in a number of the metropolitan papers, in the near future, as one of the sensational news finds of the year.

Poplar Bluff American
Poplar Bluff, MO
December 1, 1920

Chapter Twenty-Seven

ODDS AND ENDS

PERMISSION TIME IN OUACHITAS MEANS BUSY NIGHTS

Mena, AR

Missouri has its Coon Club and Kansas its Badger Club, but Arkansas has the only club of its kind on earth, the 'Possum Club.

For more than 25 years this club has survived. Based solely on the spirit of good fellowship, fun, foolishness and the eating of roast 'possum and sweet potatoes, the club has drawn attention from other clubs of a political nature, some of the recreational type, business, professional and civic, and from people from all walks of life from senators and governors to overall-clad hillbillies.

In December of every year, Mena is agog over plans for the 'Possum Club banquet, held in the National Guard Armory. The program is planned to produce a laugh every minute and anything serious is not permitted. It is possible to tell beforehand what a 'Possum Club banquet will be like since most of the entertainment is impromptu and spontaneous. An orchestra will play for dancing and hillbilly tunes will emanate from the stringed instruments of mountaineers.

Mena, a town of approximately 3,000 population, is situated in the Ouachita Mountain section of Western Arkansas. Every fall around Mena the 'possum hunters slip away after dark armed with a pine torch and accompanied by hound dogs in search of the animals in the tall timber.

Rules Listed

The club committee makes the following regulations in regard to the taking of 'possums:

"All 'possums must be on the growth and production of Polk County. Any found not to have been raised in the county will be rejected by the 'Possum Club statistician of Polk County wild life. All 'possums must be not less than three years nor more than 10 years of age, medium to extra fat, weighing not less than five pounds nor more than 15 pounds dressed. All female 'possums will be rejected. The seller must agree to keep the animals in captivity not less than five days and agree to feed the regular 'possum menu while in captivity.

'Possum fattening menu:

    6:00 a.m. – Warm water with mashed persimmons.

    9:30 a.m. – Persimmons with sour milk

    12:30 p.m. – While persimmons

    3:30 p.m. – Persimmons shredded

    6:00 p.m. – More persimmons

All 'possums must be dressed in a clean and sanitary manner. Each carcass shall pass a final inspection by the club inspector. Each invoice must bear the inspector's signature. It is preferred that 'possums be caught without the aid of dogs; however, it is permissible to use dogs that will gum 'possums instead of biting. Any carcass that shows the imprint of teeth to the extent of one-sixth-fourth of an inch will be rejected.

All live 'possums must not be less than 2 years of age, very active, not too heavy and must be of gentle disposition. If a 'possum shows a disagreeable temper, the club will not accept it. This is very important, as the club has had several damage suits in the past from members who have been bitten by quick-tempered 'possums.

The seller agrees to instruct 'possums to hang up by their tails to small bushes. This is one of the sights of the 'Possum Club banquet, and too much importance cannot be stressed on tail hanging. The club insists it must have two white 'possums with black ears. A bonus is paid for these.

The club uses from 25 to 50 dressed 'possums and from five to 15 live ones. They must be delivered one day before the banquet or the bidder bond is forfeited. The club will not take chances on its members being disappointed by not having 'possums.

On the night of the banquet, noted personages from many parts of the state and many who have come from as far north as Canada and as far south as the Gulf of Mexico will crowd into Mena to be present at one of the most famous social events in Arkansas.

Festooned With 'Possums

In the banquet hall the long tables are set. Living 'possums hand by their tails in trees, gloomily looking down on the gay throng. Statesmen, politicians, millionaires, lawyers, office holders and office seekers mingle with just plain folks.

The president's annual message is always greeted with loud applause. Telegrams from famous men who are members but unable to attend are read aloud. The initiation, giving the secrets of the order and distress signs, is always amusing.

English Baker, 85-year-old pioneer mountaineer, is president. He was elected in 1935 to serve the remainder of his lifetime as a successor of the late B.S. Petfish, after rising as the "dark horse candidate." He gave a buck and wing dance on the platform and later told tales about toting bear meat, wild turkeys, venison and furs to the Hot Springs markets more than 50 years ago.

Mr. Baker is one of the most picturesque characters in this section. He is a hunter, old time square dancer, fiddler and a singer of hillbilly tunes. Dressed in his best boots and vest, with long curls, he is a dyed-in-the-wool Ouachita mountaineer. He was born near Baker Springs resort center named for his grandfather, Elisha Baker, who settled on four sections of land in what is now the southern part of Polk County, even before homesteading days.

On the banquet program in 1927 was a young man named Chester Lauck. He served his first time, but later became active in 'Possum Club programs and, eventually, with a partner, Norris Goff, they became famous and nationally known as the radio entertainers, Lum and Abner. By "remote control" they have aided in making many of the late banquets successful.

Many of the characters in their radio skit call Mena their homes. Grandpappy Spears, Dick Huddleston and others don their best garb and taste the succulence of roast 'possum and sweet potatoes, and rub elbows with the most sophisticated cosmopolite in the country at the Polk County 'Possum Club banquet in Mena.

The Daily American Republic
Poplar Bluff, MO
November 8, 1937

HOSS DOCTORS

Two Bad Ones Do Fredericktown and One Comes to Grief

Fredericktown, Missouri does not appear to be a good field for veterinary surgeons or else we get a bad lot of them. A couple of months ago a "Dr." Wilson, an up-to-date veterinary surgeon blew into town, hung out his shingle, drove fast horses and a couple of women, killed some fine stock for some of the people of Madison County by not understanding his business, and left town between tow suns, when another veterinary surgeon named "Dr." Temple arrived in this city and whispered it around that "Dr." Wilson was minus a diploma and had no right to the title of "Dr." Exit Wilson.

Dr. Temple "practiced" around here for two or three weeks, drove fast horses, but only sported one woman, who was supposed to be his wife. While he was in this city Sheriff O'Bannon received letters from parties in Rolla, making inquiries about the doctor and his "wife." It seems the team the doctor drove was mortgaged to parties in Rolla. Before the necessary papers to take possession of the team was received by Sheriff O'Bannon, the doctor had left Fredericktown, but the sheriff overtook him in Iron County and the doctor readily turned the team over to him, the owner taking possession under the mortgage.

The woman with the doctor here is said to have a husband and three children at Rolla, and the doctor also has a wife and three children there. A man from Rolla came here for the team.

Fredericktown Democrat News
Fredericktown, MO
August 10, 1905

OZARK SAYINGS

Hot as a run-down goat.
Rough as a cow's tongue.
Beefsteak tougher than the law.
Busy as a stump-tailed cow in fly-time.
Useless as a one-horned cow!
If he gets to be a bigger liar he'll have to put on
     weight!
Ugly as a mud fence stuck with tadpoles.
Thick as crows at a hog-killin'.
Scarce as preachers in paradise.
Was so green you could scrape it off a him with
     a cob.
White as the inside of a toadstool.
Stinks worse'n a buzzard's roost!
Bare as a bird's butt!
Long as a gypsy's wagon tracks.
You look like you been a-sortin' wildcats.
Look like he'd been chawin' 'terbacker, an'
     spittin' agin the wind.
Walks like he was belly-deep in cold water.
Walked like he had a punkin' under each arm.
Millin' around like bees fixin' to swarm.
Her tongue is always waggin' like the south end
     of a goose.
Looked like the hindquarters of bad luck.
Out like Lottie's eye.
House looks like the runnin' gear of a hawk's
     nest.
So drunk he didn't know which from the other.
Squeaks like a new saddle.
Bats his eyes like a frog eatin' fire.
Sweatin' like a bound boy at a corn-shuckin'.
His teeth was a-rattlin' like a hog eatin'
     charcoal.
He came out of a chair like he had springs on
     his butt!
He's as slow as Ned in the second reader.
Land is so poor you couldn't raise a racket on it
     with five coon dogs and a gallon jug of
     whiskey.
Land is so poor, a person would have to sit on a
     sack of commercial fertilizer to raise an
     umbrella.
That feller's got four thumbs an' two left feet.

That feller looks like he was marked for a hog.
It's a good deal like climbin' a greased pole
    with two baskets of eggs.
He's lucky to come in last.
The man is so contrary, if you throwed him in
    the river he'd float upstream.
The beef was so tough, you couldn't stick a fork
    in the gravy.
The man was so drunk, he couldn't find his own
    mouth without a leadin' string.
The mother was so ugly, she had to blindfold
    the baby before it would suck.
That road is so crooked, I can't tell if he's goin'
    or comin' back.
That horse is so poor you have to tie a knot in
    his tail to keep him from slippin' through
    the collar.
So skinny you could shake his butt with a
    match.
It was so muddy you would bog a buzzard's
    shadow.
He's so stingy, he's afeard to set down.
He's so slow, they have to set stakes to see if
    he's movin'.

D. Vance Randolph and
George P. Wilson
Down in the Holler, 1953
University of Oklahoma Press
Norman, Oklahoma